Top Student, Top School?

Top Student, Top School?

*How Social Class Shapes
Where Top Valedictorians Go to College*

ALEXANDRIA WALTON RADFORD

THE UNIVERSITY OF CHICAGO PRESS   CHICAGO AND LONDON

ALEXANDRIA WALTON RADFORD is associate director of postsecondary education and transition to college at MPR Associates, Inc., a wholly owned subsidiary of RTI International. She is coauthor of *No Longer Separate, Not Yet Equal: Race and Class in Elite College Admission and Campus Life.*

The University of Chicago Press, Chicago 60637
The University of Chicago Press, Ltd., London
© 2013 by The University of Chicago
All rights reserved. Published 2013.
Printed in the United States of America

22 21 20 19 18 17 16 15 14 13   1 2 3 4 5

ISBN-13: 978-0-226-04095-0 (cloth)

ISBN-13: 978-0-226-04100-1 (paper)

ISBN-13: 978-0-226-04114-8 (e-book)

Library of Congress Cataloging-in-Publication Data

Radford, Alexandria Walton, 1980–
    Top student, top school? : how social class shapes where valedictorians go to college / Alexandria Walton Radford.
        pages ; cm.
    Includes bibliographical references and index.
    ISBN 978-0-226-04095-0 (alk. paper) — ISBN 978-0-226-04100-1 (pbk. : alk. paper) — ISBN 978-0-226-04114-8 (e-book)   1. College choice—Social aspects—United States.
2. Educational sociology—United States.   I. Title.
    LB2350.5.R333 2013
    378.1'98—dc23   2012043205

♾ This paper meets the requirements of ANSI/NISO Z39.48-1992 (Permanence of Paper).

FOR ZACHARY

Contents

Tables and Figures

CHAPTER ONE

Introduction

Three Valedictorians

Karen

By all measures, Karen was an excellent high school student.[1] Valedictorian of her class, she also received a perfect score on the verbal section of the SAT. Yet Karen did not grow up in a family or community where such accomplishment was common. Her parents never went to college.[2] Her older brother enlisted in the navy after high school. Most students from Karen's high school did not attend college, and her fellow honors students matriculated mainly at in-state public universities. Her high school peers found it "shocking" when a classmate enrolled in a most-selective private college in a different region of the country.[3]

Karen's parents wanted her to go to college, but thought she would live at home and drive to the local public four-year university " 'cause it would be affordable." They made it clear to Karen that if she wanted to enroll elsewhere, she would have to earn a scholarship.

Around the start of high school, Karen began aspiring to attend a particular Ivy League college, one of "The Big Three" comprised of Harvard, Princeton, and Yale. When asked how she identified that particular institution, Karen was not sure, but knew that she "wanted to be really smart." Still, this college was unfamiliar to her and those around her. At one point, when Karen told a community member of her plan to enroll in this institution and the listener asked her where it was located, Karen did not know.

As high school progressed, Karen's dream of attending this prestigious university began to wane. Enrolling in this type of institution
was not encouraged in her home, her community, or her high school.
Karen's parents did not see any additional benefit to attending a more-
selective college. Instead, they viewed all universities as interchangeable
because they all offered a college credential. Meanwhile, Karen started
feeling pressure from her religious community to attend the local college
affiliated with her church. Karen's high school guidance counselor might
have provided another opinion, but she could not even remember Karen's
name. Needless to say, personalized college advice that took into account
Karen's accomplishments was not forthcoming from the counseling office.

College costs also became a contentious issue in the family. Karen's
father was particularly outraged by the prices he saw for the private universities she was considering. During the only campus visit he made with
his daughter, he stated simply: "You know you're not going to be able to
[afford to] go here." He asked her repeatedly, "Why can't you go to a public school?" He did not know about the possibility of need-based financial
aid, nor did he understand that given his family's financial circumstances,
colleges would expect him to pay far less than the sticker price suggested.

The college admissions process was becoming a struggle, too. Karen
had to ask her dad repeatedly: "I'm taking the SAT; will you give me the
$25?" Then she found out that the Ivy League college she wanted to attend
required paying for another round of tests—the SAT IIs—which were not
required by the local Christian colleges she was beginning to consider.

Ultimately, Karen put aside her prestigious college aspirations. She
did not even apply to the Ivy League institution she had long imagined
attending. Instead, she matriculated at a small, regional, private Christian college with a full scholarship.

Nevertheless, Karen appeared to have lingering doubts about this
decision. In the spring of her freshman year of college, she "somehow"
found herself on the admissions website of what had been her dream
school. Only then did she learn that her family's income would have allowed her to attend for free.

Paul

Paul, like Karen, was another high achiever. He graduated first in his
class and scored in the high 700s on both the math and verbal sections

of the SAT. But unlike Karen, Paul came from a middle-class family and community. His mother and father had attended the state's flagship university as well as a community college and eventually earned an RN and a bachelor's degree, respectively. Though some of Paul's high school friends joined the military or took jobs in factories, most continued their schooling, attending either community colleges or public four-year universities around the state. Few graduates of his high school attended a private or out-of-state institution.

Early in his college search, Paul's parents told him that they could not afford to send him to a private college. They said, "We're sorry. Maybe you'd get in there, but we can't afford to have you go there." And so private colleges were "thrown right out, right in the beginning" and not explored further. To try to help with college costs, Paul applied for merit scholarships. His parents told him they did not think they would qualify for need-based financial aid, but to Paul's knowledge, they never explored the possibility or applied.

Paul's parents worked with him to try to identify possible college options, but the whole family found the process challenging. Paul had decided he wanted to study medicine, but since "there were no doctors in the family," they "had no idea of where to look." Paul turned to classmates for help, but they too were unsure of which institutions and college characteristics to consider. His high school guidance counselors did not know about out-of-state universities. If they provided any guidance, it was to steer students toward the in-state schools with which counselors were most familiar. Paul started to focus on Big Ten schools because "they had more—both academics and fun stuff." He also thought that medical school admissions officers would have heard of Big Ten schools, but might not know about smaller colleges.

In the end, Paul applied to three public universities: two in his state and one in a neighboring state. He applied to the third—a less-selective Big Ten school—on a whim, filling out the application the day it was due because a couple of his friends were applying. This out-of-state institution offered Paul a full scholarship and he enrolled.

Elizabeth

Our third valedictorian, Elizabeth, also excelled on the SATs, receiving a perfect score on the math section. In Elizabeth's family and community, however, such achievement was not particularly surprising. Elizabeth's parents had both attended prestigious private undergraduate and graduate institutions. Her older sister was enrolled in a highly selective liberal arts college. Elizabeth estimated that 99 percent of students from her prosperous suburban town's high school went on to attend college, and most students in the honors track scattered to prominent four-year private universities in the Northeast.

From the beginning of her college search, Elizabeth's parents were explicit that college costs should not influence her choice. She would not have had to pay tuition if she attended the private, not particularly selective institution where her dad worked, but her parents only "jokingly" suggested she consider it. Due to her academic credentials, Elizabeth was also guaranteed a certain amount of money if she attended the public flagship in her state. She did not apply to either of these less expensive options.

Elizabeth's family was also highly involved in her exploration of college options. Her father "fleshed out the concept" that Elizabeth should go to a university, but a "smaller one . . . that had a lot of opportunities." Her mother gave her lists of colleges that were prominent in Elizabeth's planned major and that were "just top schools in general." Her mother also organized trips so Elizabeth could visit colleges that interested her. And when Elizabeth was not "thrilled" by the prestigious private college in her state, the family simply investigated more distant colleges because Elizabeth and her family wanted her to attend a "top school."

In the end, Elizabeth applied to nine colleges, all of them private and eight of them most selective. She ultimately enrolled in a most-selective private college multiple states from home.

How Representative Are These Stories?

Karen, Paul, and Elizabeth are equal in many ways. All three are valedictorians of their high school classes and have worked hard to earn this title. They all have also taken Advanced Placement (AP) courses and performed well on standardized tests. Yet in the end, only Elizabeth— the student from the more-affluent family—enrolled in a top college.

These social class stories play out every year throughout the country, ultimately producing the national enrollment statistics observed. They repeatedly show that more-affluent students are much more highly represented at America's most prominent colleges than students who are less affluent. Consider these findings:

- Only 3 percent of students at the 146 most-selective public and private colleges in America are from the bottom socioeconomic quartile (Carnevale and Rose, 2004).
- Just 10 percent of students attending one of *U.S. News & World Report*'s top thirty public and private universities are from families with incomes of less than $30,000 (Pallais and Turner, 2006).
- Sixty-seven percent of entering freshmen at the country's 193 most-selective colleges come from the top income quartile. Twelve percent come from the second quartile and only 15 percent come from the bottom two (Leonhardt, 2011).
- At the prestigious public University of Michigan, more freshmen come from families with an annual income of $200,000 or more than from families with an annual income below the national median of $53,000 (Leonhardt, 2004).

Although some might believe that these enrollment patterns are the result of more-affluent students being better academically prepared, preparation differences by social class are unable to fully account for this phenomenon.

First, while data do show that less-affluent students are not as likely as more-affluent students to exhibit the high levels of academic preparation expected of elite college matriculants, there are many more students from less privileged backgrounds, like Karen and Paul, who have the ability to succeed at our nation's top institutions but do not attend (Hill and Winston, 2006b; Pallais and Turner, 2006). About 16 percent of students scoring in roughly the top decile of all SAT and ACT test takers are from the bottom 40 percent of the income distribution (Hill and Winston, 2006b). This finding suggests that top institutions could increase the proportion of less-affluent students in their student bodies to at least this percentage without affecting the quality of matriculants enrolled. A more encompassing, holistic review of students' abilities that considers grades, curriculum rigor, class rank, other test scores, and even essays and letters of recommendation is likely to identify an even greater percentage of promising students from less-affluent families who could thrive at America's best universities.

Second, even when students are similarly well prepared, their college destinations diverge by social class. One study found that 55 percent of upper-income students with combined math and verbal SAT scores of 1300 or above enrolled in a private, elite, Consortium on Financing Higher Education (COFHE)[4] institution compared with 30 to 39 percent of upper-middle-, middle-, lower-middle-, and lower-income students with scores in the same range (McPherson and Schapiro, 1991). A more recent analysis of students who were determined to possess the academic preparation necessary to attend a selective institution revealed that 73 percent of those in the top income quartile ultimately enrolled in such a college compared with 58, 46, and 41 percent of those in the second, third, and fourth income quartiles, respectively (Haycock, Lynch, and Engle, 2010).

This phenomenon in which students attend a less-selective college than they are qualified to attend is known as undermatching, and the evidence suggests it occurs frequently among our very brightest students—like Karen and Paul (Bowen, Chingos, and McPherson, 2009; Roderick et al., 2008, 2009). More than half of all Chicago public high school students enrolled in the system's most challenging academic programs undermatched, with more than one-third attending a two-year college or no college at all (Roderick et al., 2009).

Does Where One Attends College Even Matter?

Even when confronted with this socioeconomic status (SES) disparity among students with similar levels of preparation, some may question whether the type of college that students attend matters. Such individuals might posit, for example, that a degree from "Big State University" is just as good as one from an Ivy League school.

The research we have suggests otherwise; undergraduate alma mater is consistently found to affect later life outcomes. In fact, the benefits of attending a selective institution have been growing rather than decreasing (Brewer, Eide, and Ehrenberg, 1999; Hoxby, 2001). Bowen (1997) explains that as an increasing number of Americans go to college and become college educated—like they have in recent decades (Aud, Kewal-Ramani, and Frohlich, 2011)—it becomes more important for college graduates to distinguish themselves from others. Americans could try to use graduate school to stand out from the growing quantity of bachelor's degree recipients, but earning a greater number of advanced degrees has diminishing returns. Instead, the relevant credential becomes not the quantity of degrees possessed, but the caliber of the institutions attended.[5]

One of the most important ways that an undergraduate institution affects subsequent outcomes is in educational attainment. Students who attend more-selective colleges are more likely to receive their bachelor's degrees than students who enroll in less-selective colleges, even controlling for ability and other factors (Bowen and Bok, 1998; Bowen, Chingos, and McPherson, 2009; Carnevale and Rose, 2004; Carnevale and Strohl, 2010; Cohodes and Goodman, 2012; Kane, 1998; Long, 2008; Melguizo, 2008, 2010).[6] In addition, graduates of more-selective colleges are also more likely to obtain further education by pursuing graduate degrees (Alexander and Eckland, 1977; Bowen and Bok, 1998; Carnevale and Rose, 2004; Carnevale and Strohl, 2010; Zhang, 2005a).

Emerging research on the consequences of undermatching yields similar conclusions. Students who enroll in a college that is less selective than their academic preparation warrants are less likely to complete an undergraduate degree (Bowen, Chingos, and McPherson, 2009; Carnevale and Strohl, 2010; Nagaoka, Roderick, and Coca, 2009) or pursue a graduate degree (Carnevale and Strohl, 2010).

Research also links attending a more-selective college to greater earnings. Alumni of more-prominent universities earn larger salaries in part because they are more likely to have additional years of education.[7] But even when matched by years of schooling (as well as other characteristics), investigation after investigation indicates that on average, graduates of elite colleges enjoy higher incomes than graduates of less-elite schools (Andrews, Li, and Lovenheim, 2012; Arnold, 2002; Arnold and Youn, 2006; Behrman, Rosenzweig, and Taubman, 1996; Black and Smith, 2006; Bowen and Bok, 1998; Brand and Halaby, 2006; Brewer, Eide, and Ehrenberg, 1999; Carnevale and Strohl, 2010; Daniel, Black, and Smith, 1997; Fitzgerald, 2000; Hershbein, 2011; Long, 2008; Loury and Garman, 1995; Monks, 2000; Solmon, 1975; Thomas and Zhang, 2005; Zhang, 2005b).[8] While there are a few who question some of these studies' methods (Dale and Krueger, 2002, 2011; Gerber and Cheung, 2008), even skeptics find that at the very least, low-SES students earn more when they enroll in more-selective institutions (Dale and Krueger, 2002, 2011).

There is also evidence suggesting that selective college attendance and occupational prestige and power are related (Arnold, 2002; Arnold and Youn, 2006; Smart, 1986). President George H. W. Bush and the three U.S. presidents who have followed hold undergraduate degrees from Yale, Georgetown, Yale, and Columbia, respectively. The current Supreme Court justices' undergraduate alma maters include: Princeton (three), Stanford (two), Harvard (one), Cornell (one), Georgetown (one), and Holy Cross (one). Prestigious colleges are also well represented in the upper echelons of business. The chief executives of General Electric, Goldman Sachs, Wal-Mart, and Google attended Dartmouth, Harvard, Georgia Tech, and the University of Michigan, respectively (Leonhardt, 2011). Top companies often concentrate their recruitment efforts at elite colleges, believing these institutions are more likely to yield them the type of employees that best fit their business needs (Hansen, 2006).

Does College Selectivity Matter for Students Who Are Already Top Performers?

While the overwhelming body of research indicates that selectivity of undergraduate institution attended affects the outcomes of students at large, some might wonder if it influences top students' paths. Does it make any difference in the end that Karen went to a small, regional Christian college and Paul enrolled in a less-selective Big Ten school while Elizabeth matriculated at a most-selective private college? A planned follow-up study of valedictorians' undergraduate attainment, graduate school enrollment, and labor market outcomes will be able to address this question specifically. Until then, however, the evidence currently available suggests that selectivity of undergraduate alma mater on average does shape even our most talented students' trajectories.

To begin, top students' undergraduate attainment differs by institution attended. Bowen and Bok (1998: 380) found that white students entering college in 1989 with SAT scores of 1300 or above were 11 percentage points more likely to graduate if they had enrolled in an institution that fell in the study's top selectivity tier rather than its third selectivity tier. Using another dataset, Carnevale and Strohl (2010: 151) reported that students of all races with similarly high SAT scores were 10 percentage points more likely to graduate if they had attended a university in the study's most competitive tier of institutions rather than the study's third tier of institutions.[9] It is also important to stress that in both analyses there was no evidence that gaps in graduation rates by institutional selectivity were less pronounced for high-performing than for low-performing students. Instead, the percentage point difference in graduation rates by

institutional selectivity tended to be greater among top students, suggesting that selectivity of college attended may have a greater impact on top
students than on students at large.

Accomplished students' graduate school attainment also appears to
differ by undergraduate institution attended. Even if a top student who
attends a less-selective college manages to earn a bachelor's degree, his
or her likelihood of pursuing a graduate degree is lower. Comparing just
students with SAT scores above 1200 reveals that those who attended
undergraduate institutions in the top selectivity tier were 22 percentage
points more likely to enroll in graduate school than those who attended
colleges in the bottom selectivity tier. In fact, the percentage point gap in
graduate school attendance by undergraduate institution selectivity was
larger for students with top scores than for students with more average or
lower scores (Carnevale and Strohl, 2010: 151).

One might wonder if these advantages to attending a selective college hold when top students are identified using measures of achievement
besides SAT score. The logic might be that students who exhibit top performance in the classroom are different from students who do well on
standardized tests. For example, the former may be particularly likely
to boast noncognitive skills like drive, determination, commitment, grit,
and tenacity.

Yet even top students identified using factors other than standardized tests are found to have different career outcomes depending on the
college they attended. A qualitative longitudinal study of Illinois high
school valedictorians who graduated in 1981 found that while all achieved
respectable careers, the most important factor related to the greatest career success was attending a prestigious college (Arnold, 2002). A quantitative analysis of Rhodes scholars who are "chosen not only for their
outstanding scholarly achievements, but for their character, commitment
to others and to the common good, and for their potential for leadership in whatever domains their careers may lead" (Rhodes Trust, 2012)
produced similar conclusions. Rhodes scholars who studied at Harvard,
Yale, or Princeton as undergraduates earned more money, were more
likely to achieve professional prominence, and were more apt to become
public leaders than Rhodes scholars who earned degrees at other undergraduate institutions. These results hold even controlling for Rhodes
scholars' social class origins and SAT scores (Arnold and Youn, 2006).

In sum, studies show the following: less-affluent students are not
well represented at America's top colleges, there are a greater number of

less-affluent students with the ability to enroll who are not matriculating, and similarly well-prepared students vary in their propensity to attend by social class. When confronted with this inequity, we cannot tell ourselves that where students attend college is of no consequence and that top students will excel wherever they go. The research we have thus far suggests that college destinations can and do affect life trajectories.

Why Do Top Students' Enrollment Patterns Differ by Social Class?

Given that where students enroll has been linked to life outcomes, it is critical that we better understand why top students' college destinations continue to differ by social class. Only then can the appropriate steps be taken to address this problem. America's best students should *all* be bound for America's best colleges and universities, regardless of their socioeconomic status. All high achievers should be able to reap the benefits they have earned by virtue of their academic performance. While preparation differences might contribute to stratification by social class for students at large, if there is any group that should be able to overcome its social class origins, it should be our very brightest. The fact that social class stratification occurs even at the highest levels of academic performance demands examination.

- Does it occur because top students of different social class backgrounds simply have different aspirations?
- Does variation in student and family knowledge of college options, college costs, and financial aid explain these enrollment patterns?
- Are certain social class groups simply looking for different college attributes in deciding where to apply and/or matriculate?
- What role does the admissions process play?

This book provides fresh insight on all of these questions using original survey and interview data from a new study, the High School Valedictorian Project (HSVP). This investigation of public high school valedictorians was designed specifically to pinpoint when, how, and why similarly highly accomplished students become funneled toward different college destinations, ultimately producing the enrollment patterns repeatedly observed.

It is worth noting that HSVP data were originally analyzed by gender, race, and social class. Of the three, social class emerged as the most consistent factor shaping students' educational trajectories, even controlling for gender, race, academic preparation, and high school and community variables. This book therefore focuses on the role socioeconomic status plays in students' college destinations. Appendix B discusses how students' social class was assessed and the characteristics of students within each social class category.

The following sections of this chapter briefly describe the HSVP data, HSVP students' high level of ability, the revised framework used in this work to examine college choice, and the analyses presented in the remaining chapters.

High School Valedictorian Project Data

Appendix C explains how the HSVP sample was established and how the quantitative data for the project were assembled. Most quantitative data came from an original web survey of approximately nine hundred public high school[10] valedictorians who graduated between 2003 and 2006 in five states.[11] However, additional data on high school, community, and postsecondary characteristics were collected from various sources and integrated into the survey data as well. Survey questions are provided in appendix D.

Qualitative data were also gathered for the High School Valedictorian Project. Fifty-five in-depth interviews were conducted in person with a subsample of survey participants. Valedictorians interviewed were purposefully chosen to ensure that they came from a diversity of backgrounds and had enrolled in a variety of college destinations. At least ten valedictorians from each state were interviewed. Appendix E contains the questions that guided these interviews.

It should be noted that both the quantitative and qualitative data are based on valedictorians' retrospective accounts. While not ideal, collecting data in this way enabled information to be collected for a large group of students most efficiently and cost effectively.[12] There are several reasons to feel confident about the accounts presented. First, error in retrospective accounts has been found to occur most frequently for repetitive and unimportant events (Smith, 1984). The transition from high school to college is not repeated, nor is it likely to be seen as unimportant, particularly by students who have been highly scholastic. In fact, valedictorians' orientation toward school achievement may make them particularly good at recalling their college choice process. For example, Cole and Gonyea (2008) find that students with high test scores, where the vast majority of HSVP students fall, report their SAT scores with greater accuracy than students with lower test scores. Second, in considering HSVP students' accounts, it is important to keep in mind that valedictorians were not being asked to recall experiences from decades earlier. Rather, all respondents had been high school seniors not more than four years prior.[13] Moreover, interviews suggested that the experience was still fresh in their minds; valedictorians did not have trouble rattling off where they had applied and been admitted, nor did they express difficulty in recalling how they experienced the college choice process. Finally, those interviewed were asked questions sequentially and were allowed to take their time responding, two methods found to improve recall (Pearson, Ross, and Dawes, 1992).

Are HSVP Participants Top Students?

This book seeks to develop a better understanding of why postsecondary stratification by social class occurs even among our best students. To meet this objective, it is important that readers feel confident that the valedictorians in this HSVP sample are indeed highly accomplished.

There are many ways to operationalize top students. One benefit of using valedictorians as a proxy is that these students have had to excel on tests, papers, and projects in multiple classes over several years, reflecting both a broad and long record of achievement. While top students could be identified using standardized test scores, students selected in this manner may not exhibit the same dedication to consistent top performance in a range of subjects.

One possible concern with following valedictorians as a way of examining high achievers is that a student's ability to earn the top spot in the class depends in part on the academic ability of his or her high school classmates. As a consequence, high achievers in more-competitive high schools who are bright—maybe even brighter than valedictorians in other schools—but who do not make it to the top of their own high school class are not included in the HSVP sample. Top students identified using standardized test scores, in contrast, have a chance of being studied regardless of high school context.

This work does not suggest that it examines all top students; it does not even study all valedictorians. Undoubtedly, there are some highly able salutatorians and National Honor Society members whose slip on one calculus final, for example, precluded them from becoming valedictorian and being in the sample. Yet whether this study captures all top students is not important. More relevant is whether the valedictorians in this study can be considered top students (and thus shed light on high achievers' experiences). This section of this chapter addresses the question of valedictorians' academic performance specifically.

In assessing applicants' academic abilities, colleges use several measures, including class rank (shaped by grade point average),[14] curriculum rigor (measured by honors, AP, and International Baccalaureate or IB classes),[15] and standardized test scores[16] (Clinedinst, Hurley, and Hawkins, 2011; Hernández, 1997; Stevens, 2007).[17] By definition, valedictorians have achieved the highest grades in their class, so measured by class rank they are clearly top students.

That addressed, the participation of HSVP students in rigorous curricula is examined. An extremely high percentage, 97 percent, of HSVP students took at least one AP or IB exam during high school.[18] Moreover, this figure likely underestimates the percentage of valedictorians who participated in an AP or IB *course* while in high school because not all students sit for the official, end-of-year exams, which have a fee.[19] Yet even counting only those HSVP students who took the exam, the percentage of HSVP students participating in these rigorous courses is much higher than the 29 percent of seniors nationally who took an AP or IB course (but may or may not have sat for the exam) (Chen, Wu, and Tasoff, 2010a).

It is also important to remember that nationwide, less-affluent students are less likely to have access to college-level courses at their high schools (Clinedinst, Hurley, and Hawkins, 2011; Handwerk et al., 2008). As a result, these students' AP and IB participation results may be less a reflection of valedictorians' personal preparation and ability and more a consequence of the course offerings at their school. Nevertheless, among low-SES HSVP students, the least-affluent group in the sample and the group with the lowest participation rate on this measure, a still incredibly high 93 percent took at least one AP or IB exam.

Yet HSVP students do not just reveal themselves to be top students by enrolling in rigorous high school courses at extremely high rates. They further demonstrate their ability by scoring highly on these exams. A full 93 percent of all HSVP students performed well enough on at least one exam that graders outside of their high school felt they deserved college credit.[20] Even among low-SES valedictorians, who may have attended schools where the level of instruction was lower in order to accommodate the other students enrolled in these courses,[21] 83 percent passed at least one exam at the college level. Both these percentages are far higher than the 13 percent of all public high school graduates in 2004 who passed an AP exam (College Board, 2005a).

And most HSVP students did not pass just one AP or IB exam. More than half (55 percent) passed five or more of these tests and almost one-third (31 percent) passed seven or more.[22] Even among low-SES students who would have been more likely to encounter fewer college-level classes (Handwerk et al., 2008) and perhaps less high-level instruction, about half (45 percent) passed five or more exams. By comparison, only 15 percent of all 2006 first-time, full-time freshmen at four-year colleges (an already more-selective group than high school students in general) had taken five or more AP courses (Pryor et al., 2006), let alone passed that many exams. While direct comparisons are difficult, these national numbers suggest that HSVP students overwhelmingly pursued high school curriculums that placed them at the top part of the distribution of high school students overall.

The opportunity to take the SAT I, unlike AP and IB exams, is less dependent on school offerings. Ninety-nine percent of HSVP students reported taking the SAT I,[23] and 95 percent provided their standardized test scores.[24] The scores achieved were very high. As figure 1.1 demonstrates, 90 percent of HSVP students scored in at least the top fifth of all 2006 college-bound senior test takers, earning a combined verbal and math score of 1220 or above (College Board, 2006c). Moreover, 75 percent earned a score of 1320 or above, placing them in the very top decile of all test takers. Even more impressive, 56 percent had scores of 1400 or above, putting them among the top 5 percent of all test takers. In total, 95 percent of all HSVP students scored in the top three deciles. Even 87 percent of low-SES students, who are thought to be at a disadvantage on the SAT,[25] scored in the top three deciles; more than three-quarters scored in the top two.

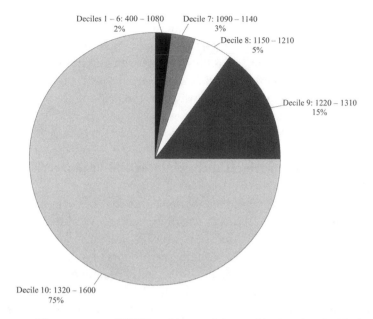

FIGURE I.I. The percentage of HSVP students receiving combined math and critical reading SAT I scores in specific ranges matched to reflect performance deciles among all 2006
college-bound senior SAT takers. *Sources:* High School Valedictorian Project Person Dataset; College Board, 2006b.

HSVP students are clearly top students as measured by their high
grades that ultimately produced their top class rank. Yet they also fare
well compared with students nationally in terms of the rigor of their high
school curriculums and their SAT scores. The vast majority of HSVP students are at the top of the distribution, even on these additional measures.

While some variation among valedictorians may occur on academic
indicators other than class rank, regressions regularly control for SAT or
AP/IB performance to prevent any differences on these measures from
affecting SES conclusions. Moreover, it is important to recognize that
some variation will always occur in samples of high-achieving students,
however defined. Not all top test scorers possess high class ranks and
have pursued rigorous curriculums, but for analysis purposes, scholars
routinely use test scores alone to make inferences about top students.

For the purpose of this analysis, it is not essential that all HSVP
students perform at the very top on all three of these indicators. Their

valedictorian status alone is a good reason to perceive them as top students worthy of consideration for admission to America's best colleges and universities. The fact that HSVP students do well on additional academic performance measures just lends further support for their designation as high achievers and their appropriateness for study in an investigation seeking to understand why top students' college destinations diverge by social class.

The College Destination Process: A Revised Framework

Students' paths to their postsecondary destinations are complex for two main reasons. First, the process usually involves several decision makers: students, parents, and admissions officers. Second, students' ultimate postsecondary institutions are usually the product of multiple decisions. While colleges with no application process may require only the decision to enroll, attending a postsecondary school with an application process requires a minimum of three choices: students have to decide to apply, admissions officers have to determine whom to admit, and students have to choose whether to enroll. These decisions are, of course, multiplied when students apply to more than one institution.

Many scholars have sought to better understand the college choice process. Some have focused on the contextual layers influencing it (Perna, 2006), while others have attempted to outline its steps (Jackson, 1982; Kotler, 1976; Lewis and Morrison, 1975). On the latter, Hossler and Gallagher's (1987) work has been particularly influential in the field. In their schema, there are three phases of college choice: (1) "predisposition," during which students develop attitudes toward attending college; (2) "search," in which students explore college options; and (3) "choice," in which students select the universities to which they will apply and the college in which they will enroll. Researchers have applied this model to explain two different decisions: (1) whether or not to attend college at all, and (2) where specifically to enroll.

While Hossler and Gallagher's (1987) framework is a very useful starting point, this project seeks to analyze not how students decide whether to attend college, but how students come to matriculate at a particular type of college. For examining this latter process specifically, it is helpful to refine Hossler and Gallagher's model somewhat. I call this revised framework the "college destination" process to distinguish it from previous models—referred to as the "college choice" process—and to emphasize that it is designed specifically to explore the type of college students come to attend (their destination) and not their decision to attend college.

The six phases of the college destination process are: (1) predisposition, (2) preparation, (3) exploration, (4) application, (5) admissions, and (6) matriculation. As table 1.1 indicates, the college destination process varies from Hossler and Gallagher's model in that their "choice" phase has been disaggregated into separate application, admissions, and matriculation phases, and the preparation stage has been added as a distinct stage rather than viewed as a factor in the predisposition stage. Figure 1.2 illustrates how the stages in the college destination process interrelate, with solid arrows indicating primary relationships and dashed arrows conveying secondary relationships.

As in Hossler and Gallagher's (1987) schema, "predisposition" in the college destination process refers to students' attitudes toward higher education in general and toward specific types of colleges. Predisposition is placed at the far left of figure 1.2 to indicate that it begins the earliest of all the stages. Predisposition's solid arrow to preparation and dashed arrow to exploration indicate that predisposition primarily influences these two stages. Its overlapping placement with preparation, and to a lesser degree exploration, is designed to help convey that predisposition is still forming while these other stages are developing. The dashed arrows from preparation and exploration to predisposition represent the

TABLE 1.1 **The Relationship between the Stages of the College Destination Process and the Stages in Hossler and Gallagher's (1987) Three-Phase Model of College Choice**

Phases in the College Destination Process	When These Phases Occur in Hossler and Gallagher's (1987) Model of College Choice
Predisposition	Predisposition
Preparation	Predisposition (Explored as student characteristics and educational activities, which are viewed as factors in shaping predisposition toward attendance)
Exploration	Search
Application	Choice (Explored as choice set within the choice phase)
Admissions	Choice (Explored as college and university courtship activities within the choice phase)
Matriculation	Choice

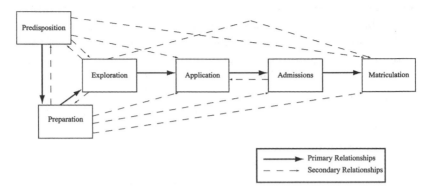

FIGURE 1.2. The college destination process.

fact that preparation and exploration can also influence students' predisposition. For example, students who discover that they are ranked first in their class can begin to form different perceptions of appropriate college destinations. Likewise, in the process of exploring different college options, students may realize that they either do or do not share the scores and characteristics of students at particular colleges, which in turn may shape the types of colleges they envision attending.

"Preparation" is pulled out as a distinct phase rather than a factor in predisposition. It first captures students' high school grades, class rank, and coursework, as well as college entrance examinations and extracurricular activities. Research indicates that differences in overall college enrollment patterns by SES are strongly related to differences in preparation (Berkner and Chavez, 1997). This phase also includes how students approach their preparation, as this too may affect their college destination process. For example, students who go through high school with college admissions very much in mind will typically act differently in the exploration, application, and matriculation stages than similarly high-achieving students who have put less emphasis on college admissions during high school. As the arrows indicate, preparation not only influences where students explore, apply, and enroll, but also where they are admitted.

Note that because this study focuses only on high achievers, quantitative preparation differences are small and already have been discussed in this chapter. Thus, in this work, the preparation analysis will focus on valedictorians' approach to their preparation. In analyses of students at large, however, scholars should analyze both of these important aspects of the preparation phase together.

The "exploration" stage is similar to Hossler and Gallagher's (1987) "search" stage. During this phase, students acquire information about the college admissions process, the financial aid process, and different college options. Exploration mainly shapes application decisions, but preferences developed in this phase can also influence final matriculation choices.

In the next phase, the "application" stage, students decide where to apply. As table 1.1 indicates, Hossler and Gallagher's (1987) model placed both application and matriculation decisions in the same "choice" stage. One reason for separating these decisions into two stages is that research shows students use different criteria in deciding where to apply and where to matriculate (Chapman, 1993: 415, 417; Choy and Ottinger, 1998: 21; Hossler and Foley, 1995).[26] For example, some students may view cost as the most important factor in determining where to apply, but once they are accepted to several schools of similar cost, campus environment may become most important in making the final matriculation decision. The opposite could be true for other students. They may decide where to apply based on a particular campus environment characteristic like size of institution, but then choose where to enroll by comparing the costs of the similarly sized institutions that accept them.

Keeping these stages separate makes it easier to identify the unique factors that influence each one. It also allows for a more sequential framework that can insert admissions as a distinct stage between these two phases. As the solid arrow leaving the application phase suggests, where students apply directly determines where they can be admitted. Yet when students learn of admissions decisions before other applications are due, admissions can affect other application decisions (noted with the dashed arrow). For example, students who apply under early action or early decision programs and learn that they are deferred rather than accepted may opt to apply to more institutions and/or less-competitive institutions before the regular admissions deadline.

The "admissions" phase is the next stage in the college destination process. It reflects universities' decisions to accept or deny students' college applications.[27] This stage is important because students cannot attend schools from which they have been rejected.[28] While the majority of students may not find admissions to be a barrier to enrolling in their first-choice institution,[29] in part because students self-select through their application choices, research indicates that about one-third of recent high school graduates attending four-year public and private colleges as freshmen were not enrolled in their first-choice institution, with half of these students not attending their first-choice institution because they failed to be admitted (Radford and Tasoff, 2009). Pryor et al. (2006) obtained similar percentages analyzing all freshmen (and not just recent high school graduates) attending four-year colleges.

Admissions decisions can even shape top students' matriculation options, especially when these students apply to America's most-selective colleges. In 2012, Harvard, Yale, Columbia, and Princeton accepted less than 8 percent of their applicants (Ellis, 2012). In recent admissions cycles, Harvard even rejected 25 percent of applicants who had a perfect score on the SAT (Menand, 2003) and more than 80 percent of valedictorian applicants (Shea and Marcus, 2001). Because admissions can have a particularly strong impact on the destinations of students aspiring to elite colleges and because this is the one stage in which actors outside of the student and family make the decisions, it is helpful to examine admissions as a distinct stage rather than view it as an organizational factor shaping choice, as Hossler and Gallagher's (1987) model does.

Lastly, in the "matriculation" phase of the college destination process, individuals choose the college they will attend from among those that have accepted them. As noted in the earlier description of the application phase, factors that students consider in deciding where to *enroll* may be different from the factors they considered earlier in the process when deciding where to *apply*. To help aid in analyzing these separate decisions that occur before and after the admissions stage, the college destination process examines the matriculation stage as its own phase rather than considering it as part of a single choice phase, as Hossler and Gallagher (1987) do.

Outline of This Book

This book examines what occurs during each stage of the college destination process in its own chapter, moving chronologically from one stage to the next. Chapter 2 explores the first stage of the college destination process: predisposition. The chapter begins by investigating what prompted the formation of valedictorians' college aspirations as well as pinpointing when these aspirations were first established. It then delves into the messages that valedictorians received from their parents about education in general, higher education, and specific colleges. It also discusses valedictorians' personal educational aspirations and their parents' educational aspirations for them at the start of high school.

Chapter 3 investigates the second stage of the college destination process: preparation. Since this chapter has already demonstrated HSVP students' high levels of preparation from a quantitative standpoint, chapter 3's discussion focuses on students' approach toward high school grades and class rank, curriculum, college entrance exams, and extracurriculars.

The third stage of the college destination process, exploration, is considered in chapter 4. The first two sections focus on the college admissions and financial aid processes. They use qualitative data to examine how valedictorians learn about these processes and quantitative data to investigate valedictorians' and their parents' understanding of these processes. The final section details how high achievers explore their college options based on interview findings. It includes discussions on when valedictorians started looking, the approach they adopted in acquiring information, the entities that influenced their search, and the reasons some failed to consider certain types of postsecondary institutions.

Chapter 5 investigates the fourth phase of the college destination process: application. The number of applications valedictorians submitted, the college characteristics they considered in determining where to apply, the individuals and resources that influenced them in deciding where to apply, and the types of colleges to which they actually applied are detailed.

The sixth chapter reports what occurs during the fifth phase of the college destination process: admissions. Using quantitative data, it first examines the acceptance rate of valedictorians' individual applications. This discussion gives particular attention to the factors related to admission at most-selective private colleges, where chances of admission are lowest. The chapter also reports which types of colleges valedictorians still had the opportunity to attend by the end of the admissions stage.

Chapter 7 explores the final stage of the college destination process: the matriculation phase. More specifically, its first two sections examine the college characteristics considered and the individuals and sources consulted in deciding where to enroll. The final portion of the chapter reveals the types of institutions in which valedictorians enrolled if they were offered admission. In this way, the role of just the matriculation choice in funneling students toward different college destinations is isolated.

Chapter 8 first presents HSVP students' ultimate college destinations. It then traces what occurs during each stage of the college destination process to clearly illuminate how, when, and why these similarly accomplished valedictorians came to attend different types of institutions. The chapter and book end by providing final thoughts about the High School Valedictorian Project's findings and possible policy implications.

CHAPTER TWO

Predisposition

Setting the Course

L ong before the brochures arrive in the mail, applications are submitted, or admissions letters are received, students begin to develop attitudes regarding college in general and specific types of colleges. This time period in which students form their outlook on higher
education is referred to as the predisposition stage of the college destination process.

Broadly, this chapter discusses the key facets of predisposition and highlights differences in students' predispositions by social class. More specifically, it first draws on the High School Valedictorian Project (HSVP)
interview data to describe what initiated valedictorians' development of
college aspirations and then uses HSVP survey data to report when these
aspirations were first established. Since parents typically play the largest
role in shaping students' predispositions (Bordua, 1960; Conklin and
Dailey, 1981; Hossler, Schmit, and Vesper, 1999; MacAllum et al., 2007;
McDill and Coleman, 1965), the next section uses qualitative data to
examine the messages students received from their parents about education, higher education, and specific colleges. The last two portions of this
chapter present HSVP survey results on valedictorians' own educational
aspirations and their perception of their parents' educational aspirations
for them.

The Inspiration behind First Postsecondary Aspirations

The events that first spark valedictorians' formation of postsecondary aspirations vary. The majority of valedictorians interviewed expressed that they always remembered planning to attend college. One student confided that it was "always in the back of my mind that I was going to go." Another felt the same way: "I guess going was always there. It was never something that I thought about."

A smaller number of valedictorians, however, did remember a specific occasion that prompted these aspirations. For some, college-related events caused them to start contemplating enrollment. For example, valedictorians in several states mentioned that they first learned about college through community members' regular discussions of prominent local college rivalries on the football field or basketball court. In other instances, an older sibling's departure for college brought the idea of higher education into the consciousness of these high achievers.[1] Career goals in childhood were also sometimes an impetus for college aspirations. Several valedictorians volunteered that they began aspiring to postsecondary education when they decided that they wanted to be a doctor or nurse and learned that such a career required education beyond high school.

HSVP interviews also uncovered social class dimensions in the development of students' first postsecondary aspirations. Valedictorians with high socioeconomic status (SES) consistently reported college attendance as "always assumed." One high-SES valedictorian born to parents who both had undergraduate and professional degrees from highly selective colleges reported: "I guess it's kind of expected that if you're in my family, you go to college." High-SES students not only expressed college attendance as expected but also as "the natural thing to do."[2]

In contrast, low-SES students seldom heard about college at home. As one such student related, "I never thought about [college] because it never came up in our house." Instead, these less-affluent students were more likely to indicate that their college aspirations began to take shape at school. For example, one low-SES valedictorian first thought about college when she took a College Board test in eighth grade in order to participate in a special academic program. Another less-affluent student recalled that it was not until her high school club took a trip to a nearby college campus, which she found "amazing" and "pretty," that she started to want to attend college.

Because college aspirations were encouraged within high-SES homes, more-affluent students tended to form college aspirations earlier than low-SES students, who generally were not exposed to the idea of college until they entered school.

The Timing of First Postsecondary Aspirations

Research suggests that students' paths to postsecondary education are smoother if they know by middle school that they want to attend college. Having college aspirations in junior high school encourages students to perform well enough in difficult classes to be placed on a college prep curriculum in high school, which in turn helps them meet college admissions requirements (McDonough, 1997). In the case of valedictorians, their high level of academic performance makes it likely that they will be placed on the college track in their schools even if they are not thinking about college or placing a lot of importance on attending. Nevertheless, even top students should be thinking about college to some degree in order to help ensure that they are taking the courses necessary for admission to the types of colleges in which they hope to enroll (McDonough, 1997).[3]

Fortunately for their college prospects, survey data suggest that the majority of HSVP students began thinking about enrolling in higher education at a young age. Consistent with qualitative results, 84 percent of valedictorians reported that they always believed they would pursue postsecondary education. Another 7 percent started thinking they would continue their education beyond high school before completing fifth grade, meaning that 91 percent of HSVP students planned on enrolling in college prior to sixth grade, or middle school. Only about 6 percent of valedictorians first contemplated pursuing postsecondary education in middle school and only 3 percent started thinking about attending in ninth grade or later.

Because having college plans by middle school is important in students' paths to higher education, this study analyzes whether propensity to have college aspirations by this point in time differs by social class. As is true throughout this work, quantitative differences discussed in the text are statistically significant at the .05 level unless otherwise noted.[4] The HSVP survey indicates that the higher a student's social class, the more likely he or she was to possess college aspirations by middle school. About four-fifths (79 percent) of low-SES valedictorians planned to attend some sort of postsecondary institution before sixth grade, compared with nine-tenths of middle-SES and almost all (97 percent) of high-SES valedictorians.

These social class differences hold even controlling for various factors. Logistic regression results shown in appendix F control for gender, race, and other variables thought to shape predisposition, such as academic achievement (Gardner, 1987; Hossler, Schmit, and Vesper, 1999), high school characteristics (Hossler, Schmit, and Vesper, 1999; Perna, 2000), and community attributes (Ainsworth, 2002; Arnold, 1995: 122; Hollinshead, 1952; Sewell and Armer, 1966). In this model, the odds of low-SES valedictorians forming college aspirations before sixth grade were about half those of middle-SES valedictorians (see appendix F, table F.2.1).[5] The odds of high-SES valedictorians doing so were about three times those of middle-SES valedictorians. These descriptive and regression results suggest that the formation of college aspirations by middle school is strongly related to social class.

One might expect these social class differences among students at large, but the fact that even very bright students exhibit such differences is illuminating. Students who do not form postsecondary aspirations until later may find their families less prepared financially, logistically, and emotionally for their enrollment in colleges matching their academic achievement.

The Shaping of Predisposition

Another important part of predisposition is the messages that students receive about higher education. These exchanges help shape a student's outlook or worldview about college attendance.

Parents play a profound role in forming students' predispositions. In fact, parents' education and parents' encouragement have been identified as two of the three most influential factors in shaping students' self-image, preferences, and inclinations (MacAllum et al., 2007). (The third factor is achievement, which is similar among HSVP students.) Hossler, Schmit, and Vesper (1999) also report that parents are the primary actors in the predisposition stage.

The influence parents exert during the predisposition phase has a lasting effect on the college destination process. One study found that

90 percent of students who reported that college attendance was taken for granted in their family attended some type of college, while only 55 percent of students who received mixed or inconsistent messages at home did so (Conklin and Dailey, 1981: 257). And parents shape not just whether students attend college but also the quality and proximity of the institutions students consider (Conklin and Dailey, 1981: 257; Flint, 1992; Hossler, Schmit, and Vesper, 1999).

Parents transmit their views on higher education to their children in different ways. Providing consistent, general "educational support in the home environment" rather than offering "specific instances of encouragement and urging" is thought to help a child internalize the idea of going to college (Conklin and Dailey, 1981: 255). Helping ensure children take the right classes, discussing the cost of college, talking about appropriate distances for college attendance, and disclosing views on the value of a college's prestige and reputation also influence children's outlooks (Smith and Fleming, 2006: 79).

HSVP interviews found that parents' attitudes and behavior regarding education in general, higher education, and specific colleges varied by social class. For example, while some low-SES valedictorians reported that their parents wanted them to attend college, their parents tended not to be as actively involved in turning that hope into reality as were more-affluent parents. One low-SES student was told by her mother to "keep up the good work" and related that her mom figured "of course I would go to college 'cause that was the path I was on," but that college was not really discussed. Repeatedly, low-SES students stated that their families did not mention specific colleges when they were growing up. As one explained, "My parents never really cared about what college I'd go to. They just said, 'If you don't go to college, you're not my son anymore!' [Laughs]." Another low-SES student indicated that she instigated her family's thinking about college options rather than the reverse. When asked if college was a topic of conversation in her family home, she responded:

Not really. [The local community college] . . . was something to aspire to. [The closest large, not most-selective private university] was "it." . . . There really wasn't an emphasis. I wish there were, but it wasn't until I started getting into the whole, "Hey, I'm going to go to college. Hey, I want to do this," that everybody started to take a look, you know?

Low-SES families that did discuss college attendance often did so in ways that narrowed rather than expanded their child's college options. First, low-SES families tended to emphasize costs much more than other families did. One low-SES student reported:

My parents always told me . . . "You're going to go to college," but where do you go to college? "You're just going to go where we can afford to send you." That kind of deal . . . It was always expected I would go to college, but they were thinking maybe [local, not most-selective public college]. Live at home and drive there, take classes—'cause it would be affordable . . . I . . . had to get a scholarship if I wanted to go somewhere else.

A second way low-SES parents reduced students' worldview of college options was by stressing attending near home. One less-affluent student reported that the colleges discussed were "always somewhere close. Out of state wasn't really [an option]. Just somewhere close." Another low-SES student confided, "Well, my mom wanted us to pursue a degree, but nothing specific. If anything, it was like, 'Oh, stay close. Don't move too far.'"[6]

Low-SES valedictorians also generally did not receive strong support for selective college attendance. In fact, the very idea of attending such schools was not taken very seriously by these students or their families. One first-generation college student reported that although she was told by an extended family member with no college experience, "You should go to an Ivy League school. You have the brains," she did not give this suggestion much consideration. Another low-SES female was similarly raised with the sense that highly selective colleges were not for her. She noted that the nationally prominent school near her hometown was the only college ever mentioned by her family, but was done so "kind of as a joke."

In sharp contrast, high-SES parents often encouraged their valedictorian offspring to attend a prestigious university. The son of an alumnus at an Ivy League institution reported that going to an elite college was not just promoted but "expected" in his family. Another high-SES student whose father went to a most-selective public college for graduate school said, "My sister went to [Ivy League college], so that gives you an idea of what the expectations were. But that had always been sort of the aim from a fairly young age."

Even when high-SES parents did not explicitly suggest attending highly selective colleges to their valedictorian children, they instilled the idea of such attendance by regularly mentioning these institutions in casual exchanges. Conversations about colleges help form students' habitus. Applying Bourdieu's (1977) original concept specifically to education, Dumais (2002: 45–46) explains that habitus shapes students' "aspirations and practices" and thus has a profound effect on how "students navigate their way through the educational system." Thus, family banter in which colleges are mentioned helps construct students' worldview about reasonable and appropriate college options.

Oftentimes, high-SES students were introduced to prestigious colleges, and then grew increasingly comfortable with the notion of attending themselves, by hearing the college stories of their parents and social network. One high-SES student whose parents had not enrolled in especially prominent universities knew about a good number of highly selective colleges through her extended family. When asked which colleges were discussed as she was growing up, she said, "mostly high-level universities," and then went on to explain that two of her uncles attended a prominent public university, two other uncles and two paternal grandparents graduated from an elite private university, and her maternal grandfather and grandmother taught at an elite private university and a private liberal arts college, respectively.

Another student had a particularly great number of family connections at a range of prominent schools, which made these institutions feel "familiar" to her long before it was time for her to start seriously exploring college options:

> Well, [most-selective private university] was obviously a big part of family discussions. Both my parents are employees of th[at] university, so—that was big. My dad did his postdoctorate at [Ivy League university] so I, we, lived in [that college's town] 'til I was five. . . . [Most-selective private liberal arts college] and [another most-selective private liberal arts college] my mom had applied to, and [my parents] both had worked at [flagship public university]. They were all very familiar places.

Since these high-SES valedictorians knew people who had attended most-selective colleges, enrolling in them did not seem outside the range of reasonable possibilities. In fact, as Mullen (2010) suggests through her research with Yale students, high-SES families create a "taste" for prestigious institution attendance in their children at an early age. Similarly gifted students whose families had no connection to these colleges, or no college experience at all, did not develop the same appetite for these schools.

HSVP Parents' Aspirations

Since students' predispositions are shaped largely at home and by parents, the HSVP survey asked valedictorians to report the aspirations their parents had for them when they (HSVP students) were entering high school.[7] Overall, results reveal that the aspirations parents had for their HSVP child tended to be high. Table 2.1 reveals that roughly four-fifths of valedictorians felt their parents viewed their college attendance as very important, two-thirds sensed that their parents perceived their enrollment in a four-year college to be very important, and one-fifth believed their parents saw their matriculation at a prestigious college as very important. Mothers tended to be a few percentage points more likely than fathers to indicate strong expectations of college and four-year college attendance to their children, but mothers and fathers conveyed prestigious college attendance as very important at similar rates.

Differences by social class were highly significant and yielded at least four interesting results. The first important pattern to note is that the percentage of HSVP students reporting that their mothers and fathers felt it very important that they attend college, a four-year college, or a prestigious college increases with social class in all cases but one: while high-SES mothers were still the most likely to view prestigious college attendance as important, middle-SES mothers were slightly less likely than low-SES mothers to share this opinion.

The second noteworthy finding is the relatively small percentage of low- and middle-SES parents of future valedictorians who indicated to their children that attending a four-year college was very important. Just 41 percent of low-SES fathers, 53 percent of low-SES mothers, and slightly less than two-thirds of both middle-SES mothers and fathers advocated this position. In contrast, about four-fifths of high-SES parents expressed these expectations. It should be noted that the survey question did not suggest that students' attendance at a four-year institution should occur immediately, but just that such attendance was very important at some point. Since four-year college attendance is usually necessary to obtain a bachelor's degree, these low percentages for such an able group of students are somewhat surprising.

TABLE 2.1 **The Percentage of HSVP Students Who Reported That Their Attending College, a Four-Year College, or a Prestigious College Was Very Important to Their Fathers, Mothers, or Themselves, by Social Class (N = 896)**

Characteristics	College (%)			Four-Year College (%)			Prestigious College (%)		
	Father	Mother	Student	Father	Mother	Student	Father	Mother	Student
Total	80.5	84.9	90.7	65.2	67.0	84.6	20.5	20.4	39.6
Social Class									
Low SES	57.5	73.8	85.1	41.1	53.2	75.2	13.5	16.3	35.5
Middle SES	79.7	83.1	90.1	60.7	61.7	83.3	14.3	14.1	31.0
High SES	90.0	91.1	93.5	79.0	77.6	89.5	29.7	28.6	50.1

Note: Results are based on HSVP students' response to the question: "Thinking back to when you entered high school, to what extent was it important to [your father, your mother, you] . . . that you attend [college, a four-year college, a prestigious college]?" HSVP students rated their parents and themselves on a scale of 1 to 5 and also were given a not applicable option. A rating of 1 represented not at all, 3 represented somewhat, and 5 represented very much. A given type of attendance was categorized as very important only if it was given a 5 on this scale. For both fathers and mothers, differences by social class are statistically significant at the .001 level for all three types of college attendance. Students differed by social class on college attendance in general at the .05 level and on four-year college and prestigious college attendance at the .001 level.

Source: High School Valedictorian Project Person Dataset.

The third aspect of these SES results worth highlighting is the difference in the viewpoints of low-SES fathers and mothers. Low-SES mothers were 16 percentage points more likely than low-SES fathers to convey college attendance as very important and 12 percentage points more likely than low-SES fathers to emphasize four-year college attendance.[8] In contrast, the difference between mother and father pairs in the middle- and high-SES categories was 3 percentage points or fewer. Thus, these more-affluent students were benefiting from more consistent messages at home, which Conklin and Dailey (1981) found was related to subsequent college decisions.

The final discovery by social class to underscore is that high-SES parents were about twice as likely as both middle- and low-SES parents to view prestigious college attendance as important. Almost 30 percent of high-SES parents conveyed this sentiment to their children compared with 16 percent or less of low- and middle-SES parents.

Logistic regressions controlling for gender, race, foreign-born parent status, selectivity of parents' postsecondary institution(s), college admissions tests, and high school and community characteristics were conducted to better understand social class differences in parents' attitudes.[9] Results revealed that while low- and middle-SES mothers did not significantly differ on any of the three college attendance measures, low-SES fathers had lower odds than middle-SES fathers of viewing college attendance in general and attendance at a four-year college in particular as very important (see appendix F, table F.2.2). Specifically, low-SES fathers' odds were 65 percent and 58 percent lower, respectively. These results are consistent with descriptive results that indicated the gaps between low- and middle-SES mothers on these two measures were smaller than the gaps between the fathers of these two SES groups.

Regression analysis also uncovered differences between middle- and high-SES parents, particularly on prestigious college attendance. High-SES fathers differed from middle-SES fathers on every outcome measure. Specifically, high-SES fathers had 78 percent greater odds of viewing college attendance as very important, 90 percent greater odds of perceiving four-year college attendance to be very important, and 134 percent greater odds of seeing prestigious college attendance as very important. High-SES mothers did not significantly differ from middle-SES mothers in the importance they attached to college in general. Nevertheless, high-SES mothers did have 55 percent and 128 percent greater odds than middle-SES mothers of indicating that attending a four-year college or most prestigious college was very important, respectively.

These large SES differences in parents' aspirations for similarly able top students are striking.

HSVP Students' Aspirations

Turning to valedictorians' educational aspirations, table 2.1 reveals that the vast majority of HSVP students had strong college aspirations. Specifically, 91 percent of valedictorians believed attending college in general to be very important, and an only slightly lower percentage (85 percent) viewed attending specifically a four-year college as very important. Far fewer HSVP students felt that attending a prestigious college was very important (40 percent). That being said, 87 percent of HSVP students regarded matriculating at a prestigious school as at least *somewhat* important.[10]

Students' aspirations did differ by social class. Like their parents, a higher percentage of high-SES than middle- or low-SES students viewed college, four-year college, and prestigious college attendance as very important. The gaps between high- and low-SES valedictorians were 7 percentage points on the college measure and 14 percentage points on the four-year college measure. In both cases, middle-SES students fell roughly in between these two other SES groups. On prestigious college attendance, the pattern differed in the same way it did for valedictorians' mothers. At 50 percent, high-SES students stood apart as most likely to indicate this as very important, but then low-SES students were slightly more likely than middle-SES students to agree, at 36 and 31 percent, respectively.

While descriptive differences by SES were statistically significant, once controls for gender, race, college admissions tests, foreign-born parent status, selectivity of parents' alma maters, and high school and community characteristics were incorporated into logistic regressions, most of these differences faded (see appendix F, table F.2.3). Specifically, valedictorians no longer differed by social class in their desire to attend college or a four-year college. Low-SES students' slightly greater propensity to identify prestigious college attendance as very important was no longer significant as well. But controls did not eliminate the most striking difference between students by SES. High-SES students still exhibited 75 percent greater odds than middle-SES students of viewing prestigious college attendance as very important.

Comparing HSVP students' aspirations with the aspirations held by their parents is also useful and yields two important conclusions. First, students were more likely to have strong college aspirations. Examining the total row in table 2.1, valedictorians were about 5 to 10 percentage points more likely than parents to view college attendance as very important and roughly 20 percentage points more likely than parents to view four-year college and prestigious college attendance as very important.

Second, differences by SES were more pronounced among parents than among valedictorians. On college and four-year college attendance measures, students' SES gap was 9 to 24 percentage points smaller than the respective SES gaps of the fathers and mothers. The only percentage point gap by SES that was larger between students than between either fathers or mothers was prestigious college attendance, and the relative size of this gap, measured by percentage difference instead of percentage point difference, was smaller for students than for parents.

These results can be viewed as positive—top students' achievement may cause social class to affect them less than it does their parents. Yet while social class differences were less pronounced for students than for parents, high-SES students still differed from their peers in their greater likelihood of aspiring to attend a prestigious college. This finding must be kept in mind as we proceed through the subsequent stages of the college destination process.

Conclusion

This chapter revealed how students of similar high ability form very different college predispositions depending on their family background. Though the initial inspiration behind valedictorians' college plans may have differed, the vast majority (93 percent) of these top students decided to pursue postsecondary education before they reached middle school. That being said, high-SES students were more likely than middle- and low-SES students to do so.

Qualitative results suggest that most HSVP students had always planned on attending college and had trouble remembering a time in which they did not intend to enroll. Others started to think about college when they began hearing about college sports, had a sibling matriculate, or developed career aspirations that required a college degree. Less-affluent valedictorians were more likely to have events outside of the home initiate their interest in college, while more-affluent valedictorians were introduced to the idea of attending college within the home.

This chapter also discussed how parents influence the predispositions students develop. Generally, parents' aspirations for their valedictorian children were high, but valedictorians' aspirations for themselves were even higher. Both the quantitative and qualitative results suggested that high-SES parents were more likely than their less-affluent peers to discuss college and encourage selective college attendance. Low-SES parents, in contrast, talked about postsecondary education less often. When they did mention college, they typically focused on cost and distance from home, which tended to curtail rather than broaden their children's worldviews of appropriate college destinations.

The final chapter of this book presents policy suggestions that may be able to change some of these differences by social class. Explaining need-based financial aid, net college costs, and differences in college quality to less-affluent parents early in their children's lives may change the messages these parents impart, and thus alter their children's views about potential college options.

CHAPTER THREE

Preparation

Paving the Way

While students' predispositions are important in shaping college destinations, their preparation for college admissions is also critical. Preparation first determines a student's ability to attend college at all. As Cabrera and La Nasa (2001: 119) highlight, a middle school student's "likelihood of continuing on to college or university rests on the completion of at least three critical tasks," two of which are preparation related: "acquiring at least minimal college qualification" and "actually graduating from high school."[1]

Second, preparation affects where students can enroll. Although the majority of American colleges accept 80 percent or more of their applicant pool (Menand, 2003) and the average acceptance rate at four-year colleges nationwide is about 66 percent (Clinedinst, Hurley, and Hawkins, 2011), most four-year public and private nonprofit institutions still have some academic requirements that applicants must meet in order to gain entry. If students have not taken the appropriate coursework or the necessary tests, they may not be allowed to enroll at four-year state universities (Berkner and Chavez, 1997; McDonough, 1997).[2] And even though private universities may not require applicants to take a specific high school curriculum, students must still prove through their high school courses and standardized test scores that they are academically prepared for college-level work (Hernández, 1997).

Demonstrating the preparation necessary to gain admission to America's most-selective colleges is even more difficult given the abundance of high-achieving applicants. For example, in 2009, more than 2,900 students with perfect verbal SAT scores, 3,500 students with perfect math SAT scores, and nearly 3,700 valedictorians applied for one of Harvard's 1,655 freshman class seats (Jan, 2009). If students want to have a chance of admission at an elite institution, they must ensure that not just their academic preparation but also their extracurricular preparation stands out among a sea of qualified applicants (Espenshade, Hale, and Chung, 2005; Espenshade and Radford, 2009; Hernández, 1997; Soares, 2007).

Third, preparation helps explain socioeconomic differences in enrollment patterns. Students with low socioeconomic status (SES) are particularly apt to have limited college options due to deficits in their high school academic preparation (Berkner and Chavez, 1997; Cabrera and La Nasa, 2001; Kahlenberg, 2006). In contrast, high-SES students' secondary school coursework and test scores tend to facilitate their admission to college in general and to highly selective four-year institutions (College Board, 2005a, 2006a; Espenshade and Radford, 2009; Mullen, 2010).

While preparation differences by SES are critical in understanding social class differences in the college destinations of students at large, variation in academic performance is less of a factor in the High School Valedictorian Project (HSVP) students' destinations. As addressed in the introduction, HSVP students are similarly well prepared on metrics like class rank, curriculum rigor, and SAT score. As high achievers, they are well equipped and positioned to attend even the most competitive colleges.

Therefore, this chapter focuses not on actual performance measures but on the other key dimension of preparation: students' *approach* to preparing for the college admissions stage of the college destination process. Specifically, this chapter uses interview data to investigate how HSVP students reached the top of their class, their reasons for pursuing rigorous coursework, their attitudes toward standardized tests, and their thinking about extracurriculars. These results will shed light on the extent to which HSVP students' expectations of certain college destinations drive their high school behavior, which in turn may make these students more committed to fulfilling their aspirations, even in the face of obstacles.

High School Grades and Class Rank

HSVP students explained their excellent high school grades in different ways. The majority indicated that becoming valedictorian, or at least receiving high grades, was something they purposefully set out to accomplish.[3] Some framed their valedictorian status as something that was expected, though they too may have sought it and expended effort to attain it. A smaller group described receiving the honor of being first in their class as something that "just kind of happened." The following discussion details these different perceptions and how social class relates to each.

Valedictorian status: purposefully sought

Those who specifically sought high grades or valedictorian status expressed several motivations. One was the positive response they received from others and felt themselves when they earned good grades. For example, one valedictorian reported: "It was always, just, I loved doing well. They [my parents] didn't push me or anything. It was just like I had to do well for myself. And it was exciting . . . when I would do well—what my classmates would say, what my grandma and grandpa would say." For others, the emotional perks were more personal. "I like achieving . . . [It] feel[s] good when you get that report card with good grades." Others talked about the sense of "personal honor" or "personal accomplishment" that comes with valedictorian status.

A second motivation that HSVP students gave for becoming valedictorian or a top student was having future opportunities. That being said, the future opportunities desired differed by social class. Students from low- and middle-SES backgrounds often sought high grades in the hopes of earning scholarships and reducing the financial burden of college attendance. A low-SES student who had little family savings for college and did not want to take on debt confided: "So it was always, 'If I'm valedictorian, I'll get more money, I'll get more scholarships, I'll be able to afford to go to college.' That was a big motivation." A middle-SES student similarly indicated that in seeking good grades, he "was trying to see what kind of universities I could get into paying the least amount of money 'cause I was trying to get rid of the burden for my parents."

In contrast, when high-SES students indicated that they sought good grades in order to have future opportunities, the first opportunity they had in mind was admission to prestigious colleges—not scholarships.[4] For example, a high-SES student reported: "I believed that in order to get into a good college you had to be the best at everything, and really have an immaculate record, so that's what I set out to do." Another high-SES valedictorian cited college admission as her primary motivator as well: "I knew that I needed to get the best grades I could possibly get in order to go on to the top [colleges]."

In the eyes of some high-SES students, good grades would not just lead to better college opportunities but to a better future. A high-SES valedictorian explained that he was driven academically by the fact that he "wanted to go to a good school [and] . . . wanted to have nice opportunities later in life." Another high-SES valedictorian suggested that attending a prestigious college was important because "the better college you go to, in theory, the better grad[uate] school you get into, which in theory leads to the better job you get, which in theory [*laughs*], you know." Thus, good grades were viewed as not just producing the short-term benefit of prestigious college admission, but also the long-term benefit of better life opportunities.[5]

Finally, a much smaller group of students so desired a high class rank that they manipulated the system to attain it. The three students who admitted to doing this in their interviews were all from high-SES families, aspired to attend a prestigious college during at least part of high school, and had high-achieving older siblings who could counsel them on how to obtain valedictorian status under their high school's valedictorian selection process.[6] Two of these students learned to take extra Advanced Placement (AP) courses offered online outside of their high school to boost their high school GPAs. Another student helped his GPA not by signing up for a greater number of challenging academic courses but by manipulating the timing of his course taking. He explained that taking gym during the regular school year could lower a student's GPA because the highest grade possible was a 4.0, while a student could earn a 5.0 or 6.0 in other courses. This valedictorian thus took gym in the summer, when grades did not count toward GPA and therefore could not lower his average. Several other HSVP students volunteered that classmates had attempted to earn high class ranks by similar means unlikely to be viewed as in the spirit of learning.

Overall, students who sought valedictorian status indicated that this was something they personally wanted and liked attaining. Many were quick to highlight that their parents did not push them into becoming valedictorians. The way valedictorians raised this point seemed to suggest they felt that others assumed their parents held their head to a book each night. While students have some power or agency in their decision to seek valedictorian status, they might not be cognizant of the ways in which parents or others have influenced their pursuit of this title. In particular, high-SES students who were motivated to earn top grades because they held elite college aspirations tended to form those aspirations with the encouragement of—or even at the instigation of—their parents. Thus, high-SES parents did not have to push their children directly to get good grades. Instead, they instilled in their children a desire to attend colleges that required good grades and then that aspiration motivated their child for them.[7] That being said, there are plenty of high-SES parents who promote prestigious college attendance to their children and yet their children do not strive to reach the top spot in their high school class. In sum, while many valedictorians take it upon themselves to become top students, their parents (as well as their peers, teachers, and community) may still have influenced their decision to pursue this goal.

Valedictorian status: expected

A second way in which valedictorians explained the high grades they achieved was that these grades were expected. As one valedictorian put it: "All my life . . . it had either been expected of me or I'd expected it of myself not to get anything less than that." The source of these expectations, however, differed by SES.

For high-SES valedictorians, expectations usually originated in the family.[8] In many cases, these students had a parent and/or an older sibling who had achieved valedictorian or salutatorian status. One student with an older sibling who had been valedictorian characterized the experience this way: "There was pressure and also sort of an expectation [to be valedictorian], and at the same time there was this nice feeling of having another valedictorian in the family." Another HSVP student similarly felt pressure to be valedictorian since her older sister had achieved this status. She explained: "We even went to the same school and everything, so it follows logically that [I] should be able to pull it off. Luckily, I could."

In contrast, middle- and low-SES students suggested that their valedictorian expectations arose from their own personal high achievement in earlier grades. Several students noted that they had been at the top of their class in middle school and felt they should achieve that status again. For example, one recalled setting her sights on becoming valedictorian in sixth grade when she received awards for all the subjects that year. Awards in earlier grades also motivated valedictorians in other ways. One reported that she felt "gypped" when she was not named the junior high valedictorian and worked hard to make sure that history did not repeat itself in high school.

An even larger number of HSVP students started to seek the valedictorian prize after early high school successes. One middle-SES student remembered

> getting this report card [in the first semester of high school] and it said I was ranked number one. . . . And [my family] was like, "Oh my gosh! . . . That's really neat." That's cool—I can say for one semester I was ranked number one. And then I just, year after year, I just kept on doing my best and I guess I got the grades for it, so maybe sometime after sophomore year, I think I realized, "Hey, I'm still number one. Maybe I'll be valedictorian."

Other middle- and low-SES students similarly learned they were capable of getting top grades and then sought to keep their high class rank. A low-SES female claimed: "I didn't set out to do it . . . and then junior year I was the valedictorian and I decided I should probably try to keep it." Likewise, a middle-SES student said: "I didn't shoot right from the beginning, but it kind of just happened that way. And once I was there I didn't really want—once I got grades good enough to be up at the top, I didn't really want to let go."

When thinking about this group, it is important to highlight the influence of schools. Some of these valedictorians may not have been as motivated toward high achievement (or may have been motivated by other factors) if they had attended more-competitive schools where their academic accomplishments did not stand out as much.

Valedictorian status: minimized accomplishment

A final group of HSVP students, around 10 percent of those interviewed, minimized the achievement of becoming valedictorian. These students did not actively seek to be valedictorian nor did they indicate that it was expected of them. They plugged along and described their being valedictorian as something that "just kind of happened." For example, one student said: "It wasn't something I set out to do. I just really liked school and I just did really well in it. So I just kind of did my thing and . . . they just told me I was going to be valedictorian." Some were particularly nonchalant about making it to the top of their class. "I could do it, so I did," one stated simply. "I wanted to get an A in every class, and I knew how to do it, so I would just do it," revealed another, without the slightest hint that it had been an arduous climb to the top.

High school characteristics and policies rather than SES seemed to most determine which valedictorians fell into this category. For example, some in this group indicated that becoming valedictorian was not that difficult because their classmates did not provide much competition. Here again is evidence of how the schools that valedictorians attend influence the way they see themselves and their achievement. For example, one student from a rural community reported:

> The school that I went to is not the best of the best . . . I think that any one of the people that I know [at not most-selective private university] could have done what I did . . . I don't feel like it was that hard. . . . It wouldn't have been that difficult for a reasonably intelligent person to stay on top of that class.

The other segment of HSVP students who minimized the achievement of becoming valedictorian did not discount their classmates' abilities, but instead the process by which valedictorian status was determined at their high school. In interviews, some HSVP students confided that at their school, all students who received A's in all of their classes were given the title of valedictorian. Other HSVP students explained that at their school, everyone who graduated with a GPA of 4.0 or above received the honor. Schools that adopted these looser policies tended to produce multiple valedictorians, and these valedictorians were often less proud of their title than valedictorians who attended schools with only one valedictorian.

To conclude this section, this investigation uncovered two important differences by social class that may impact later stages of the college destination process. First, students' motivations differed. High-SES students more frequently reported pursuing high grades with elite college admissions in mind. Less-affluent students purposefully seeking top grades were more apt to be thinking of the scholarships they could receive. It stands to reason that these differing motivations will influence not only the colleges these valedictorians explore but also where they apply and enroll.

Second, family expectations about their child's performance differed. High-SES students often had a family member with a record of academic accomplishment, making high achievement more of a family norm. In contrast, in less-affluent families, HSVP students' achievement often came as more of a surprise, with students and parents sometimes not recognizing the HSVP student's particularly strong talents until the last few years of high school. This difference affects families' abilities to prepare for their child's path after high school. High-SES parents' more frequent expectation that their child would be bright with the ability to attend a top college facilitated early emotional, logistical, and financial planning. Less-affluent families in which HSVP students' high achievement was more unexpected had less time to develop post–high school plans that reflected their child's potential. This finding suggests that when a child demonstrates great promise, it is important for schools to alert families early and not assume that families recognize the child's capabilities and know the steps worth considering accordingly.[9]

High School Curriculum

In preparing for college admission, grades and class rank are not all that matters. The difficulty of students' courseloads also shapes admissions prospects (Stevens, 2007: 191–194). Admissions officers want students to take full advantage of their secondary schools. Applicants to more-selective colleges are especially expected to enroll and perform well in the most-challenging courses available (Hernández, 1997). Chapter 1 already established that HSVP students pursued (and succeeded at) very challenging curriculums as measured by AP and/or IB exam participation and passage rates. This section therefore focuses on how and why students came to enroll in these challenging classes.

Many valedictorians indicated that they prepared for college during the school year by enrolling in honors, AP, and/or IB courses at their high school, or by taking classes at community and four-year colleges that had enrollment agreements with their high school. The majority of valedictorians took these more challenging classes without college admissions particularly in mind. For example, one student stated that taking AP and honors courses "wasn't a question whether I should do it or not because if I can do it then I should do it. And it was fun!" Another student explained that he took as many AP and honors classes as possible just to be in an environment where he could learn something and "get away from the other nonsense that was going on in school." In regular courses, this student reported, "nobody was learning anything and nobody was teaching anything." Other students explained that they took dual-enrollment courses in an effort to be challenged rather than bored.

While most valedictorians did not suggest that they took these more difficult classes to improve their chances of college admission, some— particularly those with a strong desire to attend a prestigious college— confessed that potential college acceptance letters did motivate them. For instance, when asked if there was anything she did to prepare for college admission, one high-SES valedictorian immediately responded: "I was always very conscious of what classes I was taking—so obviously, honors and AP classes." Similarly, a middle-class high achiever with as- pirations of elite college attendance quit the sport she enjoyed and had played during her first three years of high school in order to enroll in seven AP courses her senior year. Just to put that number into perspec- tive, in 2007 only 0.1 percent of all AP test takers nationally took seven or more exams in one year (College Board, 2007c). This student participated in all of these college-level classes not so much for the college credit she could receive or the academic challenge, but instead to be able to pro- claim to admissions officers: "Look at all the AP classes I've taken!"

To further prove their academic prowess to admissions officers, some students looked beyond their high school's offerings and programs. One young man took two AP courses online at the same time that he was pur- suing his IB Diploma at his high school.[10] As a result, he felt he "didn't have a life," particularly an "active social life," during high school.

HSVP students also pursued college-level courses during the summer. Some took these classes at high schools or local community colleges. This group tended to do so at their parents' urging, for their own interest, or to make up high school courses they were unable to take because they participated in extracurricular activities like the yearbook or student newspaper. Another group of valedictorians, however, attended summer programs at elite universities. The courses offered in these programs tended to be more specialized than those found at high schools and com- munity colleges: robotics instead of science, logic instead of math, and so on. Valedictorians tended to view summer programs offered at elite universities as fun and interesting and did not report enrolling for col- lege admissions purposes.

While HSVP students may have professed academic interest as their motive for enrolling in elite universities' summer programs, college admissions professionals suggest that such programs provide an admis- sions boost (Cohen, 2002; Hernández, 1997). For this reason, students' participation in these classes is worth discussing further. First, partici- pating in these programs helps applicants because admissions officers view enrolling as revealing intellectual curiosity. Second, applicants who attend prove to admissions committees that they are able to perform in a selective college course and not just their high school courses. Students who apply to the college that held their summer program can reap additional benefits as well. Institutions—particularly smaller ones with fewer spots in their freshman class—consider applicants' perceived interest in enrolling when deciding whom to admit, and spending time on campus is viewed as evidence of desire to attend (Cohen, 2002; Hernández, 1997; Mayher, 1998; Stevens, 2007: 90–91; Toor, 2001).

The alleged admissions advantage coupled with the high cost of these summer programs have caused some to question whether such programs give more-affluent students an unfair admissions advantage. Around the time HSVP students were in high school, students living on campus paid $4,792 for one four-week session at Columbia. Brown's seven-week, two-course program cost $6,775, including tuition, room and board, and other fees (Boas, 2002). Though summer programs like Upward Bound and Talent Search are available for potential first-generation college students and students from lower-income families, critics still worry that middle-class students may be excluded because they are unable to afford the cost of summer programs themselves, but also are unable to qualify for subsidized programs. Indeed, Espenshade and Radford (2009) find that middle-class applicants to elite colleges participated in college-sponsored academic programs at a lower rate than both higher- and lower-SES applicants.

A slightly different pattern emerged in the much smaller HSVP interviewee sample.[11] High- and middle-SES students were most likely to enroll, but the factor that seemed most relevant to who participated was proximity to elite institutions rather than social class. Valedictorians most often heard of these college programs through their teachers, and it seemed that teachers and families who lived closer to prestigious colleges were more familiar with these universities and their programmatic offerings. Another reason why proximity facilitated participation was that local valedictorians could often participate in these programs while commuting. Not having to incur the cost of room and board likely made enrolling a bit more financially manageable.

In sum, this qualitative analysis suggests that the majority of valedictorians took the most challenging courses available in their high school without thinking of college. For these students, their performance naturally placed them in the toughest courses their school offered and they did not question taking these courses. Nevertheless, students with strong elite college ambitions (who tended to be more affluent), were much more mindful of the classes they took, and some even enrolled in courses outside of their high school in order to further stand out to college admissions officers. This pattern was also observed in the previous section of this chapter, which found that having elite college aspirations was related to more purposefully seeking a high class rank and GPA. Finally, even though experts suggest that attending a summer program at an elite college provides an admissions advantage, no HSVP students—including those with prestigious college aspirations—reported participating for this reason or even acknowledged that they knew such a benefit existed. Valedictorians instead professed enrolling because they thought these programs would be interesting.

Standardized Tests

Former admissions officers at most-selective colleges indicate that standardized tests carry substantial weight in determining whom to accept. Hernández (1997) suggests that SAT I scores represent one-third of an Ivy League applicant's academic rating and average SAT II scores count for another one-third. Stevens (2007: 191–194) describes another scoring system at a small, elite, private liberal arts college. At this institution, students can earn up to nine points based on their academic and other accomplishments. Three points are based on SAT performance.

The fact that standardized tests play such a large role in admissions has many worried, particularly because socioeconomic status and test scores are linked (Chaplin and Hannaway, 1998; College Board, 2006d; Rothstein, 2004). More-affluent students may have an advantage because they share the culture of test writers and thus may be more likely to interpret the meaning of certain words used in test questions in the same way (Freedle, 2003). They may also score better because there is more verbal interaction in their homes (Lareau, 2003) and their parents are more likely to place them in stronger schools (Espenshade and Radford, 2009). Of greatest concern to several journalists and admissions officers, however, is that higher-SES students are better able to pay for private college admissions test preparation, which may allow them to improve their chances of admission at the expense of less-affluent students who cannot afford the high prices of these courses.[12]

It is true that private companies' courses can be costly. When HSVP students were in high school, Kaplan and Princeton Review charged close to $1,000 for thirty-five hours of class instruction (Chaker, 2005). Nevertheless, in order for high-SES students to have an advantage, private test preparation has to offer a sizable benefit not possible through other, more affordable forms of test preparation like practicing with books or computer software or receiving less-expensive instruction from high school teachers. Contrary to popular opinion, the research shows that test preparation courses taught by private companies are "hardly (if at all) more effective in improving SAT scores" than test preparation courses generally (Powers, 1993: 23). Moreover, any benefit private classes do provide is very small (Briggs, 2001, 2004, 2009). According to one analysis, scores typically only increase between 3 and 20 points on the verbal section and between 10 and 28 points on the math section (Briggs, 2004)—nowhere near the 100-point increases regularly promised in private companies' advertisements. Thus, even if some studies show that more-affluent students are more likely to take a test-preparation class through a private company (Buchmann, Condron, and Roscigno, 2010; Espenshade and Radford, 2009), the research suggests it is unlikely to provide a sizable admissions advantage.

HSVP students' participation in test preparation was only investigated in interviews, and in this fifty-five-person sample, SES differences in private test preparation enrollment were not evident.[13] In fact, valedictorians most commonly did not take a test-prep course but studied for the SAT on their own.[14] Valedictorians who studied independently for college entrance exams bought or borrowed test-prep books, took practice tests, completed prep work online or via computer software, and/or studied vocabulary. Some did it because they felt they could not afford a test-prep course, while others simply did not like the idea of paying for test prep. No particular SES group stood out as being more or less likely to use this self-directed approach to test preparation.

A much smaller set of valedictorians reported that they did not prepare for entrance exams either in a class or on their own. Students in this category did not come from a particular social class background, but they shared other characteristics. All had already taken the Preliminary SAT (PSAT) or the SAT for admission to a special academic program and so they had an idea of how they would perform. They also were confident in their test-taking abilities and/or did not aspire to attend a most-selective college. As one young man who exhibited all three of these characteristics put it:

> You know, I saw those other things out there like SAT preparation and all that stuff, and I guess that what I felt about it was as far as the SAT and tests like that go, you try your best. And the test, they're testing your scholastic ability and that's something you develop over years, you know? It's not so much the math and the writing skills as it is almost test skills really. So yeah, I just felt like, you've either got it at this point or you don't. And so again, I'll just do what I can and whatever happens, happens.

The next group of valedictorians took a test-prep class, but it was either heavily subsidized or free. Despite the lower cost of these courses, students of all SES backgrounds took advantage of them. These courses tended to be offered either through HSVP students' high schools or through academic-enrichment programs. Usually, high school teachers taught these classes, but students in special programs or in high schools that had a significant proportion of poor and/or minority students sometimes received instruction from private companies for free or at a subsidized rate.

Finally, there were HSVP students who paid full price for test preparation, though their actual costs varied depending on the length of their course. Yet again, no SES differences stood out. Two middle-SES and one high-SES valedictorian paid for a couple of days of prep and a low-, middle-, and high-SES student each signed up for courses longer in length. Despite the lack of social class variation, the students taking the lengthier prep course were all interested in attending highly selective colleges. Thus, HSVP data again indicate that students with elite college aspirations tend to approach their preparation differently than others, revealing themselves to be particularly dedicated to making themselves as competitive as possible for admission.

Nevertheless, the ultimate conclusion is that few valedictorians pay for private test preparation, those who do are not from a particular social class background, and their purchasing of this private test preparation is unlikely to provide much of an advantage regardless. Any ultimate enrollment differences in the HSVP sample cannot be fairly blamed on private test preparation.

Extracurriculars

While extracurricular preparation is not critical for admission to all post-secondary institutions, it is important to receiving an acceptance letter at America's most elite colleges. As Soares (2007: 175, 180, 194) explains, as the number of academically qualified applicants at America's more-selective colleges has grown, extracurricular involvement and perceived leadership potential have become increasingly critical in gaining admission. Extracurricular expectations are high. According to a former Dartmouth admissions officer, being the "captain of a team or two, concert mistress of an orchestra, [or] president of the senior class" places an applicant only in the middle of the elite college applicant pool. It takes "swimming at the Olympics, playing the violin at Carnegie Hall" to persuade elite college admissions officers to accept students on the strength of extracurriculars alone (Hernández, 1997: 116). It is therefore important to know how valedictorians approach extracurriculars in order to determine whether the extent of their awareness about the value of extracurricular participation contributes to admissions outcomes and ultimately enrollment differences.

In interviews,[15] HSVP students generally fell into three groups with regard to their extracurriculars: (1) those who insisted they did not get involved in activities with college admissions in mind, (2) those who did not join activities originally for college admissions purposes but later recognized that such participation could be an asset, and (3) those who fully acknowledged participating in extracurricular activities in order to receive some kind of college admissions advantage.

Students who did not become involved in extracurriculars for college admissions purposes cited other reasons for participating. For example, one student performed community service, but only because it was required for his IB Diploma. A second valedictorian joined her school's academic clubs " 'cause they really needed people." Another student reported that he wrestled because he wanted to train. Others indicated that they participated because they genuinely liked the activity. For example, one young woman served as president of the math club because she "loved it." Several joined sports teams because they simply found playing to be fun.

The next group of valedictorians indicated that when they first joined extracurricular activities they did not know doing so could help with college admissions, but realized later in the college admissions process that participating could be beneficial. For example, a low-SES student stated that for most of high school he had not thought about what would look good on his college application. "Then senior year, it was: 'Will that look good? Maybe I should put it down.'" A high-SES student from an affluent suburb whose parents obtained their higher education outside of the United States was similarly uninformed about the possible benefits of extracurricular participation: "It wasn't until I started exploring that I became aware of how much . . . extracurricular things meant." A couple of valedictorians expressed relief when they learned they had already been pursuing some of the extracurricular activities admissions officers valued.

Finally, a slim majority[16] of HSVP students acknowledged that they knew extracurriculars could be a factor in college admissions and strove to participate for that reason.[17] These students came from a variety of social class backgrounds. They also emphasized that the importance of extracurriculars was a well-known fact in their high schools. A high-SES student reported that her high school peers discussed the importance of extracurriculars at length, crying: "You need to build up your college apps [applications]! You need to build up your college apps!" Similarly, when a middle-class student was asked in a follow-up to an earlier comment, "What made you think that extracurriculars might be important in college admission?" she explained that: "Oh, just everyone hammers it down your throat. . . . It was kind of understood. You did as much as you could, as much as you could handle." First-generation college students also knew that extracurriculars could matter in admissions. One such student from a working-class high school reported that the teachers and guidance counselors conveyed the importance of extracurriculars. Another first-generation student said she knew participating in activities would help because "it's in all the magazines, even *Seventeen* magazine now. You have to do all this. So I was in every club."

Students who acknowledged that extracurricular involvement could be helpful in gaining admission still tended to value the activities in which they participated. As one explained, some of her volunteer work was "for college and some of it was because I enjoyed it." Another student who founded a club for new students explained that her motives were also mixed: part of it was "because this will look good on my college application, obviously, but, part of it was just there needed to be a place for new students." Yet another student who admitted joining clubs in order to "open doors" also reported that being involved "was fun. It was fun to have things to do rather than sit at home." Likewise, another valedictorian reported that he joined academic teams in part because he thought, "this will look kind of nice. But I think the bigger part was that my friends were in it."

Participation in community service was one activity that students tended to mention doing more strictly for admissions purposes. As one student phrased it, community service "just seemed necessary for college." One student related that he heard from teachers, websites, and older students that community service was important. Another explained that her "teachers, would just tell us: 'You need to be volunteering.' My sophomore history teacher especially, he was like, 'Everyone has a 4.0. You need to volunteer.' "

A belief in the importance of community service in college admissions has been documented elsewhere. In one newspaper story, a parent called the director of admissions to find out if his child's five hundred hours of community service were "enough" (Zernike, 2000). Though Hernández (1997), an ex-admissions officer at Dartmouth, reports that an in-depth commitment to any activity is weighed the same as in-depth commitment to community service, the belief that participating in community service increases chances of acceptance continues to persist (Sharpe, 1999). This sentiment may be well founded. Espenshade and Radford (2009) find that students who participated in a large number of community service activities were accepted at elite private universities at higher rates than otherwise comparable applicants.

Valedictorians also frequently suggested that they sought leadership roles mainly to improve their admissions prospects. One low-SES student from a working-class community explained: "My senior year I went for the editor of the literary magazine because it looked good to have the editor. So I tried to be more active getting actual positions rather than just being a part of it." Another student was quite blunt about the reason she ran for student government: "I felt it would look good when I applied to colleges." A high-SES student even fought against his natural inclinations in order to help his chances of admission at an elite college:

> I'm not a natural leader, so I don't believe that I would have normally gone for officer positions. . . . I don't like the idea of sort of imposing things upon people and I don't see myself as a leader necessarily. And I believe I went and pursued a presidency in the Math Honor Society with the explicit intention of

having something to write on my college applications. . . . And I think it definitely did help because if I didn't have any leadership, I think it would have
reflected poorly on my application.

In sum, most HSVP students were aware of the importance of extracurriculars in the college admissions process, and the majority of
them worked to ensure that their involvement would at least make them
competitive with other applicants. The valedictorians interviewed in no
way suggested that knowledge about the possible admissions advantage
of extracurricular participation was limited to a particular social class
group. In fact, even students who did not aspire to the types of colleges
that consider extracurriculars had heard about their potential role in
admissions and tried to do well in this area.[18] In sum, HSVP students did
not limit their college prospects by failing to participate in extracurriculars. Their extracurricular participation would earn them average if not
high marks at even most-selective institutions.

Conclusion

As demonstrated in the introduction to this book and the extracurricular
section in this chapter, HSVP students exhibited outstanding preparation
for college and college admissions. That being said, this chapter reveals
that valedictorians differed in their approach to preparation and this
variation appeared to be shaped most by college aspirations. Students
with more elite college aspirations were more likely to be diligent in ensuring they obtained high grades, were enrolled in challenging curriculums, and were well prepared for college admissions tests. Valedictorians
with weaker elite college aspirations were generally less deliberate about
reaching the top of their class, taking rigorous curriculums, and scoring
as well as possible on the SAT.

These results are worth discussing in the context of Morgan's (2005)
work. Morgan argues that students' prefigurative commitment ("a cognitive attachment to a future course of behavior") to attending college
influences their preparatory commitment. As he explains, "a student with
maximal preparatory commitment toward the prefigurative commitment
'I will enroll in college' will enact all possible behavior that prepares him
or her for enrolling in college and then successfully obtaining a college
degree" (103).

For HSVP students, having the prefigurative commitment to enroll in college was not an issue. All possessed it, as well as preparatory commitment. That being said, this chapter reveals that some valedictorians had a prefigurative commitment to enrolling in not just any college but an elite college. Students with a prefigurative commitment to attending a prestigious college displayed a strong preparatory commitment to making sure they met top colleges' high admissions standards—putting in extra time and effort and sometimes even making personal sacrifices in pursuit of this goal.

Based on Morgan's (2005) theory, students with this level of commitment should be less likely to abandon the idea of attending a top institution when, for example, admissions barriers like taking SAT II tests arise, financial obstacles to attending are encountered, or concerns about enrolling far from home occur. These committed students should also be more likely to explore elite college options, to follow through and apply to one or more, and enroll. This idea is discussed further in the conclusion of this book.

CHAPTER FOUR

Exploration

Investigating College

During the exploration phase of the college destination process, students research three topics: the college admissions process, the financial aid process, and potential colleges. Because these aspects of exploration are interrelated, patterns by social class will emerge across them. Yet despite their similarities, it is helpful to present each dimension separately for several reasons: each requires a different type of investigation, some students fail to explore one or more of these three facets, and variation in just one area can funnel otherwise similar students in very distinct directions.

This chapter is organized as follows: The first part uses High School Valedictorian Project (HSVP) interview data to describe how valedictorians learn about the college admissions process. Then, employing student appraisals from the HSVP survey, quantitative data are presented on students' and parents' understanding of the college admissions process. The second part of the chapter turns to the financial aid process. It scrutinizes interview data for the ways students gather information and then compares students' and parents' knowledge of the financial aid process using student survey reports. Finally, drawing on qualitative data, the third part of this chapter discusses students' exploration of college options, including when they start investigating, the approach they adopt in acquiring information, the entities that influence their search, and why some students fail to consider certain types of postsecondary institutions.

Exploration of the College Admissions Process

How HSVP students investigate the college admissions process

This study defines the college admissions process as the steps involved in applying to and being admitted to college. HSVP interviews reveal that although valedictorians learned about the basics of this process—such as required tests and coursework—through their high schools, most felt the information their high schools provided was inadequate. It is not surprising that students would expect their high schools to offer information about the next stage of education, and thus be disappointed enough by the lack of guidance received to rate their schools poorly, even if schools were their primary source of information. Dissatisfied students sought to supplement their understanding of college admissions by consulting their parents, the colleges themselves, and/or third-party college websites and books. The following discussion explores how these sources shaped valedictorians' investigation of the college admissions process.

HIGH SCHOOL.   Irrespective of their family, high school, or community socioeconomic status (SES), interviewed valedictorians invariably felt that their public high schools were not as helpful as they should have been in guiding them through the college admissions process. Many characterized the help their school provided as "not much. Not much at all."

Valedictorians gave school counselors similarly poor reviews. Counselors were described repeatedly by valedictorians as "pretty lousy" or "pretty incompetent." Poor experiences with public high school counselors—particularly those in less-affluent communities—are not atypical, as numerous studies have shown (Avery, 2009; MacAllum et al., 2007; McDonough, 1997; Perna et al., 2008; Venezia, Kirst, and Antonio, 2003; Whitmire and Esch, 2010).

The primary way valedictorians received information about college admissions from their high school was through a general meeting. Some schools offered just one session between junior and senior year, while others gave a few presentations during a scheduled class like "English" or "health." Unfortunately, valedictorians did not find these meetings to be very useful, mainly because they tended to focus on the college admissions process for average rather than top students. For example, depending on the student body, these gatherings might only discuss how to meet the local community colleges' deadlines or the coursework required to be eligible to attend local, nonselective, public four-year colleges. Since the admissions process is often different at private nonprofit[1] and more-selective colleges,[2] valedictorians who hoped to enroll in these types of institutions did not obtain much information applicable to their college admissions process during these meetings. Thus, perhaps contrary to expectations, more middling students may receive more relevant and useful college admissions information in these information sessions than high achievers do.

Further disappointing to valedictorians is the fact that even when they reached out to counseling staff outside of these meetings, they found counselors were often uninformed. Valedictorians interested in attending colleges that students in their high school did not usually consider were particularly likely to encounter unknowledgeable staff. A rural student with elite college aspirations explained: "I don't mean to be boastful here, but [the high school did not] have people going after the kind of the path that I was going to be on . . . and no one was prepared for helping me."[3] Another student from a low-SES community reported that his counselor "just couldn't give me . . . the information. . . . There weren't many students from my school [who] ever went out of state. So when I started having questions about out-of-state [and private] colleges, [the counselor] was just generally unsure."[4]

PARENTS.   While students from a range of family and community backgrounds were generally disappointed by their high school's guidance, students' appraisals of their families' help in learning about the college admissions process differed markedly by SES. In this way, valedictorians did not differ from students at large. Other research has also found that parental help in the college admissions process differs by SES (Ad Council, 2006; Arnold, 1995; Cabrera and La Nasa, 2001; Choy, 2001; College Board Advocacy & Policy Center, 2011; Espenshade and Radford, 2009; Galotti and Mark, 1994; Horn and Nuñez, 2000; Hossler and Foley, 1995; Litten, 1982; MacAllum et al., 2007; McDonough, 1997; Roderick et al., 2009; Stringer et al., 1998).

Ideally, parents should provide both encouragement and support to their children during the college choice process (Hossler, Schmit, and Vesper, 1999). Parents can convey encouragement by talking about their expectations, hopes, and dreams for their children. Support, however, is more tangible and direct. It includes saving money for college, taking children on college visits, attending financial aid workshops, and helping with forms and applications.

Low-SES and first-generation college valedictorians' parents often offered encouragement, but little support in the college admissions process. Their lack of personal experience with college contributed to their being less informed, making it more difficult to offer assistance.[5] One first-generation college student lamented that her parents "didn't really know anything . . . my dad's totally clueless." As examples, she cited that her father did not know what an AP test was and that she had to nag him about paying for the SAT.[6] Even low-SES parents who wanted to help their children sometimes did not know how to acquire information that could be useful. For example, one low-SES student declared: "[My parents] are really bad with computers. I don't even know if [my mom would] know how to go about getting an application."

Middle- and high-SES parents, in contrast, provided not just encouragement but support as well. First, they were more likely to be knowledgeable about college admissions from their own experience attending, and could advise their children on that basis.[7] They also took steps to acquire current admissions information by purchasing books and magazines on the subject. Sometimes they simply passed these resources on to their children, but other times they also read these materials themselves. Overall, they were much more likely than low-SES parents to be actively involved in the college admissions process.

These differences caused students' overall experience investigating the college admissions process to vary by SES. Lareau (2011) reports that low-SES parents did not view constant monitoring of the process as critical because they perceived that their child's path would be determined more by institutional staff than by their actions as parents. As a result, as Reay (1998) suggests, the college admissions process could be fairly solitary for less-affluent students. In contrast, the transition from high school to college was a major life event for both parents and students in more-affluent homes (Lareau, 2011). According to Lareau (2011), greater involvement by more-affluent parents may stem from their view of their high school senior as still a child, whereas less-affluent families tended to see their high school senior as grown.

COLLEGES AND OTHER SOURCES.   Valedictorians' third most common source of information about college admissions came from the colleges themselves. Use of colleges as a resource did not differ by social class or family college experience. Colleges imparted information about the process to students through several means: meetings at high schools, mailed materials, university-maintained websites, presentations during campus visits, and college open houses.

Students also cited a few additional sources as useful in their exploration of college admissions. These resources included peers, guidebooks, and third-party websites maintained by entities like *U.S. News & World Report* and Princeton Review.[8] Students mentioned these sources, however, less often than they cited high schools, parents, and colleges.

HSVP students' understanding of the college admissions process

It is important to stress that the college admissions process can be as simple or as complicated as the postsecondary institution or student makes it. Some colleges require just an enrollment process, with no application and no standardized tests. Other institutions have an application but no outside examinations. Still others insist on an application and exams, but not letters of recommendation, lists of extracurriculars, or essays.

Students shape the difficulty of the college admissions process as well. It is entirely possible for students (especially those applying to a single college, applying to a single set of state universities, or using the common application) to complete their part of the college admissions process in one sitting. Other students, however, may spend months on their part of the college admissions process: strategizing how many applications to submit and whether or where to apply early, debating how many times to take the SAT I, deciding whom to ask for letters of recommendation, trying to showcase their extracurricular accomplishments, and writing and rewriting multiple essays for multiple applications.

Despite how complex the college admissions process can be, the vast majority of HSVP students reported having a good understanding of it by the time they needed to start preparing early and rolling applications. In the HSVP survey, valedictorians were asked: "During the fall of your senior year of high school, how would you rate your understanding of the college admissions process?" They were then given a five-point scale in which a 1 reflected a poor understanding and a 5 represented an excellent understanding. As table 4.1 indicates, less than 5 percent rated their understanding as a 1 or a 2, and roughly 79 percent rated it a 4 or a 5.[9] (For ease of discussion, this chapter describes ratings of 4 or 5 as a strong or solid understanding and ratings of 1 or 2 as a poor or weak understanding.)

TABLE 4.1 **The Ratings HSVP Students Gave Their Understanding of the College Admissions Process (N = 896)**

	Rating	Percentage
	1	1.0
	2	3.9
	3	16.1
	4	45.2
	5	33.7
	Missing	.1

Note: Students were asked to rate their understanding on a scale of 1 to 5, in which a 1 reflected a poor understanding and a 5 represented an excellent understanding.
Source: High School Valedictorian Project Person Dataset.

Nevertheless, valedictorians' likelihood of having a solid understanding of the admissions process increased significantly with affluence. As figure 4.1 highlights, 72 percent of low-SES, 77 percent of middle-SES, and 83 percent of high-SES students reported that they had a strong understanding of the process. Controlling for race and gender in a logistic regression,[10] low- and middle-SES students' odds of reporting a strong understanding no longer significantly differed, but high-SES students' odds remained about 63 percent greater than the odds of middle-SES students (see appendix F, table F.4.1). Even this SES difference is no longer significant, however, once additional controls capturing parents' postsecondary education are included.

HSVP parents' understanding of the college admissions process

Students do not determine where to attend college in a vacuum. Parents in particular usually influence where their children consider attending, where they apply, and where they finally enroll. Given the role of parents, it is also important to determine how informed they are about the college admissions process. To that end, valedictorians were asked to rate their parents' knowledge as well.[11] As was true for students, parents' likelihood of having a strong understanding increases with social class. Figure 4.1 reveals that just 28 percent of low-SES students had well-informed parents compared with 51 percent of middle-SES and 69 percent of high-SES students. This social class pattern remains, even controlling for student, family, high school, community, and predisposition variables (see appendix F, table F.4.2). The odds of low-SES parents having a strong understanding of the college admissions process were

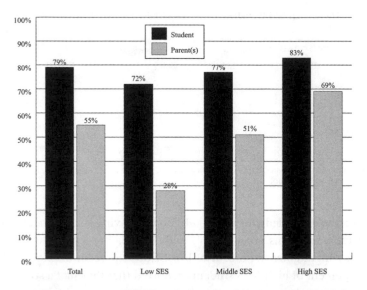

FIGURE 4.1. The percentage of HSVP students rating their own and rating their parents' understanding of the college admissions process as strong, by social class (N = 896). *Note:* Students and parents were considered to have a strong understanding if they were given a rating of 4 or 5 on a five-point scale in which a 1 reflected a poor understanding and a 5 represented an excellent understanding. Differences by social class for students were significant at the .01 level and differences by social class for parents were significant at the .001 level. *Source:* High School Valedictorian Project Person Dataset.

52 percent lower than the odds of middle-SES parents. High-SES parents' odds were 64 percent greater than those of middle-SES parents.

These results are consistent with HSVP interviews, which suggest that low-SES parents were less likely than more-affluent parents to be involved in learning about the college admissions process and to be knowledgeable about it. HSVP findings also resemble those reached by studies examining students with a broader range of academic achievement (Bloom, 2007; Horn and Nuñez, 2000; McDonough, 1997). The fact that valedictorians exhibit a pattern similar to students at large suggests that having a top student at home does not necessarily overturn traditional parental differences by SES. Even low-SES students who were first in their class usually had less-informed parents than their more-affluent peers.

Comparing valedictorians' understanding of the college admissions process with that of their parents also leads to some interesting conclusions. First, valedictorians viewed their own knowledge as strong at higher rates than they perceived their parents' knowledge as strong. About four-fifths of all valedictorians gave themselves a strong rating, but only about half awarded such a rating to their parents. The gap between students' and parents' knowledge earning a strong rating is largest in low-SES families: 44 percentage points. The divide between students and parents in middle- and high-SES families is a smaller 26 and 14 percentage points, respectively.

Second, parents differed more by SES than valedictorians did. While the range in students' understanding differed by SES by 11 percentage points, the range in parents' understanding differed by SES by 41 percentage points. Comparing the regression results for students and parents also suggests that the effect of SES is stronger on parents' understanding than on students' understanding. This finding implies that top students may be better able than their parents to limit the role of social class in shaping their understanding of the college admissions process.

Exploration of the Financial Aid Process

Before discussing this section's findings, it is important to define the financial aid process. This study views it as the steps that occur in the path to receiving financial aid for college. It is particularly focused on students' understanding of need-based federal financial aid, which is accessed by completing the Free Application for Federal Student Aid (FAFSA).[12] Examining families' knowledge of the financial aid process during the exploration stage is critical because research indicates that perceptions about financial aid (accurate and inaccurate) shape exploration of college options (Arnold, 1995; College Board and Art & Science Group, 2010; Hossler and Gallagher, 1987; Krukowski, 1985: 25; McPherson and Schapiro, 1991; Miller, 1997; Perna and Titus, 2004; Sallie Mae and Gallup, 2008). This section of the chapter first explores how students learn about financial aid and then assesses students' and parents' understanding of it.

How HSVP students investigate the financial aid process

The first thing to note about HSVP students' exploration of the financial aid process is that some students never investigate it. Valedictorians who failed to learn about financial aid included not just the most-affluent students, but less-affluent ones as well. For example, when a middle-class valedictorian with parents promoting public college attendance was asked how she explored the financial aid process, she responded: "Um, I didn't really. All I knew is that I asked my dad about it and he's like, 'No, we don't want to take any financial aid.' I guess it's like a pride thing for him. So I didn't really look into it." Other students from both middle- and high-SES backgrounds explained that they did not really explore the financial aid process because they or their families did not think they would receive any aid. For example, one set of middle-class parents told their son they could not afford to send him to a private college, but also maintained that their family would not qualify for any financial aid.

Students' and families' perceptions about their aid eligibility are often inaccurate. Several pieces of research suggest that families that should be eligible for aid do not pursue it. Recently, Sallie Mae and Ipsos (2011) found that 13 percent of families with college students and annual incomes of less than $35,000 did not apply for financial aid. The American Council on Education (2004) reported that 1.7 million low- and moderate-income students attending college at least part-time in 1999–2000 did not file for financial aid. Middle- and even upper-middle-income students can be eligible for need-based aid as well. Multiple most-selective colleges do not require parents earning less than $60,000 annually to contribute anything toward college costs (Pallais and Turner, 2006, 2007). And some of the most elite institutions provide need-based financial aid to families earning up to $200,000 a year (Jaschik, 2011). Nevertheless, according to Sallie Mae and Ipsos (2011), 18 percent of families making between $35,000 and $100,000 a year did not file a FAFSA.

While some valedictorians did not explore the possibility of receiving need-based aid, the majority of HSVP students did some investigating of the process. Nevertheless, even students who researched financial aid were unlikely to obtain comprehensive and accurate information. As with the college admissions process, students turned primarily to their high schools and families for answers to their financial aid questions, though some reached out to colleges and other sources as well. The next section uses interview data to examine the role these various entities played.

HIGH SCHOOL.   High schools varied in their ability to successfully deliver financial aid information to students and their families. Most schools that supplied information on the financial aid process did so in group meetings rather than one-on-one sessions. These meetings explaining the FAFSA sometimes were held during a class period or were presented in the evenings so that parents could also attend. In some cases, schools provided packets or the names of websites that students or families could visit to obtain further information. Schools that provided clear financial aid information helped broaden the types of colleges students explored tremendously. Two second-generation immigrant students who were not from high-SES families reported that their schools' explanation of financial aid was critical in their decision to consider and ultimately apply to elite private universities.

Other schools, however, did not adequately impart an understanding of the need-based financial aid process to their students. When asked about the involvement of their schools in the financial aid process, many HSVP students did not mention the FAFSA but instead noted that their counselors would inform them of special scholarships. While learning of individual scholarship opportunities is useful, the amounts provided are generally small. Providing understandable need-based financial aid information would have been more helpful to families in their attempt to accurately determine financially feasible college options.[13]

PARENTS. While high schools' delivery of clear financial aid information did not appear to differ by school or community characteristics, parents' knowledge of financial aid and their involvement in learning about it varied largely by social class. As observed when examining parents' support in college admissions, less-affluent parents were less involved in the financial aid process than were more-affluent parents. Other research has also found this SES difference in parents' participation in the financial aid process (Bloom, 2007; College Board Advocacy & Policy Center, 2011; College Board and Art & Science Group, 2010; Horn and Nuñez, 2000).

In interviews, no low-SES HSVP students reported that their parents were active participants in this process, but several middle- and high-SES students did. In fact, some middle- and high-SES valedictorians indicated that their parents took charge of the entire financial aid process for them. In these households, parents were the individuals attending information sessions, going online, and contacting colleges to find out about financial aid. For example, when asked, "What about financial aid? How did you learn about that process?" one high-SES student replied, "That I sort of let Dad take care of. I don't really consider the family finances to be something I've been completely privy to, which is to be expected, me being the son. So it was always more sort of like, 'Here, guys [parents], take care of this.'" Other interviews also suggested that some middle- and high-SES parents were reluctant to disclose their financial circumstances to their children. By assuming responsibility for the financial aid process, these parents were freed from having such conversations with their children.[14]

COLLEGES AND OTHER SOURCES.   Other sources of financial aid information were used less frequently. Colleges provided some details to students through websites, mailed promotional materials, or on-campus information sessions. Websites maintained by third parties like FastWeb and Princeton Review as well as message boards were also cited by students as helpful resources. Books, magazines, and peers also provided some information.

HSVP students' understanding of the financial aid process

The financial aid process is complex and intimidating at even the most basic level. A study in Southern California found that regardless of parents' education, about a quarter of seniors in low-income high schools felt that applying for financial aid was too complicated to be worth pursuing (Luna De La Rosa, 2006). The fact that the National Institute of Certified College Planners (an association that helps families repackage their finances to obtain more aid) did not exist in 2002 but had 1,200 registered members by 2007 is further evidence of the complicated nature of the financial aid process and families' lack of confidence in their ability to decipher its intricacies on their own (Farrell, 2007). Even Princeton Review now offers online courses on parts of the financial aid process (Jaschik, 2010).

Though attempts to lessen the burden of applying have been made (Dynarski and Wiederspan, 2012; Lewin, 2009; Marklein, 2010), during the time that HSVP students were applying, just doing the absolute minimum—filling out the five-page FAFSA—required answering a greater number of questions than even the longest U.S. federal income tax form (Dynarski and Scott-Clayton, 2006). Furthermore, students applying to more-selective private colleges often have to complete not only the FAFSA but an even more exhaustive questionnaire known as the CSS/Financial Aid PROFILE.

The greater complexity of the financial aid process compared with the college admissions process is reflected in students' lower levels of confidence about their knowledge. Among just HSVP students who applied for financial aid,[15] 41 percent felt they had a strong understanding of the process by the fall of their senior year of high school.[16] In contrast, nearly twice that many HSVP students believed they had a strong understanding of the college admissions process (79 percent).[17] Likewise, almost one-fourth of financial aid applicants felt their understanding of the financial aid system was poor or weak. Only 5 percent rated their knowledge of the college admissions process as similarly low.

Focusing on just the results for students in figure 4.2 indicates that at 54 percent, low-SES students were about 15 and 16 percentage points *more* likely than their middle- and high-SES counterparts, respectively, to report a solid understanding. This pattern runs contrary to the social class patterns observed for college admissions understanding, in which more-affluent students possessed the informational advantage. Regression

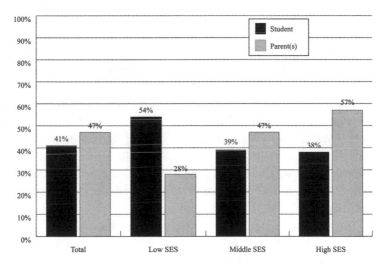

FIGURE 4.2. The percentage of HSVP financial aid applicants rating their own and rating their parents' understanding of the financial aid process as strong, by social class (N = 521). *Note:* Results are based on students who applied for financial aid. Students and parents were considered to have a strong understanding if they were given a rating of 4 or 5 on a five-point scale in which a 1 reflected a poor understanding and a 5 represented an excellent understanding. Differences by social class for students were significant at the .05 level and differences by social class for parents were significant at the .001 level. *Source:* High School Valedictorian Project Person Dataset.

results suggest, however, that this apparent low-SES advantage in financial aid understanding over middle-SES students is not significant once controls for just gender and race are incorporated (see appendix F, table F.4.3).

HSVP parents' understanding of the financial aid process

Parents' knowledge of the financial aid process may shape students' college destinations even more than parents' knowledge of the college admissions process. This can occur because families often have inaccurate perceptions about college costs and financial aid (College Board, 2011; Grodsky and Jones, 2007; Horn, Chen, and Chapman, 2003; Ikenberry and Hartle, 1998; McPherson and Schapiro, 1991) and restrict the types of universities their children can consider based on this misinformation (Arnold, 1995; College Board and Art & Science Group, 2010; Hossler and Gallagher, 1987; McDonough, 1997; Perna and Titus, 2004; Sallie Mae and Gallup, 2008; Warwick and Mansfield, 2003). One study found that 40 percent of parents eliminated *even considering* certain colleges because of concerns about costs. Middle-income families were particularly likely to do so (Sallie Mae and Gallup, 2008).

Eliminating college options based on sticker price and before receiving financial aid packages can curtail students' postsecondary opportunities. With aid, institutions that have higher sticker prices may actually cost students and families less than institutions with lower sticker prices (Roderick et al., 2009: 49). This is particularly true for low-income students. Lynch, Engle, and Cruz (2011) found that students with annual family incomes of $30,000 or less who live in Alabama, California, Massachusetts, New Hampshire, New Jersey, New York, Pennsylvania, Tennessee, Texas, and Utah would have a lower net price attending the top private university in their state than they would attending the state's public flagship. And the difference often was not small. In seven of these ten states, the families' net price at the top private university was less than half that of the public flagship.

Given these potential consequences, it is unfortunate that less than half of HSVP students who applied for financial aid felt their parents had a strong understanding of the process. This lack of parental knowledge is all the more disconcerting given that these results include only families who applied for aid. These families needed aid, and yet a minority knew the process well.

Figure 4.2 illustrates the differences in parents' knowledge by SES. Although substantial percentages of middle- and high-SES parents did not have a strong understanding, parents from these social classes were more likely than low-SES parents to earn high marks from their children for being well informed. Only 28 percent of low-SES parents had a solid understanding compared with 47 and 57 percent of middle- and high-SES parents, respectively.[18]

Regressions controlling for race and gender find that compared with middle-SES students, low-SES students had about 50 percent lower odds and high-SES students had about 50 percent greater odds of having parents who were well educated about financial aid (see appendix F, table F.4.4). This difference between high- and middle-SES parents' knowledge of financial aid is no longer significant once two related social class measures capturing family experience with college are included: first-generation college student status and whether a parent attended a most-selective college. That being said, the odds of low-SES parents having a strong understanding continue to be roughly half those of middle-SES parents, not only with additional controls for parents' education but also with controls for student's SAT score, predisposition variables, and high school and community characteristics. This result suggests that less-affluent families' socioeconomic status is highly related to their financial aid knowledge.

It is also useful to compare students' and parents' knowledge. Figure 4.1 indicated that within each SES group, a higher percentage of students rated their own knowledge of the college admissions process as strong compared to the percentage of students who rated their parents' knowledge as strong.[19] Figure 4.2 revealed that while this pattern holds for low-SES students' financial aid knowledge (low-SES valedictorians were 26 percentage points more likely to give themselves a strong rating than to give their parents a strong rating), the same is not true for middle- and high-SES students (who were about 8 and 20 percentage points less likely to view their own knowledge as strong than to view their parents' knowledge as strong, respectively). These HSVP differences in perceived knowledge of the financial aid process are consistent with related research. Horn, Chen, and Chapman (2003) find that higher-SES parents are more likely to be knowledgeable about college costs and financial aid than higher-SES students, but that low-SES parents do not have the same informational advantage over low-SES students.

Other research helps explain why these quantitative results occur. As noted earlier, HSVP interviews suggest that more-affluent parents were more involved in the financial aid process and sometimes even took over the responsibility for this process from their children. Bloom (2007) also finds that in low-SES households, students are primarily responsible for acquiring financial aid information and that their parents know and find out little about aid. A recent investigation shows that use of the new net cost calculators (which allow individuals to receive an estimate of what their net cost of attendance would be at a given institution based on their financial situation) follows the same pattern. In low-SES families, students were more likely than parents to use them, while in high-SES families the opposite was true (College Board and Art & Science Group, 2010). Here again, we see that having a top student in the household does not appear to alter parents' general social class patterns.

Exploration of College Options

During the exploration stage, students must not only learn about the college admissions and financial aid process but also investigate potential postsecondary institutions to attend. This part of the chapter first draws on qualitative interview data to illuminate when high achievers begin to explore their college options and the approaches they use in forming a list of institutions. Next, it focuses on the sources that shape students' investigations of postsecondary options, how these sources exert their influence, and the impact they have. And, finally, it explores why students fail to consider certain types of universities. As is true throughout this book, social class differences are underscored.

When HSVP students first start exploring their college options

Before discussing when HSVP students started evaluating potential colleges, it must be reported that some valedictorians never explored their college options at all. Valedictorians who failed to investigate different universities came from a variety of social class and community backgrounds, but all shared a belief that they would be admitted to their first-choice institution. Cost concerns were a major reason these high achievers did not research other colleges. For example, one middle-SES student's failure to explore different types of institutions was clearly shaped by her parents' imposition of specific cost parameters:

By the time I got to high school, I was pretty set on . . . follow[ing] in my dad's footsteps and my brother's footsteps and do[ing] computer science. So it was understood that I would go to [public in-state college] because if I went to a private institution somewhere, then I would have to pay for the difference between "State" and that. . . . That's what my parents told me—because my brother went to "State," so they knew they could afford ["State"]—and they just thought, "Well, if it's good enough for your brother then it should be good enough for you, and if you want something better, like a higher ranked institution, you need to pay the difference." And I was like, "Well, I can't do that." . . . And so it was actually the only college I applied to 'cause I knew I would get in. So I was just like, there's no point to just figure out where else I could have gotten into 'cause I wasn't going to go.

Students' self-imposed cost concerns also limited exploration of college options. For example, a high-SES valedictorian from an affluent suburban community decided in his junior year to attend his state's most-selective public flagship college and never researched other potential institutions. The university he identified had the prestige and social experience he sought, and the alumni and current students he spoke with enjoyed attending. Most important, these features came with a less imposing price tag than other elite institutions. Content with the idea of this university being his future alma mater, he did not explore other colleges that might have offered similar benefits. While this high-SES valedictorian reported that his parents did not pressure him to attend a less expensive institution, he indicated that the lower price of the flagship was the main reason he abandoned his search. He also suggested that if differences in price had not been as large, he probably would have considered and applied to out-of-state, private, most-selective institutions.

While some valedictorians did not explore multiple college options, a much larger proportion did do some investigation. Most started researching colleges during their junior year, the summer before senior year, or the fall of their senior year. Some also began looking before their junior year, but typically there was some kind of external impetus that caused them to search earlier. For example, a couple of low-SES students had a high school class that required them to investigate college options. Other students, particularly high-SES individuals, started exploring potential colleges while older siblings were doing so. One such student talked about how she would "sit in the backseat and read the Fiske Guide" as

her family toured prospective universities for her sister. A few other valedictorians began exploring their college options earlier because a family
trip took them near a university. Since they were already in the area,
these families stopped in for a campus visit.

HSVP students' approach in exploring their options

High achievers' approach to investigating potential colleges generally
took one of three forms. Some valedictorians researched only institutions that they already knew. Another group identified what they wanted
in a college and then searched for institutions that met those parameters.
The last group of valedictorians remained open to all types of colleges and
explored a wide range of college options. The approach taken by students
seemed mostly to depend on temperament rather than social class or
other characteristics.

FIRST APPROACH: INVESTIGATE ONLY KNOWN INSTITUTIONS. Many
students sought information only about colleges and universities that
were already known to them. As one valedictorian phrased it: "What I'd
heard about I looked further into." Similarly, another student described
his search as sitting at a computer and asking himself, "Uhhh, what are
the universities I know?" and then visiting the websites of those institutions. The existence of this approach begs the question, which colleges
do high achievers know?

Interviews revealed that valedictorians of all backgrounds tended to
have heard about colleges in their communities. Local and state colleges
are better known for several reasons. First, they are often integrated into
community life. Many high achievers had been on local and state college
campuses long before they started exploring college options because
their primary or secondary school athletic events or academic competi-
tions were held there. "[Public state college] and schools like that, like
[public flagship] . . . have just been around. They were just here," explained one student. A second reason students were often more aware
of state institutions was because some communities spent a considerable amount of time discussing local colleges' football and basketball
games.[20]

The third reason valedictorians were aware of local and state universities was because members of their social networks were very likely
to have considered applying to, had applied to, and/or had enrolled in

these institutions. While more-affluent students were more likely than low-SES students to know of these colleges through their social networks because their contacts were more likely to be college-educated, many HSVP students reported that teachers, neighbors, family friends, fellow worshipers, and older peers brought local colleges into their worldview:[21]

> Just growing up in this same area . . . everyone's like, "Oh, my older brother went to [public in-state university x], [public in-state university y], whatever." Those are the big schools. . . . So yeah, you just kind of grow up knowing that those are the big universities out there.

Although valedictorians were most likely to be familiar with local institutions, some had also heard of prestigious colleges before beginning their college search. Valedictorians of various backgrounds knew of some of the larger prestigious universities like Harvard or Princeton through the media, but high-SES valedictorians often knew of an even greater number of elite colleges—especially prominent, small liberal arts colleges—through their social networks.[22] High-SES students were more likely to know people in their family, in their family's social circle, or in their more prosperous school or community who attended a prestigious college.

The actual colleges to which students apply and eventually enroll are affected by using this method of only researching already familiar institutions. Students who use this approach rather than one of the following two approaches will form college lists and have college destinations that are much more shaped by both their community's postsecondary landscape and their social network.

SECOND APPROACH: SET PARAMETERS AND THEN ONLY EXPLORE COLLEGES THAT MEET THEM.   Another group of HSVP students defined aspects they wanted in their college experience and then only explored colleges that fit those requirements. Students' use of this approach did not vary by social class background, but the conditions they set often did. For example, while valedictorians of all backgrounds often used strength of proposed college major to form an initial list, low- and middle-SES students were particularly likely to require that the colleges they considered be located within a certain geographic distance from home, often within the state or closer. Low- and middle-SES families also frequently set parameters based on sticker price and would not consider institutions that exceeded the limit established. Other students, particularly high-SES individuals, restricted their search to prestigious universities.

Students frequently combined parameters to determine which universities to investigate further. Setting just two requirements typically reduced students' set of considered colleges noticeably. For example, one student who valued college major and location explained: "I decided that I wanted to look into pharmacy. And I thought at that time that I wanted to stay close to home, so that made the college application process really easy for me because there aren't a lot of pharmacy schools in this area." Several other students refined their college options based on college major and cost. Still another student described condensing her search based on college major and university prestige. This high-SES valedictorian began by:

> just kind of looking at the *U.S. News* rankings and working from there. And at the time, I thought I definitely want[ed] to do business undergrad so that pretty much narrowed down my choices because I realized that most of the Ivy Leagues didn't even have undergrad in business.

THIRD APPROACH: CONDUCT AN EXPANSIVE SEARCH. Finally, a small group of valedictorians were initially open to all colleges and then slowly and methodically eliminated institutions until they were left with a reasonable number to which they felt they could apply. Students who approached their college search in this way tended to be interested in attending highly selective colleges and yet lacked familiarity with this type of college through their families or communities. High achievers who fell into this category usually read the descriptions of a multitude of colleges in guidebooks. They also typically opened and read the college literature they received in the mail and then further investigated those institutions that sparked their interest. Some of these students also reported using third-party websites' search engines to produce a list of colleges. One first-generation college student entered so few limitations that the generated list contained the names of roughly a thousand universities. He diligently looked at each school's website and then requested information from the institutions that excited him the most. After reviewing the mailed materials, he identified the colleges he liked best and planned visits to their campuses.

Individuals and sources that affect how HSVP students
explore college options

Whichever approach students use in exploring their college options, individuals and sources shape their search as well. Specifically, this section explores how college mailings, high schools, parents, and other individuals affect HSVP students' exploration of postsecondary institutions in general, their investigation of specific universities, and their prioritizing of certain institutional characteristics.

COLLEGE MAILINGS. The majority of high school valedictorians interviewed reported that the promotional mailings colleges sent did not convince them to consider these institutions as potential alma maters. One student who attended college in his home state even found the idea absurd: "I mean, I haven't heard of anybody really saying, 'Oh, I got a letter in the mail from college [x] and that made me go there' [*Laughs*]." Many high achievers never even read the college mail they received. Those who did review their mail often suggested that the materials were unpersuasive. As one student related, the mailings "were pretty generic and sa[id] the same things."

Students who did not explore their college options or who only investigated the colleges that were already familiar to them were particularly unlikely to be swayed by college mailings:

> I remember getting this huge booklet from—Ithaca? And I was flipping though it, 'cause it was all glossy pages . . . and I was like, "Wow, this college is beautiful!" And I was like, "I've never even heard of Ithaca! I don't know where it's ranked, I don't know what they specialize in." And I knew it was out of state, so I was like, "Whatever, it's a pretty brochure, but I'm just going to throw it away."

Students who set strict parameters on their search were also less likely to be persuaded by these brochures. Those with distance criteria were particularly unlikely to be moved. For example, one student explained: "I kind of ignored [the mail] 'cause I knew I didn't want to go out of state." Another valedictorian read the material, but in the end stuck to her original criteria of in-state, public institutions: "I knew I wanted to stay in [home state], so I would get some stuff from a lot of schools on the East Coast . . . [and] yeah, they're prestigious, but I really kind of like [home state]. I think I'll stay here." High achievers also limited their exploration when they or their parents had imposed cost limits. "I got a ton of brochures from other colleges, but I was kind of like . . . I'm not going to be able to afford this, so I might as well—there's no point in applying because I'm not going to go there." Likewise, valedictorians who aspired to a prestigious college tended to ignore nonprestigious colleges' entreaties. Even the promise of merit scholarships in these mailings failed to convince these students to disregard the selective college parameter they had already established. As one high-SES valedictorian reported:

> I got a lot of those mailings . . .'cause I was [a] National Merit [Scholar]. So I would open [the mailing] up 'cause they'd always offer me money, so I'd open it up just . . . out of curiosity. I'd be like, "Whoa, that's a lot of money," and then I'd toss it away [*Laughs*]. There was some school in Texas that offered me $70,000. But I didn't want to go to an unknown school in Texas.

Nevertheless, when students received a mailing from a university that exhibited traits they wanted, the communication sometimes had an impact. For example, a low-SES student who sought to attend an elite university and had already identified several where he planned to submit applications confided: "I wasn't planning on applying to [most-selective private college] and then I received a letter from them in the mail and it said they wanted me to apply, so I was like, 'You know, why not?' And I did [apply] and that's where I ended up going." Likewise, an institution of interest that failed to send something could reduce its appeal. A high-SES valedictorian explained:

> If we begin thinking that I was probably looking at the top twenty-five to thirty schools in *U.S. News & World Report*, and then from there, whichever ones I felt more impressed by their mailings—I probably gave them an extra look. That probably did matter a lot. . . . Colleges on that list that I didn't hear anything from, I probably didn't consider very much.

In sum, mailed materials do not usually persuade students to explore an entirely new type of institution, but they can cause students to consider a college that already fits within their conception of possible institutions. In this way, mailings more often act as a winnowing tool that helps students reduce the number of schools of interest, rather than as a bridge that leads students to think about new types of universities they had not previously contemplated.

For students to contemplate applying to a different type of institution than they originally envisioned, an additional incentive typically had to be provided in the mailed materials. Offering guaranteed admission was one tactic that sometimes convinced valedictorians to apply; students liked knowing that if denied admission everywhere else, they would have at least one college they could attend in the fall. Another effective incentive for some high achievers with cost concerns was the promise of a merit scholarship. As one woman explained, a private college that was not most-selective "offered 75 percent tuition for valedictorians. That was basically the only reason I applied there." Colleges could also convince some high achievers to consider applying to their school by offering them a shortened and/or free application. Several HSVP students applied to institutions due to the brevity of the application. One low-SES student applied to four colleges in all, two of which offered free applications. She described her reaction to free applications this way:

> They would mail me an application and say, "Oh, free application!" And I would say, "Okay, let me try you 'cause I really don't know what I want to do." I received a lot of applications but . . . it was like, "Why am I going to spend $100[23] when I don't know if I really want to go there?" But when it said "Free!" it was like, well, then it leaves me another option.

Nevertheless, abbreviated or free applications could backfire. One student who applied to a college because its application was both free and short later felt: "Okay, maybe this school is not that great because this is all they're using to screen people." Another valedictorian had similar reservations about a four-year college that came to her high school's lobby and gave students a form they could fill out and immediately be accepted: "That gave me a bad impression of [public in-state university]. If anybody can go there, then why would anyone want to go there?"[24] In the end, none of the valedictorians interviewed enrolled in an institution that offered a free or shorter application.[25]

This finding suggests that if colleges want to attract students who do not typically apply to their institution, they should make initial contact earlier, before students and families have set concrete parameters. This early contact should not be focused on what the college offers in terms of specific programs, amenities, and the like, but instead on how its net costs and student outcomes compare with those of the local public institutions with which families are more familiar. If colleges can convince families that their institution is financially feasible and may even offer additional value, students may be more open to hearing details about the specific offerings of these institutions during the exploration stage.

HIGH SCHOOL.   High schools also shape students' exploration of college options by conveying messages about appropriate institutions to consider. As Espenshade and Radford (2009) describe, high school counselors and teachers influence a student's "organizational worldview," reducing the full range of colleges and universities that students could consider to a manageable subset. This subgroup is informed by the personal experiences of counselors and teachers, as well as by parental and community expectations about appropriate college destinations (Hossler, Schmit, and Vesper, 1999; McDonough, 1997: 89).

Interviewed valedictorians indicated that the primary way high schools supplied information about college options was by providing a place where students could locate information on their own, should they take the initiative to do so. These spaces were typically depositories of brochures and catalogs from local and state colleges, with maybe a few magazines or books about a broader range of institutions. One student captured the experience of many: "If you go into their office, they had a bunch of brochures and stuff, but that was about the extent of their help." While there were exceptions, most valedictorians did not use the resources in these rooms very often and did not find these spaces to be helpful overall.

A good number of valedictorians who were interviewed also reported that their high schools held their own college fairs, notified them of college fairs nearby, or brought representatives from colleges into their school. While one might presume attending such events would help students gather more information about college options, only one valedictorian reported identifying a university not previously considered as a result. These opportunities to meet with college staff were not generally useful for valedictorians because the colleges that participated tended to be oriented toward the more average student rather than the top students in the high school. Visiting institutions were mainly from within the state or region, while most-selective universities were in short supply. As a middle-SES student from one of the larger cities in his midwestern state reported, "We might have had one or two Ivies there—maybe just a single representative. It was mostly community colleges from out here."

Other research also indicates that admissions officers from selective colleges tend to concentrate their visits at schools and communities that have lots of students with the academic preparation and social backgrounds that make them likely applicants (Avery et al., 2009; Golden, 2006: 58; Stevens, 2007: 77; Zemsky and Oedel, 1983: 11). Admissions officers do not take the time to go to places where just a few students may be motivated to submit applications. Thus, valedictorians who were interested in attending more-prestigious or more-remote universities but lived in areas where such matriculation was uncommon often obtained little to no information at college fairs. Worse yet, they may have left these events feeling that more-elite or more-distant colleges were not interested in enrolling students like them.

High school counselors could compensate for the subtle message created by the absence of these institutions and broaden valedictorians' postsecondary worldview by providing personalized college advice. Unfortunately, few did so. One valedictorian reported:

> [Counselors] more helped you just make sure you had the high school credits and stuff you needed to get accepted. I think I might have gotten a brochure about [public state university student eventually attended] from high school. I don't remember exactly. There wasn't a whole lot that I did through the high school, though. It was more just kind of on my own.

The lack of personalized college counseling at high schools can be attributed in part to high student-counselor ratios (McDonough, 2004; Perna et al., 2008). In 2010, just one full-time guidance counselor was responsible for 285 public high school students (Clinedinst, Hurley, and Hawkins, 2011). The many other responsibilities counselors face also curtails their ability to offer personalized guidance (Bridgeland and Bruce, 2011; Clinedinst, Hurley, and Hawkins, 2011; Perna et al., 2008). A recent analysis indicates that public school counselors spent only 23 percent of their time on college counseling (Clinedinst, Hurley, and Hawkins, 2011).

Though counselors' time is limited, one might think that if any student could obtain personalized advice, it would be high-achieving valedictorians. Interviews, however, indicate otherwise. According to one valedictorian from a middle-class community, the counselor "could never remember my name, until she realized that I was valedictorian, and she was like, 'I should probably remember your name, right?'" Even a valedictorian from a more-affluent community lamented: "I went to see [my counselor] three times. Each time, she said it was great to finally meet me." In this way, valedictorians' counselor interactions were similar to those of students in general. Half of all young people in a recent study reported feeling like they were "just another face in the crowd" to their college guidance counselors (Johnson and Rochkind, 2010).

Thus, rather than receiving preferential treatment, valedictorians had to fight just like any student to get what little personalized time and attention their counselors could provide. A first-generation college student explained: "You had to really get to [the counselor] to get any information. You know, you had to be at her office all the [time]—Whoo! I was in her office." In fact, other research suggests that counselors may even be inclined to give high achievers less time than other students. One counselor for a low-SES school stated in a recent study: "I don't spend a lot of time on the college-bound and honors kids. . . . They're all bright, they know how to do all this, they don't need me" (Perna et al., 2008: 142).[26]

Valedictorians who did manage to arrange a meeting with their counselor indicated that they received little advice about college options. Instead, most students described their interactions with counselors about college this way: "Our guidance counselors were like, 'Whatever you want to do, we'll facilitate it,' as in, 'This is where I'm applying; I need these letters.' [To which the counselor would say] 'Okay. Got it.' It wasn't really like [the counselor would say], 'Oh, this [college] would be good for you.'"

Valedictorians also indicated that counselors felt advising students about different colleges was not part of their job. As one student reported, her counselor "was like, 'I'm not going to tell you where to go. I'm not going to push you toward anything.'" In fact, HSVP interviews suggest that counselors seemed to be quite reluctant to mention the names of any colleges at all.

When counselors did discuss particular types of postsecondary institutions, they generally did so in group settings and their college suggestions were again targeted toward the average rather than the top student. Most often, the institutions promoted were public and within the state. For example, a high-SES student in a poorly performing high school reported:

The school counselors always talked up the community colleges, because they were having to talk to people who didn't necessarily have family backgrounds in academics, or any parental emphasis on higher education. So there was also very much, "You should go to community college if you can, and if you can go to [a less-selective four-year state college], that's great!" So there was almost never any discussion of private schools and [more-selective, in-state public colleges]. . . . They figured, I guess, that people who would be [more-selective, in-state public] and private-school bound would be . . . aware of what was going on. . . . [The counselors] weren't particularly helpful—especially for someone interested in the [prestigious public] and private track. But they definitely tried to target the kind of on-the-cusp demographic.

Likewise, another student from the same state suggested that "since most of the students are interested in staying in-state, [the counselors] concentrated on the [public state] systems," discussing requirements and criteria for acceptance. Still another valedictorian reported that her school helped students complete applications to the public universities.

While making the path to in-state public colleges easier is likely to be helpful for students at large, one wonders if high schools that pave the way to this particular type of college deter high-achieving students from considering and applying to institutions that might better match their level of academic achievement. This potential downside may not outweigh the benefits of leading students to some type of college, but it still should be recognized as possibly affecting students' college destinations and causing some top students to undermatch, which on average lowers their chances of bachelor's degree completion (Bowen, Chingos, and McPherson, 2009; Carnevale and Strohl, 2010; Nagaoka, Roderick, and Coca, 2009; Roderick et al., 2009: 54). This could be easily rectified even in counseling programs that cannot offer a lot of one-on-one guidance. Counselors could organize group sessions by students' level of preparation and tailor the colleges highlighted accordingly.

Unfortunately, HSVP data suggest that counselors do not alter the colleges suggested when speaking to highly accomplished students. The few valedictorians who obtained one-on-one meetings with counselors reported that in-state public universities were generally the only institution type counselors promoted. For example, one first-generation college student applied to only one university: the in-state public flagship her counselor had always suggested she attend. When asked about her counselor's reasoning for identifying only that particular college, the valedictorian replied: "It's like the top school down here. The Harvard of the South. She thought it would be good for me." While this institution may indeed have been a good fit for this valedictorian, it is hard to believe it was the only college worth her consideration. Valedictorians almost never reported that their counselor volunteered considering an out-of-state, private, or most-selective private college.

Even when valedictorians personally raised the idea of attending a private or out-of-state institution, they received little support from their counselors. Counselors sometimes even tried to dissuade those who expressed interest in more-selective or private institutions. One student reported that when students would talk to the counselor about their interest in attending private colleges, the response would be: "Oh. Okay. Well, have you looked at [in-state public university *x*, in-state public university *y*]?" A high-SES student in Florida, which has a large merit aid program, received a similar lack of encouragement from his counselor, even though they had good rapport.

HSVP STUDENT: My guidance counselor—she really loved me. And she would kind of push me more towards applying toward the local [public] schools where I would get . . . reduced tuition and stuff. But . . . there wasn't as much of a push for competitive schools.

INTERVIEWER: Why do you think that was?

HSVP STUDENT: I mean, she definitely would support me when I would apply to these schools, and write good [recommendations] . . . and would go out of her way to help me, but . . . [the counselors are] more, I guess, familiar and used to kids going to the local [state] schools. . . . And she wanted to make sure that I at least had some options open in case I [did not] get into whatever schools I wanted.

Counselors may be less likely to suggest private college for several reasons. First, they may be less familiar with these colleges since enrollment in them is less common.[27] Second, they may be unsure about private colleges' application requirements. (Admissions procedures vary at private colleges and are generally more involved than those at public colleges.) Third, counselors may be reluctant to suggest colleges with higher sticker prices.[28] Of course, counselors could be trained to teach families that their net price may be far lower than the sticker prices observed and that private colleges may offer other benefits—like higher graduation rates—that make them worth considering.

Though counselors typically did not promote valedictorians' elite college attendance, high school teachers sometimes did.[29] The first group of teachers who occasionally offered college advice included those who led the clubs in which students participated. Unlike counselors, these teachers often had downtime with students, which allowed them to both get to know their charges well and casually discuss colleges and offer suggestions.

The second group of teachers who sometimes provided helpful college insight included those who regularly taught the high school's best and brightest. Unlike counselors, these instructors saw the talent and potential of the valedictorians day after day in their classrooms. These teachers also tended to be more knowledgeable about selective colleges than counselors because they often knew previous students who had continued to top institutions. Some of these teachers may even have developed close enough bonds with former high-achieving students to know how they fared at different institutions. Teachers could then apply prior students' experiences in providing advice to their newest crop of bright students. For example, one valedictorian reported that the head of her IB program "pushed me to go to a good school and try to get out of state if you can." Another top student reported that his IB teachers would tell him: "Go! Go! You're a great student—apply for the highest possible college or the most prestigious possible college."[30]

Teachers may also be more likely than counselors to get to know high achievers' personal backgrounds and tailor their guidance in light of that information. For instance, a first-generation college student had an AP teacher who would tell everyone to go to college and then pull her aside and push her personally: "You're going to a good school, right?" This valedictorian felt the teacher knew about her family's low-SES background and wanted to ensure she attended an institution more aligned with her achievements than her social class. As others have highlighted, first-generation college students frequently do not know many college-educated people other than their teachers, which makes teachers' opinions and counsel particularly influential (Mullen, 2010; Sagawa and Schramm, 2008).

When considering some teachers' willingness to get involved in students' college choice process and offer advice, it is important to keep in mind that teachers generally do not receive official training in college counseling. Without college advising instruction, any suggestions teachers give are likely to be based more on personal experience than professional best practices. Casual counseling by teachers should thus not be viewed as an adequate substitute for more-formal college advising. It is also important to keep in mind that students who participate in few school activities or exhibit less-impressive performance in the classroom may have less access to teachers' college suggestions.

In sum, HSVP interviews suggest that most public high schools are not broadening the view of high achievers with regard to possible college options. Instead, the conduct of schools and counselors is more likely to discourage than encourage valedictorians' consideration of institutions that match their academic achievement. Because of this, students who aspire to attend private, out-of-state, or most-selective colleges generally receive the inspiration to attend these universities from another source. In some cases, a teacher steps in, but most of the time it falls to nonschool entities like parents to promote this type of college destination. And, as the next section demonstrates, the likelihood that parents will encourage attendance at these institutions varies dramatically by social class.

PARENTS.   As with college admissions and financial aid, parents' support to valedictorians in exploring college options differed strongly by SES. Compared with low-SES parents, high-SES parents were more involved in helping their children gather information about specific colleges. This involvement tended to take two forms. The first is best described as helping give children the tools for them to conduct their own college search. Such parents, for example, bought their children college guidebooks and facilitated college visits. They also suggested to their children that they talk to others about their alma maters, with some making a special effort to put their child in contact with relatives, friends, or coworkers who attended particular colleges. As one high-SES student explained, my parents "constantly encouraged me to . . . call people, talk to people who were alumni, get to know people—just ask questions."[31]

Other high-SES parents went a step further and embarked on their own exploration of college options for their child. These parents tended to perform their own research by reading college guidebooks and other college materials and then offered suggestions to their children about promising colleges to consider. For instance, one high-SES mother used her experience hiring college interns for the software company where she worked to help identify institutions with good engineering programs for her son, an aspiring engineer. Similarly, another high-SES mother made her child a list of colleges to explore based on institutions that had strong programs in her child's intended major and were well regarded in general.[32]

The involvement of low-SES parents stands in sharp contrast. First, low-SES students never reported that their parents took it upon themselves to personally research universities. The aunt and mother of a first-generation college student encouraged her to attend Harvard or Princeton simply because of these universities' reputations nationally. According to this valedictorian, "I think that they figured that those were the top schools and so that was where I [as a top high school student] should go." These family members had not spent any time finding out this student's actual odds of admission at these colleges or exploring other college options that might be a better fit.

Also in contrast with high-SES parents, low-SES parents often impeded their children's ability to investigate college options. Low-SES parents were less likely both to give their children college materials and take them on visits to college campuses.[33] For example, one low-SES valedictorian with parents who wanted him to attend the college located closest to home, which happened to be a community college, reported: "My parents didn't want me to go anywhere else, so they didn't want to drive anywhere [to visit]."[34]

Parents differed by SES not just in the assistance they gave their child during their college search, but in their likelihood of suggesting particular colleges and the types of institutions they promoted. Again, high-SES parents were most involved and tended to be most specific in their advice. When asked, "Did your parents have certain colleges or types of colleges in mind that you should apply to? What were their suggestions?" the daughter of two PhDs responded:

> Well, colleges like [most-elective private college]. You know, private universities that have a population of 2,600 undergrads. Smaller, not like [public state universities]. Not as small as [most-selective liberal arts college], which I think has about eight hundred people in it. Kind of, large enough so it has opportunities like clubs, overseas studies, that sort of thing, but small enough that you weren't just a number in a crowd.

While few high-SES parents were this specific about desired college traits, they did commonly promote elite college attendance. Prestige was often more important than any other factor; many high-SES families indicated that even if their child had to be farther from home and/or was charged more to enroll, attending an elite university would be worth it. This sentiment came from high-SES parents with prestigious alma maters as well as from those without. High-SES parents who had not personally attended an elite college often worked with and knew individuals who did attend and concluded that such attendance was valuable. As one high-SES student reported, "My mom was in love with [Ivy League college]. . . . She was like, 'Oh, you should apply there!' " Their parents' emphasis on prestigious colleges struck many high-SES students, particularly those in high-SES communities, as normal and commonplace. "Obviously, your parents want you to go to the best that you can get into," said one. "They were suggesting all Ivy Leagues, obviously, because that's what every parent does," explained another. As is discussed below, however, not every parent emphasizes institutional prestige, especially not parents of more modest means.

In comparison with high-SES parents, middle-SES parents were far less likely to offer detailed opinions as to the type of college their children should attend.[35] Completing a four-year degree at an accredited school was emphasized much more than attending a particular type of four-year college. As one student with family college experience at Historically Black Colleges and Universities (HBCUs) and public universities reported, "They didn't give—they were more of the type that as long as you go and get a degree, we don't really care where you go. Go there and do your best." Another student explained: "I know [my parents] wanted us all to go to college and get a degree. But as far as where I went, my parents kind of left up to me . . . wherever I feel comfortable. That was about it."

While middle-SES parents were unlikely to name specific colleges, many did convey preferences for certain college characteristics. The college qualities middle-SES parents valued, however, differed from those espoused by high-SES parents. First, middle-SES parents were more likely to focus on an institution's distance from home, which high-SES parents were less likely to stress. High-SES parents who did mention distance to their children tended to have more expansive geographic boundaries than did middle-SES parents. For example, high-SES parents residing on the East Coast might suggest that their children stay on the East Coast rather than go to the West Coast for college. In contrast, middle-SES parents tended to prefer that their children be within a few hours by car. Yet while distance from home was a consideration for middle-SES parents, these parents did not assume that the closest college was the best college. Rather, colleges were expected to be within a certain mile radius, and then additional judgments could be used to choose between them.

Middle-SES parents also differed from high-SES parents in their greater focus on cost. The cost concerns their parents voiced often stopped middle-SES children from even exploring the possibility of attending a private institution. While a couple of middle-SES parents encouraged their children to apply to at least one prestigious private institution, a larger number of middle-SES parents discouraged even considering these universities, frequently citing cost. It is important to highlight that these cost fears may be based on lack of adequate knowledge of financial aid. Many private colleges offer generous merit aid to top students and even some of the most-selective private universities offer generous need-based aid that can free even middle-class parents from paying anything for their child's education.[36] These cost concerns, warranted or not, affected students' exploration of college options.

Low-SES parents were the least likely to have suggestions of specific colleges or types of colleges for their children. For example, when asked about whether her parents had any suggestions, a rural, first-generation college student explained: "Not really, they were just, I guess, really proud to have me go anywhere because neither one of them had really had that experience." Other scholars have also found that low-SES parents are less likely to have specific suggestions about where their children should attend, and hypothesize that this is partially due to low-SES parents' lack of personal college experience and college-educated contacts (Espenshade and Radford, 2009; Lareau, 2003; McDonough, 1997; Rowan-Kenyon, Bell, and Perna, 2008).

When low-SES parents expressed any college preferences, they tended to center around their child attending college close to home. For example, one student described her mother's attitude this way: "She wanted me to stay in-state, but aside from that she was pretty open—whatever I wanted to do." For these low-SES parents, proximity was more important than a university's reputation or whether the college was a two- or four-year institution. One mother who had attended college for a year did not care if her daughter attended a two- or four-year college, but did care about location: "She didn't want me to go too far away. She didn't want me out of driving distance. That was really the only thing she said to me about where to go." Another family valued proximity so highly that they wanted their valedictorian son to attend a two-year college down the street rather than a four-year college twenty minutes away.[37]

Though middle-SES parents also valued location, it was not the primary factor that it was for these low-SES families.

A few low-SES parents wanted their children to live at home while attending college. Parents from a rural community had concerns about partying at colleges. In the other two cases, the families had recently emigrated from Latin America and were not accustomed to the idea of children living away from home while pursuing undergraduate studies.[38] While middle-SES parents also valued having their children close to home, they generally wanted them to have a residential college experience.

In addition to preferring colleges closer to home, low-SES parents also favored colleges they thought would be less expensive. That being said, they were less adamant than middle-class parents that their children heed this preference. There are several factors that may contribute to this difference. Low-SES parents' milder insistence on where their children considered applying may first be symptomatic of their lower level of involvement throughout the entire exploration stage. As noted, low-SES parents tend not to have personal experience with four-year colleges and thus may be reluctant to dictate their children's education decisions, particularly when their children have done well in school. Middle-SES parents, however, may be more confident in their college advice because they are more likely to have personal experience as undergraduates. Lareau's (2011) aforementioned conclusion that low-SES parents are more likely to see high school seniors as adults whereas more-affluent parents are more apt to view them as children may also contribute to this difference in parents' imposing of cost restrictions.

Middle-SES parents may be more likely than low-SES parents to prohibit their children from considering institutions with sticker prices above their budget for a third reason as well. Because middle-SES parents assumed they would be shouldering much of the college costs themselves, they may have felt more empowered to place certain limitations on the colleges their children considered. In contrast, it was more understood in low-SES households that the child would be taking on a larger part of the financial burden because of the parents' limited resources.[39] This dynamic may cause low-SES parents to leave the decision of where to apply more up to their child, after giving them a warning that more-expensive universities could be out of reach. For example, a low-SES valedictorian reported: "I guess [my parents] kind of assumed I'd apply to public schools, but I didn't. . . . My mom was kind of like, 'Do whatever you want, but I'm not going to be able to pay for it.'" Another low-

SES student reported that her parent did not care whether she attended a public or private college, but made it clear that if she went to a private college, she "would have to get the full scholarship to go there."

Of the three explanations, middle-SES parents' concern for their bank accounts seemed to contribute most to their greater insistence that their children consider colleges that met their cost parameters. Even middle-SES parents who were not involved in other aspects of the college admissions process were often resolute that their child should not apply to institutions deemed too expensive. Similarly uninvolved low-SES parents were less likely to be so unyielding on this point.

SOCIAL NETWORK. Finally, valedictorians received college suggestions from other members of their social network as well. HSVP students most frequently talked about universities with their classmates. These discussions centered on where peers were thinking of submitting applications and did lead some valedictorians to explore institutions they had not previously considered. Nevertheless, advice was not usually received in such exchanges because classmates lacked personal college experience just as valedictorians did.

Instead, guidance on where to apply was more typically given by older peers who had already been to college. Older siblings and their friends commonly served as sources of information. Fellow church members and job supervisors also provided suggestions to a couple of valedictorians. Of course, the advice these social network members gave was based on their own experiences, which were shaped by their own social class background. And, because valedictorians' social networks differ by socioeconomic status the suggestions received from social network members varied as well.

Lastly, it is worth noting that despite reports about the growing use of private college consultants (McDonough, 1997; Worth, 2000), particularly among high-SES students (Cabrera and La Nasa, 2001; Cole, 2006; McDonough, 1997; Worth, 2000), none of the fifty-five valedictorians interviewed reported receiving suggestions about colleges to consider from private college consultants.[40]

Why HSVP students fail to explore certain types of colleges

Additional qualitative data shed further light on valedictorians' exploration of college options. In interviews, HSVP students were asked to list the colleges to which they applied and were then asked whether they had ever *considered* applying to any of the types of institutions not represented in their list. For example, valedictorians who only reported applying to public colleges were asked if they had ever considered a private college. Such probing is important because the types of institutions students consider is not necessarily reflected in where they apply. To better understand how students reach their college destinations, it is helpful to assess if the opportunity to attend certain types of colleges was eliminated during the exploration stage, and if so, how and why.

CONSIDERING TWO-YEAR INSTITUTIONS. Only a couple of valedictorians reported considering two-year colleges. Both were from low-SES families, had older siblings who had attended community colleges, and stated that attending a two-year college was a last resort—to be exercised only if they did not receive enough aid to enroll in a four-year institution.

Other high achievers appeared to give momentary thought to the idea of attending a two-year college before rejecting it for one of the following two reasons: First, the most common explanation these students provided was that they sought a four-year college degree ("there's no way I would have stopped at the two-year") and had heard that transferring credits from a two-year to a four-year college could be difficult. "I knew eventually I would be getting my four-year [degree] so I just wanted to get right into it," explained a student otherwise sensitive to college costs. Second, they reported that they felt attending a four-year college would offer more advantages than a two-year college due to four-year institutions' stronger academic reputation. One student described the sentiments of many: "It just seemed like a four-year college would get me farther than a two-year."

Most HSVP students, however, never even allowed themselves to consider the idea of attending a two-year institution. For low-SES students in this category, their proven academic ability prevented them from feeling that they personally should attend a two-year college. As one low-SES student from a poor community reported, "Not to be biased or anything, but because I felt as though I was number one in my class . . . why limit myself to a two-year college?" Similarly, a first-generation college student related that since she could attend a public, in-state, four-year college for free due to her state's merit aid program, she and her mother felt she should just "go for it [the four-year college]," instead of a two-year college.

For high-SES valedictorians, two factors combined to make considering a community college inconceivable. First, like low-SES students,
they had demonstrated that they had the academic preparation to be successful at a four-year college. But second, two-year college enrollment
was not as common in high-SES students' social networks, which made
it even more difficult for them to envision attending. As a result, more-
affluent valedictorians tended to report that they had never—or even
never ever—contemplated attending a community college. One high-SES
student from a high-SES community even laughed at the idea of considering a two-year college.

CONSIDERING PUBLIC FOUR-YEAR INSTITUTIONS.   Most HSVP students
considered public colleges, but some did not. Valedictorians who dis-
missed the idea provided three reasons. First, some felt they could manage the costs of a private college. In fact, many high-SES students were
told not to worry about costs whatsoever. For example, a high-SES student ignored a public college's offer of a merit scholarship because her parents always said, "Go where you want to go. It doesn't matter." But a few
low-SES students also ignored public colleges because they felt confident
that they would receive the financial aid they needed to enroll in a private college. For instance, one stated: "When it came to [most-selective
private college], I was aware of all of their financial aid initiatives, so I
figured I would definitely qualify because my family doesn't have any
money, so I didn't worry about it."[41] Similarly, another low-SES student
reported:

> I read up about financial aid . . . [and thought] maybe this wouldn't be out
> of reach. They appear to be generous. They say they're going to commit to
> meeting 100 percent of your demonstrated need. And they talk about median
> income of the students and it's $150,000 and here my mom's making $45,000 a
> year. And I'm like, "I think I'll get a lot of financial aid." So I don't think it'll
> be out of reach to attend a private school.

A second reason students did not consider public colleges was because they were simply not impressed by the academic quality of public
institutions. One low-SES student confided: "I'd always gone to public
schools my entire life . . . I didn't really leave with a very favorable impression. So I was like, maybe I should try a private college." Another
low-SES student felt that attending a public college was "small time . . . I

really wanted something bigger than that—not bigger in size, but bigger in the esteem or something. . . . So it never really crossed my mind."

Several low-SES female students also indicated that they did not explore public colleges because of concerns about the social atmosphere at such institutions. When asked the main reason she did not want to enroll in a public college, one such valedictorian replied:

> I wouldn't say it's because I have a higher view of private colleges, necessarily, but it's just that, I didn't like the partying. I didn't want to get into any of that kind of stuff. I didn't want to be around any of that stuff because in [hometown] I wasn't around it . . . so I didn't really want to have to deal with that.

These female first-generation college students felt that this behavior was less likely to occur at private colleges, particularly Christian-oriented ones. "It's just a lot healthier. There's a lot less pressure to do things that people our age should not be doing," explained one.[42]

CONSIDERING PRIVATE FOUR-YEAR INSTITUTIONS. Students from a range of SES backgrounds cited higher costs as the main reason they did not contemplate private colleges or stopped exploring them almost immediately. "I did [consider private colleges] for about five minutes and then I realized how expensive it was going to be," explained a low-SES student. A middle-SES student felt and acted similarly: "It was like—the private schools—I can't afford that, you know? And so it wasn't an issue of could I get in or not. [Private colleges were] thrown right out."

These students who cited higher costs as their reason for failing to consider private institutions never found out what the net cost would be with financial aid. Instead, the sticker price turned these students away. These valedictorians or their families apparently found it easier to explore public colleges with lower prices that they knew they could pay for, or at least afford more easily, than to invest any time or energy exploring and applying to private colleges that ultimately might not be economically feasible to attend.[43] For example, one middle-SES student related:

> I wanted it to be where I could get a lot of scholarships . . . and then not have to pay that much after scholarships. So a private college, they may cost a lot and people say, "Yeah, they give out a lot of scholarships," but I didn't want to risk it, I guess? So—I went for public school [*Laughs*].

Some valedictorians also suggested that relative—and not just absolute—costs influenced their decision to forego investigating private institutions. These students felt they had good public college options in their state, and thus potentially spending extra money to attend a private college was not worth exploring. One valedictorian captured the sentiment of several top students: "I just never really thought about [private colleges]. I guess 'cause I knew over in California we have UCs,[44] which [are] already good, so I felt like, 'Why should I bother applying to another college if I feel the education here is great?'"

Spending extra money on a private *undergraduate* degree was particularly derided by some high achievers, particularly those anticipating future graduate school expenses. Both low- and high-SES students expressed this general sentiment: "I don't think it's necessary to pay the amount for a private institution just for an undergrad degree. Graduate school, for sure, I'm thinking of going to a private college or university."

CONSIDERING MOST-SELECTIVE INSTITUTIONS.   Although low-SES students sometimes report feeling out of place socioeconomically at elite universities (Ewers, 2005; Kaufman, 2001) and McDonough (1997: 112) suggests that low-SES parents may counsel their children to attend colleges where "people are more like us," HSVP students did not express reservations about attending elite colleges because of the social class background of students attending.[45] Instead, many failed to investigate most-selective colleges because of concerns about cost. A lack of desire to attend college farther from home also worked to deter some valedictorians who did not live near a prestigious institution. These reasons are common among students at large as well. A recent study of students of all levels of preparation found that cost was the primary reason lower-income students stopped considering harder schools (College Board Advocacy & Policy Center, 2011). "Too far from home" was selected the next most often.

Yet high-achieving students also gave a couple of additional reasons for not exploring most-selective colleges. First, they were concerned about the academic environment at such institutions. One middle-SES student who wanted to pursue engineering was particularly intimidated by the students at elite colleges. "I would kill myself if I [went] to MIT [Massachusetts Institute of Technology] 'cause everybody there is a genius and I've just heard it's so stressful when you go there." This student had watched a video about robots made by MIT students in her high school science class and so she wondered, "If I go there, am I going to have to make a robot? 'Cause I'm not smart enough to make a robot. I don't know the first thing about making a robot. And I was like, 'Well, I'm not going there.'"

Others talked more about how they felt that the social experience they wanted during college did not exist at such institutions. "I didn't want to be focused on academics 150 percent of my time," reported a middle-SES student. A low-SES student had the same worry. "I wanted to go to a quality school without wanting to kill myself. I want to get a good education but . . . I want to mix it with a social life. You know what I mean?" A black male valedictorian with a perfect score on one section of the SAT had similar concerns that the nonacademic aspects of his college experience, particularly school spirit, would be lacking at an elite school:

> I actually got a call from Harvard my summer of my senior year. They wanted me to apply there. But . . . that just didn't really sound too fun . . . it just didn't sound like an environment for me. I know I have a lot of energy and I couldn't see myself. I feel like I'd go bored out of my head . . . I probably would have gone crazy up there.

Students who worried about the academic and social environments at elite colleges tended not to know anyone who was attending or had attended such schools. Their families and high schools also generally had not encouraged them to enroll in an elite institution, and in some cases, even discouraged them from doing so. In contrast, valedictorians who knew individuals who had attended most-selective colleges were less likely to think undergraduates at these schools were out of their league academically or lacked a social life. And without these concerns, they were more apt to apply. Not surprisingly, high-SES valedictorians interviewed were more likely than their less-affluent peers to know someone with elite college experience. This finding highlights how students' social networks play a critical role in shaping their opinions about different types of institutions, and ultimately the set of colleges they consider.

Conclusion

During the exploration phase of the college destination process, students investigate three things: the college admissions process, the financial aid process, and college options. To synthesize this chapter's most important findings, first, the nature of the help high schools and parents provided was similar in each of the three aspects of the exploration stage. HSVP interviews suggested that guidance from high schools in providing information on college admissions, financial aid, and college options was woefully lacking, even in more-affluent communities. Some counselors did not even mention the existence of need-based aid. Counselors also generally did not explain the admissions process at out-of-state, private, and most-selective institutions or note the possible educational and career benefits of such attendance.[46]

In the absence of sufficient guidance from high schools, valedictorians frequently turned to their families for information. Yet parents' knowledge about and involvement in the college admissions and financial aid processes, as well as their college preferences for their child, differed by SES. Compared with other parents, those who were more affluent were better informed about college admissions and financial aid and more actively involved in their child's navigation of these processes. In fact, in some higher-SES families, parents took the lead in tackling the financial aid process, freeing their children to concentrate on the other dimensions of the exploration stage. To summarize parents' college preferences, lower-SES parents typically favored less-expensive universities that were closer to home, while more-privileged parents tended to value more-prestigious institutions.

This chapter also unveiled critical differences in how valedictorians investigated their college options. In some cases, top students' college opportunities were limited because they failed to explore possible colleges and instead focused on one institution almost immediately. In other cases, students were funneled in a particular direction because they only researched colleges that were already familiar to them. These familiar colleges varied substantially depending on valedictorians' communities and social networks, which are shaped by SES. Other times, students were pushed toward certain types of universities and away from others because of the parameters they established in determining which institutions to consider. Low- and middle-SES students were particularly likely to limit their search on the basis of cost or a university's distance from home, while high-SES students often restricted their exploration of colleges to prestigious institutions. Parents often encouraged the setting of these particular constraints.

It is also important to note that some valedictorians failed to truly contemplate pursuing certain types of institutions. Focusing on just the

two ends of the college spectrum in this conclusion, it should first be
highlighted that few valedictorians considered public two-year colleges.
Valedictorians of all backgrounds felt community colleges did not match
their academic abilities or educational aspirations, yet more-affluent valedictorians also had an additional reason for not exploring these institutions: members of their social network did not attend. This made it especially difficult for high-SES valedictorians to see themselves enrolled
in this type of institution. Attending was incompatible with high-SES
students' sense of self.

On the opposite end of the college spectrum, some valedictorians
did not consider attending most-selective colleges. Regardless of social
class background, valedictorians in this camp often cited cost and distance as explanations. Yet the two other concerns mentioned by some,
the academic and social environment of such institutions, had a social
class dimension. High-SES students were less apt to be worried about
these elements of campus life because they were more likely to know
others who had attended prestigious institutions and survived academically while enjoying themselves socially. Less-affluent valedictorians, in
contrast, were less likely to know someone who had enrolled in such an
institution and thus had a harder time envisioning their own attendance.

The overarching finding of this chapter is that lack of comprehensive
counseling about college admissions, need-based aid, and different college options enables social class to strongly impact the exploration phase
of valedictorians' college destination process.

CHAPTER FIVE

Application

Choosing Potential Destinations

A pplication is the fourth phase of the college destination process. While decisions made in the predisposition, preparation, and exploration stages are important and influential, they are not irreversible. In contrast, students' actions by the end of the application stage have permanent consequences. If students do not apply to a given institution, they cannot enroll in that institution. This chapter discusses the number of applications High School Valedictorian Project (HSVP) students submitted, describes both the college characteristics and the sources that influenced where they applied, and analyzes the actual types of universities at which HSVP students filed applications. The many differences by social class in application behavior are highlighted throughout.

Number of Applications Submitted

The number of colleges to which HSVP students applied varies greatly. First, as figure 5.1 depicts, about 15 percent of valedictorians reporting where they had applied submitted only one application. Of these students who applied to just one institution, more than two-thirds (68 percent) applied through an early decision (ED) or early action (EA) program. By submitting applications through either of these early admissions programs, these students would have learned whether they were admitted before regular college application deadlines. Those admitted under ED would have been bound to enroll and not allowed to apply elsewhere.

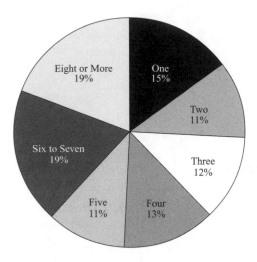

FIGURE 5.1. Percentage distribution of the number of applications HSVP students submitted (N=715). *Note:* Results are based on students with application data. *Source:* High School Valedictorian Project Person Dataset.

Students admitted under EA would have had the option of applying to other institutions, but may have decided not to do so if their EA college was their first choice and they were confident that they could afford to attend.

The other 32 percent of HSVP students who applied to only one college did not apply under an early admissions program. They seemed to be confident enough about their chances of admission that they did not feel the need to file other applications. When one such student was asked whether she was nervous about only applying to one institution, a not most-selective private college, she answered, "No. . . . That may sound mean, but I'd seen people get in who had lower grades." Even a student who applied only to a most-selective in-state public university felt very confident he would be accepted given that he was first in his class and typically fifty students from his affluent high school were admitted to this institution each year.

In considering the riskiness of this second group of students' application behavior, it is important to keep a couple of facts in mind. First, because of their outstanding academic preparation, HSVP students have an excellent chance of admission at most colleges. Second, this group usually was not applying to highly competitive colleges. Specifically, less than one-quarter of these students sent their application to a most-selective college and less than one-tenth sent their application to a most-selective private college, where admissions rates tend to be the lowest. Thus, the decision by these valedictorians to only apply to one institution probably did not put their chances of attending a four-year college the following fall in great danger. Nevertheless, because most in this group did not apply to a most-selective institution, these high achievers may have been putting themselves at risk of the consequences of undermatching.

Returning to figure 5.1, most valedictorians clearly applied to more than one college. Eleven percent filed two applications and 36 percent submitted between three and five. Finally, about 19 percent sent applications to six or seven colleges and another 19 percent put forward applications to eight or more. Comparing these results with those for freshmen at four-year colleges nationally in 2003 indicates that valedictorians tend to apply to a greater number of universities.[1] Specifically, HSVP students were 5 percentage points less likely to apply to one or two colleges, 9 percentage points less likely to apply to three to five colleges, and 14 percentage points more likely to apply to six or more (Ewers, 2004). The U.S Department of Education's Education Longitudinal Study (ELS) also highlights how valedictorians differ from students at large. In ELS, only 13 percent of 2003–2004 high school seniors who planned to continue their education beyond high school filed five or more applications their senior year (Chen, Wu, and Tasoff, 2010b) compared with 49 percent of HSVP students.

There are several reasons that more than one-third of HSVP students applied to six or more colleges. First, interviews suggest that valedictorians sent applications to a large number of colleges because they were informed by numerous sources that doing so was appropriate. The College Board's (2009) website states: "In this climate of competitive admissions . . . five to eight applications are usually enough to ensure that a student is accepted into a suitable institution."[2] The behavior of peers also persuaded valedictorians to apply to numerous schools. One HSVP student who submitted applications to nine colleges reported that her classmates' behavior encouraged her to do so. "That's what everyone was doing," she stated. Similarly, an HSVP student who applied to eleven colleges explained that she did so in large part because one of her friends had "taken a college prep class and [the course] recommended that you apply to at least nine schools. So I figured that eleven was reasonable."

High aspirations also caused valedictorians to apply to a large number of colleges. Other research shows that top students are more likely to aspire to an elite college (Chapman and Jackson, 1987; Litten, Sullivan, and Brodigan, 1983: 89) and that students with prestigious college aspirations tend to submit a greater number of applications (Finder, 2007; Sax et al., 2003). Given the low acceptance rates of elite colleges, students with elite aspirations likely file more applications in an effort to improve their chances of gaining admission to at least one prominent university. In the HSVP survey, students who reported that it was very important to them that they attend a prestigious college were 13 percentage points more likely than others to apply to eight or more institutions.

A less common but third reason valedictorians applied to a long list of colleges was to learn whether they would be admitted—a phenomenon known as "trophy hunting." Students who trophy hunt apply to colleges they do not plan to attend in order to find out whether they would be accepted. Valedictorians who practiced this were craving validation after years of working to reach the top of their class. They wanted a source outside of their family, high school, and community to appraise how their abilities and accomplishments compared to students elsewhere. Even more important, these high achievers wanted to be able to point to the fact that they could have attended prestigious college x, even if they did not enroll. They felt that this elite college acceptance letter, if not diploma, would give them a lasting sense of pride and help rid themselves of any doubts as to their abilities. One student captured the sentiment of trophy hunters well: "I thought it would be worth applying just to see what would happen . . . I wanted to know if I could get in, you know? I didn't want to not apply to someplace and then wonder—always, forever."

While HSVP valedictorians from all socioeconomic status (SES) backgrounds applied to a greater number of institutions than students in general, key differences still emerged by social class. High-SES valedictorians were noticeably more likely than their less-affluent high-achieving counterparts to apply to more institutions. High-SES HSVP students applied to an average of 5.4 schools. For both low- and middle-SES students, the average was 4.5 applications. As figure 5.2 illustrates, 27 percent of high-SES valedictorians sent applications to eight or more schools, more than double the percentage for low- and middle-SES valedictorians (13 percent for both groups). Meanwhile, low- and middle-SES HSVP students were 10 percentage points more likely than high-SES HSVP students to apply to just two or three institutions. Even after controlling for race, gender, SAT score, foreign-born parent status, and family college experience, high-SES valedictorians applied to a signifi-

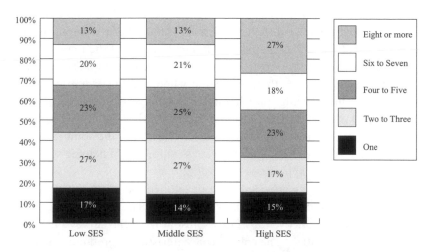

FIGURE 5.2. Percentage distribution of the number of applications HSVP students submitted, by social class (N=715). *Note:* Results are based on students with application data. *Source:* High School Valedictorian Project Person Dataset.

cantly greater number of institutions than their middle-SES counterparts (about 0.5 more applications overall) (see appendix F, table F.5.1). When high school and community variables were incorporated, however, this difference between middle- and high-SES students was no longer statistically significant.

To put these social class results in context, other research has also found that high-SES students apply to more institutions (Avery and Turner, 2008; Bryan et al., 2011; Chen, Wu, and Tasoff, 2010b; Hossler, Schmit, and Vesper, 1999; Sanderson et al., 1996). Aside from being better able to afford multiple application fees,[3] high-SES students may apply to more colleges because they are more committed to prestigious college attendance. These HSVP findings suggest that high achievement fails to eliminate these general SES patterns and cause less-affluent top students to adopt the application behavior of their more-affluent peers.

College Characteristics HSVP Students Considered When Making Application Decisions

This section discusses how valedictorians selected the universities to which they applied. To this end, the HSVP survey supplied a list of twenty-three college characteristics and asked students to select the five that most influenced their application decisions. It is important to highlight that the survey did not ask students to report the reasons they applied to a specific set of colleges, but instead requested that they indicate the college features they considered when deciding where to apply. Because of this wording, the characteristics the students selected may have helped them eliminate institutions to which they did not want to apply, as well as identify those institutions to which they did want to apply. For example, campus visits may be just as important in helping students decide where *not* to apply as where to apply.

The characteristics provided were developed based on an extensive review of the literature and previous surveys. Interviews conducted after the survey did not uncover any factors absent from the survey's list that were highly influential.[4] The college characteristics offered in the survey were categorized for analysis purposes as follows: academic, reputation,[5] cost, distance from home,[6] and campus environment.

Table 5.1 reveals that the characteristics students selected varied greatly. Only one item, academic reputation/prestige of institution, was chosen by more than half of all students. In all, 79 percent of respondents reported that this factor influenced where they applied.[7] The next most often selected item was campus visit, picked by almost 44 percent of all students. Other characteristics were not as overwhelmingly popular,[8] and are discussed by category.

Social class differences did not occur on either academic characteristic: faculty attention/involvement in teaching or special academic programs. Nevertheless, it is worth noting that one-third or more of the students in all three social classes indicated that special academic programs like a particular field of study, joint degree program, or honors program influenced their application decisions. Others also report that the types of degrees or programs offered (Warwick and Mansfield, 2003: 117) as well as quality of major (Maguire Associates, 2009) tend to be very important to students in evaluating colleges. Litten (1982) states that high-ability students are particularly likely to view academic programs as important in deciding where to apply.

The students' selection of reputation characteristics differed more by SES than did their selection of academic factors. Overall, high-SES students were repeatedly more likely than their counterparts to choose reputation items. Specifically, at 89 percent, they were 18 percentage points more likely than middle-SES valedictorians and 20 percentage points more

TABLE 5.1 **The Percentage of HSVP Students Reporting That the Following College Characteristics Were among the Five That Most Influenced Where They Decided to Apply, by Social Class (N = 515)**

Factor by Category	Total	Low SES	Middle SES	High SES	Significance
Academic					
Special Academic Program (Major, Honors)	34.8	37.3	35.7	33.0	—
Faculty Attention/Involvement in Teaching	18.8	16.0	20.4	18.3	—
Reputation					
Academic Reputation/Prestige of Institution	78.6	69.3	71.3	88.8	***
Rankings in National Magazines	32.8	17.3	30.1	40.6	**
Graduates Have Good Employment Outcomes	19.8	10.7	20.4	22.3	—
Graduates Admitted to Top Graduate Schools	18.3	17.3	13.0	23.7	*
Cost					
Cost of Attendance	26.2	41.3	31.9	15.6	***
Merit Aid Opportunities	21.0	21.3	26.9	15.2	*
Financial Aid Availability	20.2	48.0	27.3	4.0	***
Distance from Home					
Desire to Study Away from Hometown	25.6	33.3	26.4	22.3	—
Desire to Study Near Hometown	16.5	20.0	20.4	11.6	*
Desire to Attend College While Living at Home	5.2	12.0	6.5	1.8	**
Campus Environment					
Campus Visit	43.7	38.7	39.8	49.1	—
Campus Location (State or City/Community)	34.2	22.7	34.7	37.5	—
College Size	32.2	29.3	31.5	33.9	—
College Setting (Rural, Urban, Suburban)	23.9	17.3	20.8	29.0	*
College Facilities	19.6	13.3	18.1	23.2	—
Special Extracurricular (Abroad Program, Sport)	12.8	9.3	10.2	16.5	—
Other People I Know Will Also Be Attending	7.8	12.0	9.7	4.5	*
Religious Affiliation	4.5	6.7	3.2	4.9	—
Presence of Students of My Ethnicity/Race	1.9	4.0	0.5	2.7	—
Presence of Students of My Social Class	1.4	2.7	0.9	1.3	—
Desire to Attend a Single-Sex College	.2	.0	.5	.0	—

Note: Results are based on students with application data who selected five factors as influential, as requested in the survey question. $*p < .05$; $**p < .01$; $***p < .001$
Source: High School Valedictorian Project Person Dataset.

likely than low-SES valedictorians to select a university's academic reputation as important. Likewise, as compared with middle- and low-SES students, respectively, high-SES students were 11 and 24 percentage points more likely to select rankings in national magazines,[9] and 11 and 7 percentage points more likely to choose alumni admitted to top graduate schools. A composite variable of reputation factors leads to the same conclusion as these individual reputation results. About 57 percent of valedictorians in the highest social class category chose two or more reputation factors compared with 42 percent of middle-SES and 32 percent of low-SES valedictorians.

The greater emphasis by high-SES students on institutional prestige was also observed in qualitative HSVP data. In interviews, valedictorians of this social class background repeatedly expressed the following sentiment: "I guess I would say that the most important factor in my applying to certain colleges was the question of which college is considered the most prestigious, which one is considered the top." In fact, in many cases, high-SES HSVP students could not come up with reasons for applying to elite colleges other than the prestige of these institutions, which they felt would improve their future graduate school and employment prospects.

Placing these findings in a broader perspective, other research has shown that high-ability students as well as high-SES students at large put greater emphasis on prestige (Duffy and Goldberg, 1998; Finder, 2007; Flanagan, 2001; Ingels, Planty, and Bozick, 2005; Litten, 1982; Mayher, 1998; McDonough et al., 1998). The fact that valedictorians from more-affluent backgrounds were so much more likely than their counterparts to choose reputation factors again suggests that becoming a top student does not eliminate social class differences in college preferences.

Cost is another factor that influences students' application decisions (Hu and Hossler, 2000: 685; Warwick and Mansfield, 2003). Not surprisingly, the importance valedictorians attached to college costs differed strongly by social class. While 20 percent of middle-SES and 35 percent of low-SES students selected two or more cost criteria, less than 5 percent of high-SES students did so. As for the specific cost factors selected, high-SES students chose financial aid availability at a rate that was 44 and 23 percentage points below low- and middle-SES students, respectively. High-SES valedictorians were also less than half as likely as middle- and low-SES high achievers to pick cost of attendance as influential.[10] Finally, high-SES valedictorians were 6 to 12 percentage points less likely than their peers to consider merit aid opportunities in choosing where to apply.

It is worth highlighting that while low-SES valedictorians were most likely to select financial aid availability and cost of attendance, middle-SES valedictorians were most likely to choose merit aid opportunities. As Espenshade and Radford (2009) discuss, middle-SES students may be more sensitive to merit scholarships because they do not receive as much need-based financial support as low-SES students, and yet the amount they are expected to pay takes a bigger toll on their families' finances than it does on the finances of high-SES families (Avery and Hoxby, 2004: 268; Bowen, Kurzweil, and Tobin, 2005: 110; Collison, 1993; Gose, 1998; Herring, 2005; McGinn, 2005).

HSVP qualitative results regarding cost and social class are consistent with these survey findings. First, it was clear in interviews that high-SES valedictorians placed less attention on cost. As one high-SES valedictorian recounted, "My parents always said, 'We want the best education for you and we don't really care how much it costs. We've saved up for it.' So that was not an issue." High-SES students also frequently explained that their family viewed a college education as an "investment" and perceived enrolling in a more prestigious college, even if it was more expensive, as offering greater financial returns in the long term than attending a less expensive, less prestigious institution.

Interview results also revealed that cost factors affected middle- and low-SES valedictorians in multiple ways. Some valedictorians indicated that cost helped them decide where *not to* apply. In this case, institutions' sticker prices scared students and families away. For others, cost helped them decide where *to* apply. For these students, types of institutions believed to be cheaper or more likely to provide greater amounts of financial aid or grants were more likely to receive an application. It is also worth noting that some low- and middle-SES valedictorians reported that costs did not affect their application decisions. They typically elaborated in the same breath, however, that costs *did* influence their enrollment choice. Thus, costs were a concern to this subset of low- and middle-SES students, but they decided not to eliminate colleges until after they received financial aid packages and learned their official net costs.[11]

The relative importance of cost on valedictorians' application decisions by SES generally mirrors patterns among students at large. Other research also shows that poorer students are more likely than high-SES students to take cost into account when deciding where to apply (Avery and Turner, 2008; College Board Advocacy & Policy Center, 2011; Litten, 1982; McDonough, 1997). Valedictorians' potentially very bright financial futures did not eradicate this general SES pattern. Even given their promising prospects less-affluent valedictorians did not adopt the view of their high-SES peers that more-expensive, prestigious institutions were worth the extra cost in the long run. Costs in the short run were still very much relevant to less-affluent valedictorians and their families, who had fewer financial resources at their disposal.

The next category of results regarding a college's distance from home also exhibits some quantitative differences by social class. Middle- and low-SES students were about 8 percentage points more likely than high-SES students to report that their desire to attend college near their hometown was influential in their application decisions.[12] Moreover, 12 percent of low-SES and 7 percent of middle-SES students indicated that the desire to attend college while living at home was important, compared to just 2 percent of high-SES students.[13] Valedictorians did not differ significantly by SES in their desire to attend college away from hometown, though about one-quarter indicated that this was important to them.

HSVP interviews help explain these distance results obtained through the survey. While high-SES students did not generally value attending college away from home in and of itself, they were much more comfortable than their peers with the idea of attending a college farther from home if doing so would enable them to attend a more prestigious college. As one high-SES valedictorian put it: "If I'm going to be far away, it needs to be at a really good school. I'm not going to go to University of Kansas or something just to go far away."

High-SES students' greater comfort with distance seemed to derive in part from the fact that they were more likely to have traveled and lived outside of their state as well as have relatives and family friends in other states.[14] High-SES valedictorians were also willing to fly between their home and college, and viewed doing so as not particularly burdensome. Generally, for high-SES students, a college's distance from home was not deemed a potential logistical hassle until it required traveling to the other side of the country.

In contrast, for less-affluent valedictorians, attending a college most easily reached by plane was often perceived as too inconvenient to be worthwhile. Though some low-SES students preferred colleges where they could commute from home, middle- and low-SES valedictorians more typically sought to enroll in a university within a few hours' drive of their hometown. They were not as keen as high-SES students on the idea of having to fly between home and school, in part due to the greater costs of air travel, but also because of the greater advanced planning that such transport typically requires. Repeatedly, middle- and low-SES students reported wanting to be able to get in a car and drive home within a few hours if necessary. They frequently discussed the possibility of something "crazy happening," something "going wrong," or "emergency situations" in which being able to drive home would be important.

High-SES valedictorians, in contrast, did not express concerns about problems arising and not being able to get home. Perhaps their greater affluence made them feel secure enough in their personal and family situation that they did not envision an emergency occurring. They also may have believed that if there was a crisis, flying home would not be a significant hurdle, as their family was accustomed to plane travel and had the resources to fund a last-minute trip if necessary.

The fact that not all states have a top college within their borders and not all communities have a top university within a few hours by car means that these distance preferences can have significant consequences on where students attend. More-affluent students' greater openness to attending a college farther away facilitates their applying to a most-selective college (or even several of them), which in turn assists in their admission to and matriculation at an elite institution. In contrast, less-affluent top students' more frequent desire to attend college closer to home may prevent those in certain locations from applying to, and later being able to enroll in, a most-selective institution.

Campus environment is the final category of influential college characteristics analyzed. As mentioned, campus visit was the second most popular choice of all the options listed. It was also the most commonly picked campus environment factor. Campus location and college size came next, receiving votes from about one-third or more of all valedictorians. Selection of these top three environment factors did not differ significantly by SES, but interviews revealed that students who chose campus location and college size often had very different preferences within these valued criteria. For example, students who attached importance to the community in which an institution was situated varied in the type of community they wanted. One student who was interested in pursuing acting wanted to be in a city known for its theater. Another student enjoyed colonial history and for that reason decided to apply to institutions in communities steeped in that tradition. Still another student liked to sail and so she sought to attend a college on the water. Likewise, size of institution was often mentioned in interviews, though the actual size valedictorians perceived as ideal varied. Some were adamant about attending a big university, others favored medium-sized institutions, and still others preferred small colleges.

Chosen by almost a quarter of all students, college setting was also commonly selected. That said, its popularity differed somewhat by SES. High-SES students were at least 8 percentage points more likely than low- and middle-SES students to pick this factor as important. The particular type of campus setting students wanted often mirrored where they were raised. Students from urban communities talked about wanting to be in an urban area for college, while students from nonurban areas sometimes stated specifically that they did not want to attend college in a city.

Other campus environment factors received fewer votes and did not differ by social class with one exception. These characteristics included facilities, special extracurricular, knowing other people attending, college's religious affiliation, presence of students with respondent's racial or ethnic background, presence of students with respondent's social class background, and desire to enroll in a single-sex institution. The one item where differences by social class did occur was: other people I know will also be attending [this college]. Only 5 percent of high-SES students chose this option, compared with 10 percent of middle-SES and 12 percent of low-SES students. HSVP interviews suggest that high-SES valedictorians may have been less likely to pick this factor because they were more comfortable with the idea of being on their own. They were more likely to have traveled, lived in other communities, and to know people from other areas. Having already personally entered environments in which they knew no one, as well as having friends or family members who had done so, likely encouraged these high-SES students to give less weight to whether they already knew people at a particular institution.

Overall, high-SES students were more apt than other SES groups to consider a college's environment. Sixty-four percent selected two or more campus environment characteristics compared with 48 percent of low-SES and 56 percent of middle-SES groups. Less-affluent valedictorians' more pressing cost concerns likely made it harder for campus environment criteria to emerge as one of the five most important factors influencing where they applied. Avery and Turner (2008) also find that campus life factors are less important to top students from low-income backgrounds.

Individuals and Resources That Influenced HSVP Students' Application Decisions

Not just college characteristics shape where students apply. Individuals and resources consulted can also have an impact. Figure 5.3 presents the percentage of valedictorians who reported that a particular entity was influential in their application decisions. The figure clearly depicts that valedictorians were most likely to report being shaped by their parents (70 percent), followed by information from colleges (62 percent). Interestingly, high school guidance counselors and teachers were about as likely as peers and college guidebooks to sway valedictorians; between 41 and 46 percent of HSVP students reported that any one of these sources was

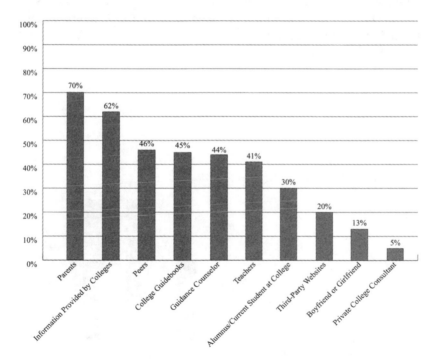

FIGURE 5.3. The percentage of HSVP students reporting that the following individuals or resources influenced their application decisions (N = 647). *Note:* Results are based on students with application data who selected at least one individual or resource as influential. Students could choose more than one category. *Source:* High School Valedictorian Project Person Dataset.

influential. About 30 percent of high achievers were persuaded by an alumnus or current student at a college they were considering, 20 percent were affected by third-party websites (run by entities like *U.S. News & World Report* or Princeton Review), and 13 percent were influenced by their boyfriend or girlfriend. Only 5 percent claimed that a private consultant shaped their decision to apply to specific colleges.[15]

No significant social class differences could be detected in the percentage of valedictorians reporting that they were influenced by information provided by colleges, peers, guidance counselors, teachers, alumni or current college students, or private college consultants. The four sources that were selected at different rates by SES are presented in figure 5.4. The first of these sources is boyfriend or girlfriend. In this case, middle-SES valedictorians chose this category more frequently than their peers; 18 percent considered their boyfriend or girlfriend as influential, compared with 11 percent of high-SES and 7 percent of low-SES students.

Selection of the other three sources exhibited a different pattern by SES. High-SES students were more likely than both middle- and

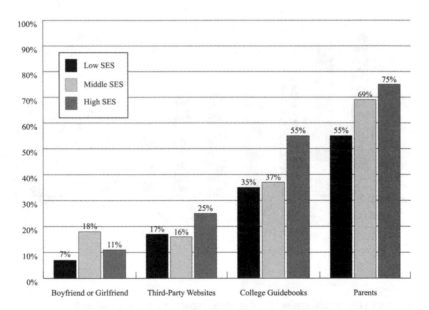

FIGURE 5.4. Social class differences in the individuals and resources influencing HSVP students' application decisions (N = 647). *Note:* Results are based on students with application data who selected at least one individual or resource as influential. Students could choose more than one category. *Source:* High School Valedictorian Project Person Dataset.

low-SES students to report being influenced by parents, college guide-books, and third-party websites. These gaps by SES are particularly large for parents and guidebooks. Specifically, 75 percent of high-SES students selected parents, compared with 69 percent of middle-SES and 55 percent of low-SES students. Likewise, 55 percent of high-SES students chose college guidebooks, in contrast with 37 and 35 percent of middle- and low-SES students, respectively.

As noted in chapter 4 on exploration, more-affluent parents were more actively involved than less-affluent parents in exploring college options. The results presented here suggest that this pattern of parental involve-ment continues in the application stage. Chapter 4 also indicated that more-affluent students were more likely to report that their parents bought them college guidebooks. Having these resources permanently in the home likely facilitates student use during the application stage, helping to explain the SES results observed here. High-SES valedictorians may also have been more likely to use guidebooks and third-party websites because they were more likely to consider colleges farther away from home, for which information would be more difficult to gather locally.

Where HSVP Students Applied

The heart of the application stage is where students actually apply. In discussing this topic, differences by social class are again underscored.

This analysis proceeds as follows. The HSVP survey asked students to list all of the institutions at which they filed applications. Since less than 1 percent of valedictorians applied to a less-than-four-year college and this percentage did not differ by social class, only four-year colleges were studied.[16] Four-year colleges were placed into four distinct categories that combine both control and selectivity dimensions: regular public, regular private, most-selective public, and most-selective private institutions. In-stitutional control was determined using Integrated Postsecondary Edu-cation Data System (IPEDS) data and "private" refers to private nonprofit institutions only.[17] As for selectivity classifications, colleges were consid-ered "most selective" if *U.S. News & World Report* (2006) gave them this highest selectivity rating and "regular" if *U.S News* gave them any other selectivity rating. These are the same selectivity designations used throughout the book. Appendix A provides a complete list of the seventy-two public and private colleges *U.S. News* considered most selective.

In examining where students apply, this chapter focuses on whether or not valedictorians sent at least one application to one of these four institutional categories. The logic behind this approach is that students who do not apply to a certain type of college foreclose the opportunity to attend that kind of college. But those who submit at least one application keep the option of attending that type of institution open for at least a little longer in the college destination process.

Valedictorians applied to different types of colleges at varying rates. At 66 percent, HSVP students were most likely to apply to a most-selective private college. Regular public colleges, which are typically less expensive and more available locally than most-selective private institutions, were applied to the next most frequently, at 61 percent. Valedictorians applied to the other two types of institutions—regular private colleges (plentiful, but generally more costly) and most-selective public colleges (less numerous, but usually cheaper)[18]—at a lower rate: 45 percent.

There were also large social class differences in where students applied. As figure 5.5 depicts, the percentage of students applying to a most-selective private college increases monotonically with social class. Just half of low-SES and 58 percent of middle-SES valedictorians applied to this type of college compared with 80 percent of all high-SES valedictorians—a 30 percentage-point gap. The pattern is the same at most-selective public colleges, though the gap by SES is somewhat smaller at 19 percentage points.[19] Application rates to regular private colleges follow the opposite pattern, with likelihood of applying falling with increased SES. Sixty percent of low-SES students applied to a regular private college compared with 35 percent of high-SES students. Finally, while the pattern by SES at regular public colleges is not monotonic, less-affluent low- and middle-SES students at 65 and 70 percent, respectively, were more apt to apply than high-SES students at 52 percent. Throughout, differences between low- and middle-SES students were consistently smaller than differences between high-SES students and the next SES group.

Regressions produce a similar pattern by SES. The results reveal that once controls for race and gender are added, low- and middle-SES students did not significantly differ in their odds of applying to any of these four types of institutions. High-SES students, however, continued to stand apart. Compared to their middle-SES counterparts, high-SES valedictorians had significantly greater odds of applying to a most-selective public college controlling for gender and race, and significantly

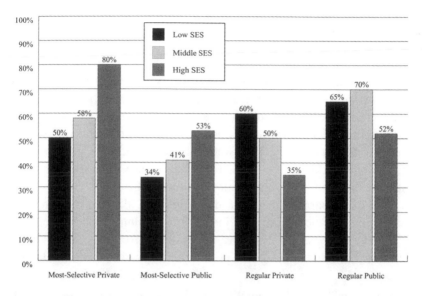

FIGURE 5.5. The percentage of HSVP students applying to at least one college of this type, by social class (N=715). *Note:* Results are based on students with application data. Differences by social class were significant at the .001 level for each institution type. *Source:* High School Valedictorian Project Person Dataset.

greater odds of applying to a most-selective private college even with additional controls like SAT score and other family characteristics. For regular colleges, the opposite pattern prevailed. Compared to middle-SES valedictorians, high-SES valedictorians exhibited significantly lower odds of applying to a regular public college controlling for gender and race, and significantly lower odds of applying to a regular private college controlling for gender, race, SAT score, family characteristics, high school and community characteristics, and total number of applications submitted. (For more details on these regression results, see appendix F, tables F.5.2–F.5.5.)

Conclusion

More than any of the prior stages discussed in this study, the application stage sets the course for students' ultimate college destinations. Like the lotto slogan "you can't win if you don't play," the message in the college destination process could be "you can't attend if you don't apply." With this adage in mind, the most important findings of the chapter are highlighted below.

First, there was significant variation in the number of colleges to which students apply. At the two extremes, 15 percent of valedictorians applied to only one institution, while 38 percent applied to six or more. Valedictorians who applied to six or more universities did so mainly because they were informed that doing so was appropriate and/or they sought to attend an elite college where chances of admission are less assured, even for valedictorians. High-SES students were more likely than their peers to apply to a large number of universities.

By a large margin, valedictorians were most likely to indicate that academic reputation/prestige of institution was important in their application decisions. The next most commonly selected factor was campus visit. Though these two most popularly chosen characteristics did not differ by SES, other differences by SES did emerge. High-SES students were more likely to pick reputation and campus environment items, while middle- and low-SES students were more likely to select cost and distance from home criteria.

This chapter also examined the individuals and sources that shaped application decisions. Parents and information provided by colleges were chosen most often by valedictorians. Similar to what was observed in the exploration stage (see chapter 4), the higher the valedictorians' SES, the more likely they were to indicate that their parents were involved in their application choices. The assistance of these more-affluent parents may also have been more helpful because they could likely offer advice based on their personal college experience and/or the experiences of their greater number of college-educated contacts.

Finally, the chapter investigated the types of institutions to which valedictorians applied. Valedictorians may have been headed toward different college destinations in previous stages, but they still had the power to alter their trajectories through their application decisions. By the end of the application stage, however, doors close. And when they do, some SES groups are more likely than others to have jettisoned certain college options.

Given that HSVP students are among the most accomplished high school students in the country, the extent to which they forego attending some of the best universities in the country is of particular interest. Results indicate that 50 percent of low-SES and 42 percent of middle-

SES valedictorians have abandoned the possibility of attending a most-selective private college by not filing an application to at least one such institution. In contrast, only 20 percent of high-SES valedictorians have similarly eliminated this type of elite college from contention. This pattern by SES is also present at most-selective public colleges, where cost concerns should be less of a barrier. By the end of the application stage, 66 percent of low-SES and 59 percent of middle-SES valedictorians no longer have the chance to enroll in a most-selective public college compared with 47 percent of high-SES valedictorians. Chapter 8 will examine how the magnitude of these SES differences in the application stage compares with the extent of SES differences in the admissions and enrollment stages.

CHAPTER SIX

Admissions

Gaining Permission to Enter

A s explained in chapter 5, the application stage is extremely important in shaping where students enroll. Yet college destinations are also affected by college admissions, as students cannot enroll in colleges that reject their application. In the admissions phase, control shifts away from students and to institutions, as it is institutions that decide whether or not to offer students acceptance letters.

In thinking about admissions, it is important to remember that rejections occur infrequently in the United States. The majority of American colleges accept 80 percent or more of their applicant pool (Menand, 2003) and the average acceptance rate at four-year colleges is about 66 percent (Clinedinst, Hurley, and Hawkins, 2011). In fact, fewer than 150 colleges have acceptance rates of less than 50 percent (Carnevale and Rose, 2004). Moreover, depending on the specific student population examined, between two-thirds and nine-tenths of students are even admitted to their first-choice institution (Hoover, 2008; Lederman, 2009b; Pryor et al., 2006).

Thus, most students—and particularly top students like valedictorians—are able to attend the institutions to which they apply. Of course, students' success in gaining admission, particularly at their first-choice institutions, occurs in part because students self-select in where they apply; less-qualified students do not bother to apply to more-competitive schools where their chance of acceptance is low. If these less well-prepared students did start applying to more-selective colleges, admissions would become more of a hurdle for them.

That being said, for high-achieving students like valedictorians, admissions is unlikely to be a barrier to entry at most institutions. Only at a handful of the most-selective universities do admissions committees routinely reject applicants,[1] including valedictorian applicants.[2] Still, because it is possible for the admissions stage to constrain students' college options, it is important to include admissions decisions in order to fully understand the college destination process.[3]

This chapter details the admissions stage of the college destination process by discussing both colleges' objectives during the admissions process and High School Valedictorian Project (HSVP) students' admissions outcomes.[4] The opening two sections of the chapter use the HSVP *application* dataset to assess how *valedictorians' individual applications* were received at different types of colleges. This type of analysis reveals whether an application tied to a given set of student characteristics received an offer of admission to a particular school. It is thus most closely tied to a university's acceptance rate.

While it is important to know how students' individual applications fare at various types of colleges, to understand the college destination process it is also valuable to know whether admissions decisions foreclosed the opportunity of students to attend a particular type of college. To assess this, the next section of the chapter returns to the HSVP *person* dataset used in the rest of this book and analyzes how *valedictorians as individuals* fared. Specifically, it reveals how likely valedictorians were to have an offer of admission from a particular type of college if they submitted at least one application to this type of institution. The motivation behind doing this second type of analysis is that from the college destination perspective, it does not really matter if a student applied to Harvard, Princeton, and Yale and had a 100 percent application acceptance rate (all three applications accepted) or a 33 percent application acceptance rate (just one application accepted). What matters is that in both cases the student had the opportunity to enroll in a most-selective private college and reap the benefits that studies show come from attending.[5]

How HSVP Students' Applications Fare

As Espenshade and Radford (2009) discuss, while individual colleges may have particular preferences in deciding whom to admit, college admissions decisions are generally guided by one or more of the following three institutional priorities: (1) enroll sufficient numbers of students to meet bottom-line budget targets, (2) obtain students of sufficient quality, and (3) ensure variety and diversity among the student body (Duffy and Goldberg, 1998). Colleges that are less selective or not selective focus primarily on meeting the first of these three objectives (Kirp, 2003). More-selective institutions, in contrast, are able to take all three criteria into consideration because of the abundance of applications they receive.[6]

Examining how applications submitted by valedictorians are received in the admissions process requires shifting the unit of analysis from individual valedictorians to applications submitted by valedictorians.[7] The HSVP dataset contains admissions outcomes for 3,035 valedictorian applications. In order to capture the varying admissions policies used at different types of institutions to evaluate these applications, applications were disaggregated into six categories: regular in-state public, regular out-of-state public, regular private, most-selective in-state public, most-selective out-of-state public, and most-selective private.

Acceptance rates and admissions policies at these six types of institutions differ along three lines. First, they vary in college selectivity. Compared with other colleges, most-selective institutions not only admit a smaller percentage of applicants but their accepted applicants exhibit higher test scores and grades (Morse and Flanigan, 2006). Admissions policies also differ by control. In general, public colleges tend to rely more on a combination of grade point average (GPA) and standardized test scores in determining whom to admit, while private colleges typically employ a more holistic review in which letters of recommendation, extracurriculars, and essays play a role. Finally, residency can be a factor in admissions decisions, particularly at public universities. Generally, the admissions offices of private colleges do not pay much attention to whether an application is submitted by an in-state or an out-of-state student.[8] Public institutions, however, are charged specifically with educating the people within their state borders (Tobin, 2009), and thus usually have lower admissions standards for in-state than for out-of-state students (Groen and White, 2003).

HSVP applications were sent to different types of institutions at varying rates. By far the greatest percentage of all HSVP applications (48 percent), were filed at most-selective private colleges. The next three largest percentages of filed applications (at 19, 16, and 11 percent, respectively) went to regular in-state public, regular private, and most-selective in-state public colleges. Relatively few applications were submitted to out-of-state public universities, regardless of whether they were most selective (3 percent of all applications) or not most selective (also 3 percent of all applications).[9]

As expected, admit rates at these types of colleges vary, particularly along selectivity lines. As figure 6.1 clearly depicts, acceptance rates were highest for applications filed at regular in-state public institutions; 99.7 percent of all applications to such schools received offers of admission. At 96 and 97 percent, respectively, acceptance rates were also extremely high for applications submitted at regular out-of-state public and regular private institutions.

Acceptance rates at most-selective institutions varied more. While the 97 percent acceptance rate at most-selective in-state public institutions was comparable to that of regular institutions, admission to other most-selective institutions was less assured. At most-selective out-of-state public colleges, 85 percent of HSVP applications were accepted. But by far the lowest admit rate for HSVP applications was at most-selective private colleges (54 percent).

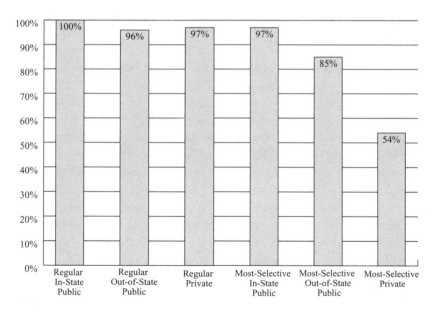

FIGURE 6.1. The percentage of HSVP applications accepted at different types of colleges (N=3,033). *Source:* High School Valedictorian Project Application Dataset.

The lower acceptance rates at these last two institution types should not be surprising, however, when considered in context. Admissions standards at most-selective public universities are high in general. For example, students admitted as freshmen to the prestigious public University of Virginia in the spring of 2009 had an average combined math and verbal SAT score of 1390 and a mean high school GPA of 4.14. Ninety-one percent were in the top tenth of their high school class (Heuchert, 2009). When one considers that gaining admission to a most-selective public college as an out-of-state resident typically requires exhibiting even higher levels of performance (Groen and White, 2003), this 85 percent HSVP acceptance rate starts to look more impressive.

Even the seemingly low 54 percent admit rate at most-selective private colleges is quite high considering the admit rate of applications in general at such schools. Recent admissions data made publicly available through the U.S. Department of Education (2011)[10] reveals that eight of the private institutions deemed most selective by *U.S. News* had acceptance rates of 10 percent or below, sixteen had rates between 11 percent and 20 percent, and another sixteen had rates between 21 percent and 30 percent. The average acceptance rate for all 61 most-selective private institutions was 24 percent. Valedictorian applications' 54 percent acceptance rate was more than twice as high.

We already know from chapter 5 that many lower-SES valedictorians do not apply to more-selective schools. But among those who do, how do they fare? HSVP data reveal that most of the time, SES differences in acceptance rates do not occur. No significant admissions difference could be detected by SES at regular in-state public, regular out-of-state public, regular private, or most-selective in-state public institutions. At most-selective out-of-state public colleges, where acceptance rates were slightly lower, a significant difference by social class did emerge, but only 3 percent of all applications were filed at such institutions and only three applications total came from low-SES students.

By far the clearest social class difference in acceptance rates occurred at most-selective private institutions. Low-SES students enjoyed the highest rate of success: 63 percent of their applications were accepted. Applications submitted by middle- and high-SES valedictorians, in contrast, were admitted at rates of 50 and 54 percent, respectively. Thus, when low-SES valedictorians do submit applications (which they do less frequently than their more-affluent peers), their applications have a better probability of admission than those sent by their more-affluent peers.

This apparent low-SES admissions advantage holds, controlling for gender, race, SAT score, number of passed AP and IB exams, as well as other variables known to influence acceptance at most-selective private institutions, like applying under an early admissions program,[11] as a legacy applicant,[12] or as an athletic recruit.[13] Applications submitted by low-SES students had more than twice the odds of admission as applications submitted by middle-SES students (see appendix F, table F.6.1). This finding suggests that most-selective private college admissions officers do give a preference to low-SES valedictorians, particularly when they are otherwise similar to middle-SES valedictorians. Given the greater socioeconomic hurdles less-affluent students face, admissions officers may be more impressed when low-SES students reach the top of their class than when middle- or high-SES students manage to do so.

It is important to put this preference for low-SES valedictorians in the context of other research findings. First, low-income or low-SES students have been found to represent just 10 to 11 percent of all undergraduates at the nation's most-selective public and private colleges (Bowen, Kurzweil, and Tobin, 2005; Espenshade and Radford, 2009; Heller, 2004). These statistics have led to calls for greater social class diversity at these institutions (Bowen, Kurzweil, and Tobin, 2005; Kahlenberg, 2004, 2010a). One way to increase the representation of low-SES students is through admission. Yet thus far, investigations examining all applicants, and not just valedictorians, have found that low-SES and first-generation college students receive only a negligible to modest advantage in elite college admissions, all else equal (Bowen, Kurzweil, and Tobin, 2005; Espenshade, Hale, and Chung, 2005). That being said, there is some evidence that most-selective private colleges are more likely to show low-SES students preference than are most-selective public colleges, particularly if these low-SES students are from nonwhite backgrounds (Espenshade and Radford, 2009). Admitting less-affluent students who are nonwhite bolsters not just the number of low-SES students enrolled but also helps universities achieve their diversity goals. Similarly, low-SES valedictorians may be more attractive than low-SES students generally because they are able to help colleges' profiles in two ways: by increasing the percentage of students from low-SES backgrounds and by raising the percentage of students with high class ranks. This benefit may cause admissions officers to give more of an advantage to low-SES valedictorians than they do low-SES applicants at large.

How HSVP Students Fare Personally

While acceptance rates for valedictorians' applications are important, they do not reveal what happens to valedictorians as individuals. As noted in this chapter's introduction, valedictorians who submitted three applications to three different most-selective private colleges and were accepted by only one would have an application acceptance rate of 33 percent. While this rate is low, the fact that these valedictorians have even one offer from a most-selective private college means that they can still attend this type of institution and enjoy the educational, financial, and career benefits that appear to be connected to this enrollment. In fact, if they matriculate, they will be just as able to receive the advantages of most-selective college attendance as students who had a perfect 100 percent application acceptance rate at most-selective private colleges. For this reason, it is critical that this chapter examine whether individual valedictorians had at least one offer of admission from a given type of institution if they applied to that type of institution.

To determine how *valedictorians* rather than *applications* fare at the six types of institutions identified at the outset of this chapter, this section shifts the unit of analysis from applications back to valedictorians. This valedictorian analysis assesses whether students who submitted at least one application to a given institution type received at least one offer of admission from this institution type. Acceptance rates for valedictorians as individuals did not differ significantly by social class at any of the six types of institutions examined and therefore only results for valedictorians as a whole are discussed here.

The overall pattern is very similar to that observed with valedictorians' applications. Valedictorians who applied to an institution that was not most selective were almost guaranteed an acceptance letter. About 99 percent of valedictorians who applied to a regular in-state public, regular out-of-state public, or regular private college were accepted by at least one college of this type. Valedictorians also had a 99 percent admit rate at most-selective in-state public institutions. HSVP students were slightly less embraced at the two other types of most-selective institutions. Ninety percent of valedictorians who applied to a most-selective public out-of-state university and 83 percent of valedictorians who applied to a most-selective private college received at least one acceptance letter from this kind of university.

Though valedictorians' acceptance rate of 83 percent at most-selective private colleges is lower than those at other institution types, it is important to stress that this HSVP *students'* admit rate is much higher than the HSVP *applications'* admit rate of 54 percent. It is also much higher than the average acceptance rate of 24 percent for applicants at large at America's sixty-one most-selective private colleges (U.S. Department of Education, 2011), and significantly higher than the acceptance rates of less than 10 percent exhibited at seven or so of the most elite private universities (Ellis, 2012).

For valedictorians who wish to have a greater than 83 percent chance of admission to an elite private college, HSVP results suggest that applying to a greater number of institutions of this type may help. While 83 percent of students who applied to one or more most-selective private colleges were admitted to at least one, 89 percent of those who applied to two or more, 93 percent of those who applied to three or more, 96 percent of those who applied to four or more, and 98 percent of those who applied to five or more received at least one letter of acceptance. Though the pattern is clear, this strategy of applying to more elite colleges should not be viewed as foolproof; valedictorians who applied to a greater number of most-selective private colleges may have had a better chance of acceptance due to other aspects of their application.[14]

Conclusion

This chapter revealed that at most types of institutions, valedictorians' college applications enjoy a very successful reception. The generally high admit rate of applications submitted by valedictorians is to be expected given their level of academic performance and the fact that academic achievement is a primary factor in college admissions. The one type of institution where valedictorians' applications do not have as high an acceptance rate is most-selective private colleges, where just 54 percent of all HSVP applications submitted were accepted. This lower admit rate occurs because most-selective private colleges have an abundance of high-achieving applicants, which in turn allows these institutions to consider additional criteria in deciding whom to admit.

While applications' acceptance rates did not differ by SES at most institution types, they did at most-selective private colleges. Sixty-three percent of low-SES, 54 percent of high-SES, and 50 percent of middle-SES applications received a positive response in return. Moreover, applications from low-SES students were more likely to be admitted, even controlling for an array of factors that have been linked to odds of admission, suggesting that when other traits are equal, most-selective private colleges give low-SES valedictorians an advantage over other valedictorians.

The final section of this chapter examined how individual valedictorians fared (rather than how their applications fared). The analysis indicated that even at most-selective private colleges where gaining admission is more difficult, valedictorians were very likely to be accepted if they applied. This finding was true regardless of social class. Low-, middle-, and high-SES students were similarly likely to be accepted at a given type of institution if they simply applied to that type of institution. This result suggests that the admissions stage does not funnel valedictorians of different social class backgrounds toward particular types of institutions. The next chapter will explore the role the matriculation phase plays in shaping HSVP students' ultimate college destinations.

CHAPTER SEVEN

Matriculation

Selecting among Offers of Admission

Eventually, the notices arrive (accepted, rejected, wait-listed), costs are defined (expensive, inexpensive, manageable; scholarship, no scholarship), and the matriculation stage of the college destination process begins. What happens during this phase? More specifically, how do high achievers decide between the types of institutions that accept them and where do they ultimately enroll?

This chapter answers these questions using the following structure. The first two sections tackle how students make their enrollment decisions. It employs both qualitative and quantitative High School Valedictorian Project (HSVP) data to highlight both the college characteristics and the individuals and sources that influenced valedictorians' decisions. The third section of the chapter uses survey data to reveal the actual types of institutions in which valedictorians enrolled based on their offers of admission. By examining where students decide to enroll given the offers of admission they receive, this chapter is able to isolate the role the matriculation stage plays in leading students toward various college destinations. The next chapter will discuss where students attend as a result of the decisions made throughout the stages of the college destination process.

College Characteristics HSVP Students Considered
When Making Matriculation Decisions

Students take into account a variety of factors in deciding where to enroll.
The HSVP survey asked valedictorians to select the five college characteristics that most influenced their enrollment decisions from a list of twenty-
three options. The options presented correspond with those provided in
an earlier question that asked students to select the five factors that most
influenced their application decisions. These items were developed after
an exhaustive literature review of works examining the characteristics
that students value in selecting a college.

Valedictorians were particularly likely to identify two factors as important in their matriculation choice. As table 7.1 reveals, just over two-thirds
of all HSVP students selected academic reputation/prestige of institution
and nearly 62 percent chose campus visit. These two factors were also
selected most frequently as influential in students' application decisions.[1]
Because other characteristics were not selected nearly as often, they are
presented by the categories outlined and explained in chapter 5, which
discusses application. These categories are: academic, reputation, cost,
distance from home, and campus environment.

As explained in chapter 5, there is some overlap between academic and
reputation factors and so these characteristics are discussed together.[2]
While 67 percent of valedictorians picked academic reputation/prestige
of institution as one of their five most influential factors, one-third of
HSVP students selected special academic program and roughly one-fifth
picked faculty attention/involvement in teaching, rankings in national
magazines, and/or graduates have good employment outcomes. These
findings are consistent with other research, which finds that students in
general[3] and high-achieving students[4] put emphasis on academic and
reputation factors when selecting an institution.

Comparing the results in table 7.1 with table 5.1 (which shows the factors students selected as influential in their application decisions) reveals
that the percentage of HSVP students selecting special academic programs, faculty attention, graduates' employment outcomes, and graduates'
admission to top graduate schools as influential in their application choice
does not differ substantially from the percentage selecting these items
as important in their matriculation choice. Nevertheless, the percentage selecting two items (academic reputation/prestige of institution and

TABLE 7.1 **The Percentage of HSVP Students Reporting That the Following College Characteristics Were among the Five That Most Influenced Where They Decided to Enroll, by Social Class (N=434)**

Factor by Category	Total	Low SES	Middle SES	High SES	Significance
Academic					
Special Academic Program (Major, Honors)	32.7	31.2	33.0	33.0	—
Faculty Attention/Involvement in Teaching	20.1	18.0	18.7	22.0	—
Reputation					
Academic Reputation/Prestige of Institution	66.8	59.0	61.0	74.9	**
Rankings in National Magazines	20.5	14.8	13.7	28.8	**
Graduates Have Good Employment Outcomes	20.1	16.4	17.6	23.6	—
Graduates Admitted to Top Graduate Schools	16.8	13.1	12.6	22.0	*
Cost					
Cost of Attendance	29.5	42.6	39.0	16.2	***
Merit Aid	24.9	19.7	30.8	20.9	—
Financial Aid Package	29.0	63.9	36.8	10.5	***
Distance from Home					
Desire to Study Away from Hometown	17.5	19.7	14.8	19.4	—
Desire to Study Near Hometown	18.7	16.4	23.1	15.2	—
Desire to Attend College While Living at Home	6.0	14.8	7.1	2.1	**
Campus Environment					
Campus Visit	61.8	54.1	61.0	64.9	—
Campus Location (State or City/ Community)	28.3	16.4	29.7	30.9	—
College Size	32.3	32.8	29.1	35.1	—
College Setting (Rural, Urban, Suburban)	21.4	23.0	22.0	20.4	—
College Facilities	24.2	13.1	20.9	30.9	**
Special Extracurricular (Abroad Program, Sport)	10.8	6.6	8.8	14.1	—
Other People I Know Will Also Be Attending	9.7	8.2	12.6	7.3	—
Religious Affiliation	4.6	8.2	3.3	4.7	—
Presence of Students of My Ethnicity/ Race	2.1	4.9	1.1	2.1	—
Presence of Students of My Social Class	1.6	3.3	1.7	1.1	—
Desire to Attend a Single-Sex College	.7	.0	1.7	.0	—

Note: Results are based on students with matriculation data who selected five factors as influential, as requested in the survey question. $*p < .05$; $**p < .01$; $***p < .001$
Source: High School Valedictorian Project Person Dataset.

rankings in national magazines) does vary between these two stages. On both, valedictorians were 12 percentage points less likely to indicate that these items affected their matriculation decision as they were to report that these items shaped their application decision.[5] In other words, prestige and rankings were less likely to be critical to students when making their final enrollment choice than when they were determining where to apply.

HSVP interviews suggest that these two reputation items may be less important during the matriculation phase because students frequently only applied to (or only seriously considered attending) colleges that already satisfied their prestige requirements. Put another way, students who felt their college options in the matriculation stage were similarly reputable tended to find factors other than reputation to help them make their enrollment choice.

A focus on differences by social class during the matriculation stage reveals that while valedictorians did not differ by socioeconomic status (SES) in their propensity to select academic factors as important in deciding where to enroll, they did vary in their propensity to choose reputation items. When asked about their enrollment decision, high-SES valedictorians were about twice as likely as both their low- and middle-SES peers to select rankings in national magazines, 14 to 16 percentage points more likely to choose academic reputation/prestige of institution, and 9 percentage points more likely to pick graduates admitted to top graduate schools. Moreover, 45 percent of high-SES students selected at least two reputation items as among the five that most influenced their matriculation choice. Only 26 percent of low-SES and 30 percent of middle-SES students did the same. The greater emphasis high-SES students place on institutional prestige was also observed in the predisposition, preparation, exploration, and application chapters. Other investigations find that high-SES students at large are also more focused on reputation (Duffy and Goldberg, 1998; Flanagan, 2001; Mayher, 1998) and even rankings specifically (McDonough et al., 1998). Being a high achiever does not appear to eliminate these general SES differences, as social class differences clearly appear even among HSVP students.

The way academics and reputation shape students' enrollment choices was also explored qualitatively. Interviews revealed that an interest in pursuing graduate school funneled HSVP students toward two very different types of colleges. The first group of students' graduate school plans encouraged them to attend less-expensive, less-prestigious public colleges. There were two main reasons these students moved in this direction. For one, they generally emphasized in interviews that graduate school could be costly, and knowing this, they purposefully enrolled in a lower-cost college for their bachelor's degree in order to save money and minimize their undergraduate debt. Middle- and high-SES students who followed this path sometimes even struck explicit deals with their parents, in which any remaining funds that their parents had designated for their undergraduate education could be used to cover graduate school expenses. Other times, parents made more implicit offers in which they hinted that they would be more able to help cover graduate school costs if their child opted to enroll in a less expensive undergraduate institution. Either way, such arrangements encouraged some valedictorians with graduate school aspirations to enroll in less-expensive colleges for their bachelor's degrees.

A second reason some valedictorians with graduate school plans opted for less-costly, less-selective public institutions was because they were told by parents, teachers, and/or individuals working in their career field of interest that the reputation of their undergraduate college would not have a strong impact on their careers if they planned to attend graduate school. A middle-SES aspiring doctor identified both this and the above cost rationale as influential in her decision to forego a more expensive Ivy League university's offer of admission and instead matriculate at a regular public college:

If [regular public college *x*] is giving me this amount of money, where I'm basically not going to have to pay anything after the scholarship, why not do it, because I know I'm going to med[ical] school and I'm going to have to take out loans then, so why take out loans now? And I was talking to people . . . in terms of how much does your undergraduate education matter? And if you're going to be a physician, no one looks at your undergraduate school; they want to look at where you went to med[ical] school. So I'm like, "Okay, if that's the case, then I can go to [regular public college]." And that's basically how I went there.

The second group of valedictorians with graduate school aspirations made very different matriculation choices. They enrolled in the most prestigious undergraduate institution they could attend in an effort to improve their chances of admission at an elite graduate school. Even when enrolling in a more prestigious college as an undergraduate was more expensive, valedictorians in this camp, who tended to come from high-SES and/or immigrant backgrounds, felt that it was worth paying more if it might improve their graduate school prospects.

This second group of valedictorians conveyed that they did not just want to attend *a graduate school*, as students in the first faction professed. Rather, this second cluster wanted to attend *one of the best graduate schools*. These students believed that enrolling in a stronger undergraduate institution would increase their chances of acceptance at a better graduate school. While students in this category may not have believed that a prestigious undergraduate institution would provide a guaranteed path to a better life, they felt, at the very least, that attending a prestigious college as an undergraduate could not hurt. They reasoned that if they had the opportunity to enroll in an elite college for their undergraduate education, they should do so irrespective of the cost.[6]

Generally, research supports the latter group's position. Studies find that controlling for a range of factors, students from more-selective undergraduate alma maters are more likely to go to graduate school, attend more-selective graduate institutions, and finish graduate degrees (Bowen and Bok, 1998; Eide, Brewer, and Ehrenberg, 1998; Zhang, 2005a). Attending a most-selective undergraduate institution may also encourage students' interest in applying to graduate school and facilitate their admission to graduate programs—particularly elite ones (Bernstein, 2003; Weiss, 1997)—and provide the academic preparation helpful in successfully completing.

Not just academic and reputation factors shape matriculation decisions. Cost is another important consideration for many. Between 25 and 30 percent of valedictorians indicated that cost of attendance, merit aid, or financial aid package influenced their enrollment decision. Other research shows that factors related to college costs, including low tuition, price, expenses, and financial aid/scholarship assistance play a role in where students submit their enrollment deposits (Archer and Bailey, 2000; Chapman, 1993; Choy and Ottinger, 1998; College Savings Foundation, 2010; Gardner, 1987; Kim, DesJardins, and McCall, 2009; Sanderson et al., 1996; Sax et al., 2003; Shank and Beasley, 1998). A recent study found that 58 percent of all families considered cost during the matriculation stage (Sallie Mae and Gallup, 2008).

A comparison of the percentage of valedictorians selecting cost factors as influential in the application and matriculation stages reveals that cost factors were selected at higher rates in the matriculation stage. Specifically, students were 3 percentage points more likely to choose cost of attendance, 4 percentage points more likely to pick merit aid, and 9 percentage points more likely to select financial aid in the matriculation than application stage.[7] Thus, though cost factors play a role in both stages of the college destination process, they seem to be more likely to have an influence once students receive their aid packages and know their net costs.

Social class differences in valedictorians' likelihood of selecting cost factors as important in their matriculation decisions are stark. As table 7.1 displays, about 64 percent of low-SES and 37 percent of middle-SES valedictorians picked financial aid package as influential in their matriculation choice compared with just 11 percent of high-SES valedictorians. Similarly, low- and middle-SES students picked cost of attendance at higher rates (43 and 39 percent, respectively) than high-SES students (16 percent). Differences by SES in the selection of merit aid fall short of statistical significance at the .05 level but are statistically significant at the .1 level. The SES pattern on this measure, however, is distinct. One-fifth of both low- and high-SES students identified merit aid as important compared to about one-third of middle-SES students. Possible implications for middle-SES valedictorians' more frequent selection of merit aid will be discussed in greater detail later in this chapter.

Overall, 8 percent of high-SES valedictorians selected at least two cost factors as important in their enrollment choice, compared with 36 percent of low-SES and 28 percent of middle-SES valedictorians. This finding further underscores that less-affluent valedictorians tend to weigh cost more than their high-SES peers in making their matriculation decision. Less-affluent students' greater emphasis on cost has been found in other research as well.[8] Having high potential does not appear to eliminate cost concerns for low- and middle-SES valedictorians.[9]

In interviews with HSVP students, the importance of cost varied. Some high-SES students indicated that cost was never a consideration in their college destination process, and that the matriculation stage was no exception. These valedictorians tended not to consider cost because their parents: (1) indicated that they would cover all college costs, (2) instructed them not to worry about money, and/or (3) told them they could attend any college they wanted. Having no personal financial incentive to attend a cheaper school and having permission from their parents not to consider cost implications for their family, these students based their enrollment decisions on other criteria.

Parents who gave their children carte blanche in selecting their undergraduate institution tended to convey to their offspring that education was an investment and that the greater returns received from attending a more prestigious college would be worth the higher costs of attending. The adults who imparted this message were frequently both graduate school educated and of high socioeconomic status. The fact that these parents invested in their own education beyond the bachelor's degree and achieved high socioeconomic status may make them more likely than parents whose incomes are not as tied to an advanced degree to perceive a relationship between educational investment and economic returns.[10]

While some valedictorians did not think about costs during the matriculation stage because they were told by their parents not to take costs into account throughout the entire college destination process, another group of valedictorians did not consider costs during the matriculation stage precisely because they had kept costs in mind in previous stages. This latter group, which was especially likely to include middle-SES students, tended to eliminate cost differences between institutions through their exploration and/or application decisions. Typically, such students never explored or applied to private colleges, and the public colleges to which they applied and were accepted all exhibited the same or similar price tags. As a result, cost was a moot point in their matriculation decisions.

Though the previous two groups of valedictorians did not consider cost in their matriculation choice, many HSVP students' enrollment decisions were influenced by cost to some degree. Although some such valedictorians decided to enroll in a college solely because it was the cheapest one to which they were admitted or because they received a scholarship from that university, a greater number reported that cost was just one of several reasons they chose their college. For example, campus environment and lower cost combined to make one student choose a most-selective public college instead of a most-selective private college. Another student accepted by two similarly prestigious universities chose the cheaper of the two. All else equal, "Why not also help my parents a little bit?" was her feeling. Some HSVP students chose the intermediate-priced institution at which they were admitted because it was still financially feasible and they liked it better than their cheapest option. Better academic program offerings at another college convinced several to forego less-expensive options. Another institution's greater prestige persuaded others, especially high-SES valedictorians, to reject cheaper college options.

To further explore the role of cost in matriculation decisions, HSVP students were asked in interviews whether they or their families had set a specific dollar limit on the amount they were willing to pay—or go into debt to pay—for college. Low-SES students were particularly likely to give debt-averse statements like: "I definitely didn't want to take out any loans . . . I didn't want to go into debt." They were also more likely than their peers to report that they or their families had established limits to the amount they were willing to spend or borrow for their undergraduate education.

Students and parents from more-affluent families, in contrast, were less likely to have created a definitive budget and tended to view cost as just one of many factors to consider in choosing a college. Such families were often willing to pay more for a degree from a college with a better reputation, especially if that reputation was world renowned. For example, one high-SES valedictorian explained that while he turned down a most-selective private college to enroll in his state's flagship, which offered him considerable merit aid, if he had been accepted to a particular "Big Three" Ivy League college,[11] he and his family would have obtained the loans and done "whatever would have been necessary to go." Another high-SES student whose parent had just been laid off at the time of her matriculation choice, enrolled in a regular in-state public college for free rather than attend one of two most-selective public colleges to which she was admitted. Still, she reported that "if I had gotten into ['Big Three' Ivy League college x], then I would have paid for the entire thing." Yet another student who declined a most-selective private college and a most-selective public college to enroll in a less-selective college that offered her merit aid related: "If I had gotten into ['Big Three' Ivy League college y], even with no scholarship, I would have taken out as much money as I needed to 'cause I feel like it's something that's worth it. If you're going to spend that much money on something, it might as well be an education at [Big Three Ivy League college y]." In sum, the überelite colleges, but not elite colleges just a few ranks lower, were perceived to offer a heightened and distinct return on investment.[12]

A college's distance from home also shapes students' matriculation choice (Choy and Ottinger, 1998; Gardner, 1987; Sanderson et al., 1996; Sax et al., 2003). HSVP survey results also find that some students felt this to be an important consideration. Slightly less than one-fifth of students indicated that a desire to study away from their hometown influenced where they decided to enroll, while almost another one-fifth reported just the opposite: that a desire to study near their hometown affected their matriculation choice. Relatively few valedictorians reported that a desire to attend college while living at home shaped their decision (6 percent).

HSVP qualitative findings were consistent with these quantitative results. When students were asked in open-ended interview questions what influenced their matriculation choice, they raised factors related to a college's distance from home far less frequently than other items. Moreover, none of the fifty-five students interviewed suggested that a college's distance from home was the primary reason they decided to enroll in a given institution.

Desire to attend college while living at home and desire to study near hometown were selected by comparably low percentages of students as important in both the matriculation and application stages. Desire to study away from hometown, however, was selected as influential less frequently during the enrollment choice than in the application decision. In the application stage, 26 percent of students chose this factor, whereas only 18 percent did in the matriculation stage.

Interviews suggest a couple of reasons for these results. First, distance from home preferences tended to be evaluated and addressed during the exploration and application stages of the college destination process. As a result, any colleges seriously under consideration during the matriculation phase were typically already viewed as an acceptable distance from home, making distance less useful as a tiebreaker. Second, some students changed their minds about wanting to attend college away from home over the course of the college destination process. They usually decided that it was not important to them or no longer as important to them as they originally anticipated. Low- and middle-SES students were more likely than more-affluent students to have second thoughts about attending college farther away. Their concern about attending more-distant institutions was largely the same as that given in the application stage: they wanted to be able to drive home in cases of emergency (see chapter 5 for more detail on this SES difference).

Examining just quantitative matriculation data by social class indicates that HSVP students differed by SES on only one distance factor: desire to attend college while living at home. As table 7.1 reveals, the importance of living at home steadily declines as social class increases. Fifteen percent of low-SES, 7 percent of middle-SES, and 2 percent of high-SES students chose this option. Other investigations also observe an SES difference with regard to distance preferences. Several scholars report that low- and middle-SES individuals are more apt than more-affluent students to favor attending a college close to home (Choy and Ottinger, 1998; Sanderson et al., 1996; Turley, 2006). Even in studies of just high achievers, low-income individuals were more likely than their high-income peers to value being able to live at home (not just close to home) while attending college (Avery and Turner, 2008).

Campus environment represents the final category of factors that influenced students' enrollment choice. At 62 percent, campus visit was picked second out of all twenty-three factors listed and was selected first out of all the campus environment options. The high percentage of students identifying campus visit as important mirrored what students revealed in interviews. Valedictorians reported that they both accepted and rejected offers of admission based on the feeling they had on campus. Some got "a bad vibe" when visiting a particular college and decided against attending, while others immediately felt "at home, safe, happy," and enrolled.[13]

After campus visit, college size and campus location were selected the next most often, with 32 percent and 28 percent of students' votes, respectively. College facilities and college setting were also popular, at 24 percent and 21 percent, respectively. College setting and college size were also noted as important in interviews. The remaining campus environment items (special extracurricular, knowing other people attending, college's religious affiliation, presence of students with respondent's racial or ethnic background, presence of students with respondent's social class background, and desire to attend a single-sex institution) were selected by fewer than 11 percent of valedictorians and were not commonly mentioned in interviews.

Research shows that while students at large value a friendly atmosphere, the campus visit, already having friends at the institution, security and safety on campus, a college's size, and campus social life,[14] high achievers appear to give more weight to the campus environment than other students do (Choy and Ottinger, 1998). More than half of all high achievers in one study indicated that appearance or atmosphere of college influenced their matriculation choice (Randall, 1999). Another study of top students found that college size was one of the four most important factors in students' enrollment decisions (Archer and Bailey, 2000).

HSVP students chose campus environment factors at similar rates in both the application and matriculation stages, except in three cases. First, students were about 6 percentage points more likely to select campus location during the application phase than during the enrollment phase. A college's campus location is relatively easy to ascertain and would be simple to use in coarsely sorting colleges in determining where to apply. And if all of the college options left by the matriculation stage already meet students' campus location expectations, this factor is less likely to play a decisive role in enrollment choice.

The other two exceptions flow in the other direction, with factors more likely to be selected during the matriculation stage. First, students were about 5 percentage points more likely to choose college facilities during the later stage. Facilities represent a more specific characteristic for which comparable data on a long list of colleges may be difficult to obtain, making it a less practical measure on which to compare schools during the application stage. Once the number of college options has been culled down through the application and admission stages, however, facilities at potential alma maters may be easier to compare and thus more influential in deciding where to enroll.

The second campus environment factor chosen at a higher rate during the matriculation stage was campus visit. Specifically, valedictorians were 18 percentage points more likely to pick this item as influential during enrollment than during application. Students may select campus visit more frequently during the enrollment stage because some wait to make visits to institutions until after they have been admitted. Though the HSVP survey did not ask students about the timing of their campus visits and HSVP interviews did not question students explicitly about this either, Avery, Fairbanks, and Zeckhauser (2003) note that less-affluent students tend to delay visiting campuses until after they have found out where they have been admitted. This way, they do not spend money traveling to a college that they have not been permitted to attend.

Campus visits may also be more influential in the matriculation stage in that they can help break ties between institutions that otherwise rank similarly on the factors students consider important. For example, one valedictorian wanted to attend a prestigious college and used this as a key consideration in deciding where to apply. Once she received her offers of admission, she decided between these prestigious colleges based on her campus visit. Specifically, she explained that she enrolled in a different elite college than her parents' prestigious alma mater because she had the sense that at her parents' college, "if you weren't always upset at plastic containers and 'Corporate America,' then you weren't OK [accepted or welcome on campus]."

Examining just matriculation choice, there were some SES differences in the importance of campus environment. First, students' likelihood of selecting college facilities steadily increased as their social class rose. While this is the only specific campus environment factor that differed by SES, low-SES students' weaker interest in the campus environment is observed again when analyzing the percentage of students who chose as influential two or more campus environment factors. Fifty-four percent of low-SES valedictorians, compared with 67 percent of middle-SES and 71 percent of high-SES valedictorians, selected at least two campus environment factors.

This HSVP result is consistent with other studies. One investigation found that low-SES students were less likely than their high-SES counterparts to report that a college's campus affected their matriculation choice (Choy and Ottinger, 1998). Another study that was focused on just high achievers observed that lower-income individuals were less apt than their higher-income peers to be influenced by activities and on-campus life (Avery and Turner, 2008). It seems that being a valedictorian does not alter these general SES patterns. Even low-SES students who reached the top of their class put more emphasis on other factors.

Individuals and Resources That Influenced HSVP Students' Matriculation Decisions

In addition to institutional characteristics, individuals and resources shape students' matriculation decisions. Other research has found that parents are especially powerful (Arnold, 1995; MacAllum et al., 2007), and figure 7.1 depicting HSVP survey data illustrates the same. About 84 percent of all valedictorians selected parents as influential. It is important to remember, however, that parents' influence may lead students toward very different types of colleges. Specifically, other research and HSVP interviews suggest that low- and middle-SES parents may be motivated to push their children toward in-state public institutions as a way of reducing college costs, while high-SES parents may promote private, more-selective colleges because they believe such attendance will facilitate their children's future success (Chinni, 2006; Duffy and Goldberg, 1998; Easterbrook, 2004; Flanagan, 2001; Glater, 2006; Lareau, 2003; Mayher, 1998; McDonough, 1997; Rowan-Kenyon, Bell, and Perna, 2008; Soares, 2007).

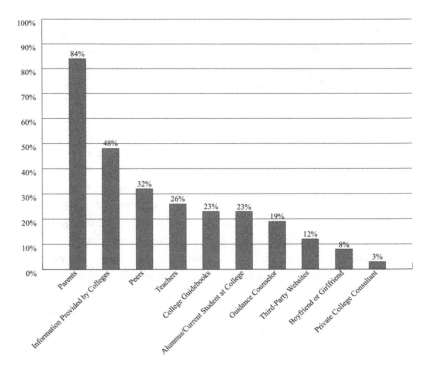

FIGURE 7.1. The percentage of HSVP students reporting that the following individuals or resources influenced their matriculation decisions (N=536). *Note:* Results are based on students with matriculation data who selected at least one individual or resource as influential. Students could choose more than one category. *Source:* High School Valedictorian Project Person Dataset.

Compared with parents, other sources were chosen far less frequently. Less than half of students selected colleges as influential in the matriculation stage, fewer than one-third selected peers, and about one-quarter picked teachers, guidebooks, or alumni. Not even one-fifth chose guidance counselors.

Since HSVP students were given the same list when identifying those influential in their application decisions, it is useful to compare the findings of figure 7.1 to those presented in figure 5.3. Doing so reveals that of all the entities listed, valedictorians were most likely to select parents in both stages. That being said, valedictorians were more likely to identify parents as influential in the matriculation stage (84 percent) than in the application stage (70 percent). In contrast, HSVP students picked all other sources at a lower rate during the matriculation decision than during the application decision.[15] These findings are consistent with Choy and Ottinger's (1998) research and HSVP interviews, which suggest that once students reach the matriculation phase they have established their preferences and are less susceptible to influences outside of the family.

Returning to just matriculation results, the likelihood of students selecting parents increased with SES: 74 percent of low-SES, 82 percent of middle-SES, and 89 percent of high-SES students did so. The same pattern by SES was observed during the application stage. As noted in chapter 4 on exploration, HSVP interviews and Espenshade and Radford's (2009) quantitative data indicate that low-SES parents are less likely than high-SES parents to have specific suggestions about where their children should attend. This result is probably partially due to low-SES parents' lack of personal college experience and college-educated contacts.

Though guidebooks were selected less often than parents, the likelihood of students selecting them also differed significantly by SES. This item was chosen by 16 percent of low-SES, 20 percent of middle-SES, and 29 percent of high-SES students. This SES pattern also occurred in the application stage. HSVP interview results discussed in chapter 4 suggest that consultation of guidebooks may increase with SES because more-affluent parents were more likely to buy these resources for their children, which may in turn facilitate their use. Other sources were not chosen at significantly different rates by SES.

Where HSVP Students Enroll

This section examines differences by social class with regard to where students enroll *given the offers of admission received*. The purpose of analyzing matriculation decisions in this context is to isolate the role these decisions alone play in funneling students toward certain destinations. As noted in the introduction, the next chapter will present students' final college destinations and explain how actions in multiple phases produced the differences observed by social class.

Valedictorians' matriculation preferences are clear. Seventy-one percent of all HSVP students accepted by a most-selective private college enrolled in a most-selective private college. In contrast, 44 percent of those admitted to a most-selective public college, 42 percent accepted by a regular public college, and 36 percent admitted to a regular private college chose to matriculate at that type of institution.[16]

While valedictorians did not differ by SES in their likelihood of accepting an offer of admission from a regular private college or a most-
selective public college, valedictorians did vary by SES in their likelihood of accepting an offer of admission from a regular public college
and a most-selective private college. Among HSVP students admitted to
at least one regular public college, 31 percent of high-SES students enrolled compared with 51 percent of low-SES and 48 percent of middle-SES
students. The lower propensity of high-SES valedictorians to enroll in a
regular public college if admitted holds controlling for gender and race,
but fades once other personal characteristics like SAT score and parents'
postsecondary alma maters are incorporated (see appendix F, table F.7.1).

Among HSVP students admitted to a most-selective private college,
a different matriculation pattern by SES occurred. About 78 percent
of high-SES and 76 percent of low-SES students chose to matriculate,
while middle-SES students (60 percent) were far less likely to do so.
The lower propensity of admitted middle-class students to enroll in
most-selective colleges has also been observed elsewhere (Espenshade
and Radford, 2009; Gose, 1998; McPherson and Schapiro, 1991: 94).
Middle-class students may be less likely to accept offers of admission
from most-selective colleges because less-selective universities woo them
away with merit scholarships that more-selective colleges will not match
(Bowen, Kurzweil, and Tobin, 2005: 110; Collison, 1993; Gose, 1998;
Herring, 2005; Jesse, 2011).

While low- and high-SES students are also offered merit scholarships, middle-SES students are thought to be more influenced by them.
Merit aid is less important in the enrollment choice of low-SES students
because they tend to receive enough need-based aid that the merit aid
they could receive at less-selective colleges would not make a large difference in their net costs (Avery and Hoxby, 2004: 268; Bowen, Kurzweil,
and Tobin, 2005: 110). High-SES students are less influenced by merit aid
because their family's greater resources and preference toward more-
selective colleges make the lower costs of less-selective colleges offering merit aid less enticing to them than it is to middle-class families,
for whom meeting expected family contributions may be more daunt-
ing (Avery and Hoxby, 2004: 268; Duffy and Goldberg, 1998; Flanagan,
2001; Gose, 1998; Herring, 2005; Mayher, 1998; McGinn, 2005).

To further explore this result, multivariate analysis is useful. Compared with their middle-SES counterparts, high-SES students have 2.4
times the odds of enrolling at a most-selective private college if admitted

with just gender and race as controls, 2.2 times the odds of enrolling with the addition of SAT score and family background, and 1.9 times the odds of enrolling once high school and community characteristics are further incorporated (see appendix F, table F.7.2). Only after the numbers of offers of admission from each college type category are included is this difference between middle- and high-SES students no longer significant.

Differences between the odds of middle- and low-SES students enrolling at a most-selective private college waver depending on the controls used. The two groups do not significantly differ in their propensity to enroll in a most-selective private college when gender and race are the only controls, yet low-SES students have 186 percent significantly greater odds than middle-SES students of enrolling in a most-selective private college once matched on SAT score and family characteristics. That being said, once high school and community variables are incorporated, differences between low- and middle-SES students in likelihood of matriculating again fade from statistical significance.

Conclusion

The first important observation of this chapter is that the college characteristics and individuals important in the application decisions of HSVP students were also prominent in their subsequent matriculation decisions. In both stages, parents were most likely to be selected as an influential source. As for institutional characteristics, academic reputation/prestige of institution and campus visit were particularly likely to play key roles in shaping decisions. That being said, certain institutional traits like cost and facilities were more likely to be selected as important in the matriculation stage than in the application stage, while academic reputation, rankings in national magazines, wanting to attend college far from home, and campus location were more likely to be chosen as influential in the application stage.

Second, students' social class background was related to the college characteristics that were most important in their matriculation choice. High-SES students were more likely to concentrate on reputation and, to a lesser extent, campus environment, while both low- and middle-SES students were more likely to focus on cost. Though a relatively small percentage of low-SES students valued attending college while living at home (15 percent), they were more likely to choose this item than other SES groups.

Third, as for the actual matriculation choices students made given their offers of admission, valedictorians exhibited a preference for most-selective private colleges. Seventy-one percent admitted to such an institution enrolled in one. Middle-SES students, however, were not as likely as low- and high-SES students to accept offers of admission from these colleges.

CHAPTER EIGHT

Integrating It All

College Destinations and the Paths That Lead to Them

The goal of this book is to reveal why similarly able students attend different types of colleges. To that end, this chapter presents valedictorians' ultimate college destinations and draws upon findings from the previous six chapters on each stage of the college destination process to explain these enrollment outcomes. Results are first discussed for valedictorians as a whole, and then by social class. The chapter concludes by synthesizing this work's overarching findings and highlighting areas that may be ripe for reform.

HSVP Students' College Destinations

Figure 8.1 depicts where valedictorians enrolled by both control and selectivity. It reveals that most-selective private colleges were valedictorians' most popular college destination: 39 percent matriculated at this type of institution. The next most popular college type was regular public institutions, which enrolled 26 percent of the valedictorians in the study. Most-selective public and regular private colleges followed behind, receiving 19 and 16 percent of all High School Valedictorian Project (HSVP) students, respectively. Examining the results just by control indicates that a majority of valedictorians (55 percent) attended a private college. Analyzed just by selectivity, a majority (58 percent) of HSVP students also matriculated at a most-selective college.

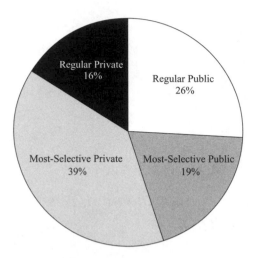

FIGURE 8.1. Percentage distribution displaying the selectivity and institutional control of HSVP students' college destinations (N=622). *Note:* Results are based on students with enrollment data. *Source:* High School Valedictorian Project Person Dataset.

Figure 8.2 helps illustrate how this enrollment pattern for valedictorians as a whole was produced.[1] The first set of bars showing application results indicates that students were most likely to apply to a most-selective private college (66 percent). This application preference can be traced back to the predisposition stage. Forty percent of valedictorians agreed that when they were entering high school they felt it was very important to enroll in a prestigious college. For many valedictorians, these prestigious college aspirations served as a primary motivator to succeed during high school. Moreover, the extra effort they expended in pursuit of the high grades that they felt were needed for admission to an elite college made them all the more committed to the idea of attending. Thus, it is not surprising that in the exploration phase, valedictorians heavily considered university prestige, relying a great deal on reputation and/or rankings in devising a list of prospective schools. In fact, when asked to select the college characteristics that most influenced where they applied, HSVP students were more likely to pick "academic reputation/prestige of institution" than any of the twenty-three other options listed.

While valedictorians were most likely to apply to a most-selective private college, they applied to a regular public college at almost as high

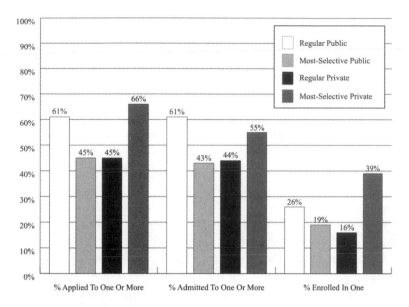

FIGURE 8.2. The role the application, admissions, and matriculation stages played in HSVP students' paths to regular public, most-selective public, regular private, and most-selective private institutions (N=622). *Note:* Results are based on students with enrollment data. *Source:* High School Valedictorian Project Person Dataset.

a rate (61 percent). The reasons for this high application rate at regular public colleges, however, are very different than the reasons for the high application rate at most-selective private colleges. First, in contrast to most-selective private colleges, regular public colleges are available in every state. Therefore, valedictorians who specifically wanted to stay in state for college would have had a regular public college to which they could apply, but might not have had an in-state most-selective private college option.

Second, because regular public colleges are more ubiquitous, HSVP students were more likely to know about them. Valedictorians were particularly likely to have heard of local regular public colleges because community or high school events were held at these institutions. Students were also more familiar with regular public colleges because they tended to know people who had attended or were attending them.[2] Since some valedictorians only researched the colleges with which they were already familiar, this greater awareness of regular public colleges contributed to the high application rate observed.

Finally, the lower selectivity and lesser costs of regular public colleges made them appealing places to apply; valedictorians often applied to at least one in order to have a "safety school." The admissions results show that valedictorians were right to believe that by submitting an application to such an institution they were virtually assured an acceptance letter in return. Valedictorians also often applied to at least one regular public college because doing so helped them guarantee a low-cost college option in case family financial circumstances changed or the financial aid expected from preferred institutions did not materialize.

At 45 percent each, application rates for most-selective public and regular private colleges were lower than application rates for most-selective private and regular public colleges. The lower likelihood of HSVP students applying to a most-selective public college occurred for several reasons. First, in 2006, only six states in the country had a most-selective public college within their borders. Thus, students who did not reside in one of these states and did not want to attend college out of state or pay out-of-state tuition did not have a most-selective public college option. As discussed in chapter 4 on exploration, even students who had a most-selective public college in their state sometimes did not apply to it because they thought private colleges offered a stronger academic reputation or a more favorable campus environment.

While regular private colleges are more numerous and accessible than most-selective public colleges, valedictorians' application rate to regular private colleges was similarly low. This likely occurs because HSVP students were often uncomfortable with regular private colleges' high sticker prices, especially when those price tags did not come with an elite diploma.

Turning to the second set of bars in figure 8.2, at three types of institutions (regular public, regular private, and most-selective public colleges) the percentage of students admitted to at least one college of this type is nearly identical to the percentage who applied. The exception occurs at most-selective private colleges, where the percentage of valedictorians with an offer of admission is 11 percentage points lower than the percentage who submitted an application.

This pattern occurs because nearly all valedictorians who applied to the first three types of institutions were accepted by at least one college from that category. In contrast, only 83 percent of HSVP students who applied to at least one most-selective private college were accepted by one, reducing the share of valedictorians who had a most-selective private college option by the end of the admissions stage. In fact, the admissions stage shrunk the percentage of valedictorians who could enroll in a most-selective private college to such an extent that the percentage with this opportunity (55 percent) became lower than the percentage with the opportunity to attend a regular public college (61 percent). This represents a reversal from the order present in the application stage, in which a higher percentage of valedictorians had a most-selective private college option than had a regular public college option. Nevertheless, at the end of the admissions stage, valedictorians were still more likely to have the opportunity to attend a most-selective private college than a most-selective public or regular private college because valedictorians applied to most-selective private colleges at such a higher rate.

The final set of bars in figure 8.2 reveals that the percentage of valedictorians in the most-selective private college category rebounds from the admissions stage to become valedictorians' most popular enrollment destination. This change occurs as a result of students' matriculation choices. About 71 percent of all valedictorians admitted to a most-selective private college decided to enroll in one. In contrast, just 44, 42, and 36 percent of students offered the chance to attend a most-selective public, regular public, or regular private college chose to matriculate, respectively. This difference in enrollment rates can be attributed to the fact that valedictorians were most likely to select "academic reputation/ prestige of institution" as influential in their matriculation decisions and that most-selective private colleges typically have the greatest prestige of these four college categories. Valedictorians' strong predispositions toward most-selective private colleges and the fact that many had spent their high school years devoted to reaching this type of college also made them inclined to accept offers of admission from these schools.

Thus, in sum, though the admissions stage reduced valedictorians' opportunity to attend a most-selective private college, their higher application and enrollment rates compensated for this decrease, and caused the plurality of valedictorians to ultimately matriculate at a most-selective private college. Regular public colleges, in contrast, enrolled a smaller proportion of valedictorians than most-selective private colleges. This occurred not because valedictorians failed to apply in high numbers (almost as high a percentage applied there as to a most-selective private college) or were not admitted (almost all were), but because they did not choose to matriculate as frequently. As for the lower proportions of valedictorians enrolled at most-selective public colleges and regular private colleges, this can be attributed to lower application and matriculation rates. The admissions stage did not play a role in funneling valedictorians away from these institutions.

HSVP Students' College Destinations by Social Class

Other investigations of students at large (Baum and Ma, 2007; Pallais and Turner, 2006) and just high achievers (Avery and Turner, 2008; Haycock, Lynch, and Engle, 2010; McPherson and Schapiro, 1991) find that college destinations vary by social class. Valedictorians were no exception; reaching the top of one's high school class does not negate the role of socioeconomic status (SES). As figure 8.3 reveals, the difference by SES in attendance at most-selective private universities is particularly stark. More than half (53 percent) of all high-SES valedictorians enrolled in this type of institution compared with 32 and 28 percent of low- and middle-SES valedictorians, respectively. And while differences by social

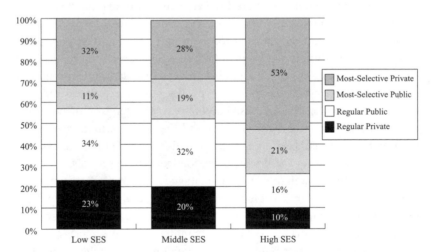

FIGURE 8.3. Percentage distribution showing the control and selectivity of HSVP students' college destinations, by social class (N = 622). *Note:* Results are based on students with enrollment data. Differences by social class in the percentage of HSVP students who enrolled in a most-selective public college are not statistically significant at the .05 level, but differences in the percentage who enrolled in a regular private college are significant at the .01 level and differences in the percentage who enrolled in a regular public college or a most-selective private college are significant at the .001 level. Percentages may not sum to 100 due to rounding. *Source:* High School Valedictorian Project Person Dataset.

class in the percentage enrolled in most-selective public colleges were not statistically significant, examining colleges just by selectivity and not institutional control reveals that nearly three-fourths (74 percent) of all high-SES valedictorians attended some type of most-selective college compared with 47 percent of middle-SES and 43 percent of low-SES valedictorians.

Because such a large percentage of high-SES students were enrolled in most-selective institutions—public and private—it is not surprising that they were about half as likely as other students to attend a regular private or regular public college. Ten percent of high-SES valedictorians were enrolled in a regular private college compared with 20 percent and 23 percent of middle- and low-SES students, respectively. Sixteen percent of high-SES students were enrolled in a regular public college in contrast with 32 percent and 34 percent of middle- and low-SES students, respectively. As observed in other phenomena along the college destination process, these final enrollment results indicate that high-SES valedictorians stand apart, varying more from both their middle- and low-SES peers than middle- and low-SES valedictorians differ from one another.

The forces behind these statistically significant SES differences in enrollment at regular private, regular public, and most-selective private institutions are examined and explained in depth through the three figures that follow. Figure 8.4 helps clarify why high-SES valedictorians were less likely than other SES groups to attend regular private colleges. At 35 percent, high-SES HSVP students were 28 percentage points less likely than their low-SES counterparts and 14 percentage points less likely than their middle-SES peers to apply to these institutions. High-SES students were probably less apt to submit an application because they placed a stronger emphasis on university prestige, which regular private colleges, by definition, tend not to have in as great a quantity as most-selective colleges.[3]

The 28 percentage-point gap by SES in the application stage increases by only 1 percentage point by the end of the admissions stage. This negligible expansion occurs because gaining admission at such institutions is not difficult for valedictorians. Between 98 and 99 percent of valedictorians who applied to a regular private college were admitted to at least one, regardless of SES.

In the matriculation phase, the SES gap shrinks from 29 percentage points to just 13 percentage points. This reduction occurs because all SES groups with an offer from a regular private institution opted to

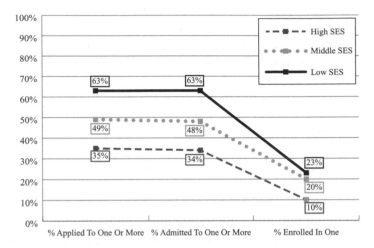

FIGURE 8.4. The role the application, admissions, and matriculation stages played in HSVP students' paths to regular private institutions, by social class (N=622). *Note:* Results are based on students with enrollment data. Differences by social class in the percentage of HSVP students who applied and were admitted are statistically significant at the .001 level. Differences by social class in the percentage of HSVP students who enrolled are statistically significant at the .01 level. *Source:* High School Valedictorian Project Person Dataset.

enroll in one at similarly low rates. The low propensity of valedictorians to attend if admitted irrespective of SES likely occurs because regular private colleges tend to cost more than public colleges and do not offer as much prestige as most-selective colleges.

In sum, the lower enrollment of high-SES students at regular private colleges is best explained by their lower application rate. High-SES valedictorians who applied to a regular private college were accepted and enrolled as frequently as their low- and middle-SES peers did.

Figure 8.5 illustrates how high-SES valedictorians became less likely than less-affluent high achievers to attend regular public colleges. First, high-SES students apply at a lower rate than low- and middle-SES students (53 percent vs. 64 and 68 percent, respectively). Though this 15 percentage-point gap in application rate is not as large as it is at regular private colleges (28 percentage points), it is still substantial. This difference by SES in application to regular public colleges can be partially explained by diverging preferences. The predisposition, exploration, and application stages revealed that high-SES students were more interested than other groups in university prestige. The preparation stage

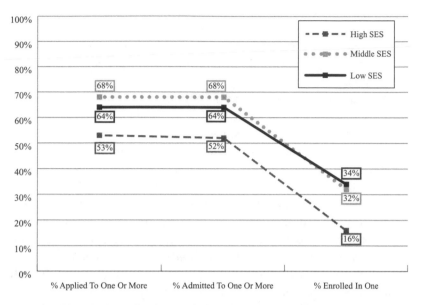

FIGURE 8.5. The role the application, admissions, and matriculation stages played in HSVP students' paths to regular public institutions, by social class (N=622). *Note:* Results are based on students with enrollment data. Differences by social class in the percentage of HSVP students who applied and were admitted are statistically significant at the .01 level. Differences by social class in the percentage of HSVP students who enrolled are statistically significant at the .001 level. *Source:* High School Valedictorian Project Person Dataset.

revealed that students with elite college aspirations, many of whom were from high-SES backgrounds, also exerted a lot of effort in high school to ensure they had the credentials to realize these aspirations. Since regular public colleges are not most selective by definition, it is not surprising that high-SES students were less interested in applying to such schools. Meanwhile, low- and middle-SES students' exploration and application decisions tended to be more shaped by cost concerns. Because regular public colleges' sticker prices are low, particularly when students qualify for in-state tuition, it is not surprising that low- and middle-SES students were more inclined than high-SES students to apply.

The SES differences established in the application phase largely remain unchanged by the close of the admissions stage. After admissions decisions are rendered, the SES gap stands at 16 percentage points, just 1 percentage point greater than the 15-point gap that existed in the application stage. This gap is almost identical because valedictorians of all SES backgrounds were equally likely to be admitted to a regular public college if they applied; at least 99 percent of valedictorians from each SES group who applied to this type of institution were accepted by at least one. HSVP students' high admit rate occurs because they are extremely strong academically within the regular public university applicant pool.

Matriculation choices expand the SES gap in regular public college enrollment by 2 points, to a total of 18 percentage points. This gap grows because low- and middle-SES students were more likely than high-SES students to matriculate if admitted (54 percent and 48 percent vs. 33 percent, respectively). It is worth noting that because low-SES students enrolled if admitted at a higher rate than middle-SES students did, the order by SES in the enrollment stage changes from the order present in the application and admissions stages. Low-SES students become the SES group most likely to attend, even though they were the second most likely SES group to apply and be admitted. Low- and middle-SES valedictorians were probably more apt to enroll because they were less likely than high-SES students to consider a university's reputation and more likely to consider cost during the matriculation phase. Interviews also suggest that high-SES students who applied to a regular public college frequently did so just to have a safety school. They were much less likely than middle- and low-SES applicants to seriously consider attending such institutions when making their enrollment decision, in part because they were more likely to be strongly committed to attending a prestigious college. For those who felt they had devoted their high school years to additional studying, more rigorous course taking, and securing extracurricular accomplishments mainly for the purpose of attending a prestigious college, it was difficult to forget about the extra toil and sweat and enroll in a college where that effort was never required to gain admission.

In sum, the weaker representation of high-SES valedictorians at regular public colleges was primarily due to their lower application rate. That being said, high-SES students' lower propensity than their peers to enroll if admitted also contributed to the gap. The admissions process did not play a role.

Most-selective private colleges represent the third and final type of college destination where valedictorians' enrollment differed by SES. Figure 8.6 reveals that the divergence by SES is set in motion in the application stage. Seventy-nine percent of high-SES valedictorians applied to a most-selective private university compared with 50 percent of low-SES

and 59 percent of middle-SES valedictorians. High-SES students probably submitted applications at a higher rate because they tended to value
university prestige more than other students. They revealed this preference for elite institutions not just in the application phase but in the
predisposition, preparation, and exploration stages as well. High-SES
students were more apt to have alumni and current students from these
institutions within their social networks, which in turn helped them feel
that such universities were not just appropriate but also beneficial and
enjoyable places to attend. They also appeared more committed to the
idea of attending, often taking very deliberate steps to ensure that they
were competitive for admission. Putting in this concerted effort during
their high school years likely made high-SES students all the more determined to apply. They were eager for their reward: an offer of admission. Of course it is important to note that high-SES valedictorians were
also probably more comfortable exploring and applying to most-selective
private colleges because they were less intimidated than less-affluent
students by potential costs.

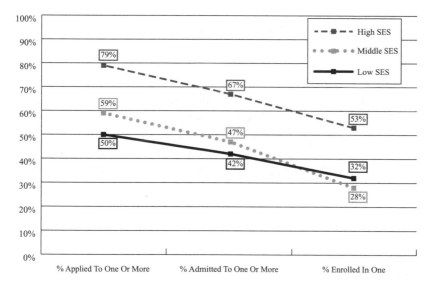

FIGURE 8.6. The role the application, admissions, and matriculation stages played in HSVP
students' paths to most-selective private institutions, by social class (N = 622). *Note:* Results
are based on students with enrollment data. Differences by social class in the percentage of
HSVP students who applied, admitted, and were enrolled are statistically significant at the
.001 level. *Source:* High School Valedictorian Project Person Dataset.

The next panel in figure 8.6 depicts what occurs in the admissions stage. Specifically, the gap between high- and low-SES students closes 4 percentage points to become a 25 percentage-point gap while the gap between high- and middle-SES students remains at 20 percentage points. The chances of valedictorians having an offer from a most-selective private college if they applied to at least one did not differ significantly by SES.[4]

SES differences did occur, however, in the matriculation stage. First, the gap between high- and low-SES students decreased another 4 points to 21 percentage points. This occurs because these two groups are similarly likely to enroll if admitted. In contrast, the gap between high- and middle-SES students increased 5 points to 25 percentage points because middle-SES students were 18 percentage points less likely than high-SES students to enroll in a most-selective private college if admitted. As a result of this enrollment behavior, the position of middle-SES valedictorians relative to low-SES valedictorians switches during this last phase, making middle-SES HSVP students least likely to attend a most-selective private college. Compared with low-SES students, middle-SES students were probably less likely to enroll because they were more likely to consider merit aid in making their final matriculation choice.[5] The percentage of middle-SES students who indicated that reputation was important in deciding where to enroll was about the same as the percentage for low-SES students, and thus is probably not as responsible for this difference in enrollment behavior.

In sum, these results indicate that high-SES students were more likely than low-SES students to attend a most-selective private college because they applied at much higher rates. Events during the admissions and matriculation stages did little to change the gap between these two groups. The difference in representation at most-selective private colleges between high- and middle-SES valedictorians, however, should mainly be attributed to differences in application rates, though differences in propensity to enroll also contributed.

Overarching Findings

Several important conclusions can be reached by stepping back from these specific results and considering the book as a whole. First, high-SES valedictorians' college destinations were distinct from those of low- and middle-SES valedictorians, who had more-similar enrollment patterns. These results underscore that even exhibiting repeated high achievement and ultimately reaching the top of one's class does not render social class moot. Having a top student as a child may affect parents' encouragement, but it does not appear to alter parents' tangible support. In fact, comparing HSVP results with results from studies of students at large suggest that parents of valedictorians exhibit similar levels of involvement and college preferences.

While it might not be surprising that parents would find it difficult to cast off the influence of socioeconomic status even when they have a particularly bright child, one might assume that schools would intervene, ensuring that at least top students are not held back by their social class. Yet the notion that valedictorians might receive more or better college counseling from their schools because of their high achievement is not supported by this analysis. In fact, there is some evidence that top students may actually receive more-limited, less-appropriate college advice from schools than students at large.

A second key finding from this work is that application decisions did the most to produce the ultimate variation in students' college destinations. Admissions did not play a role and enrollment choices sometimes contributed, but not to the same extent as application decisions.

These results suggest that in devoting so much of their coverage to the admissions process, the popular media is missing other important aspects that shape where students ultimately enroll. It may not be surprising that admissions fails to be a big hurdle for high achievers, but it is important to recognize that even the enrollment patterns of students with lower levels of achievement are shaped more by application than by admissions decisions. The majority of American colleges accept 80 percent or more of their applicant pool (Menand, 2003). Nationwide, the average acceptance rate at four-year colleges is about 66 percent (Clinedinst, Hurley, and Hawkins, 2011). In fact, fewer than 150 colleges have acceptance rates of less than 50 percent (Carnevale and Rose, 2004). Depending on the specific student population examined, between two-thirds and nine-tenths of students are even admitted to their first-choice institution (Hoover, 2008; Lederman, 2009b; Pryor et al., 2006; Radford and Tasoff, 2009).

It is worth highlighting that the relatively greater importance of the application stage over the admissions stage is due in part because students self-select. If students with very low levels of preparation started applying to our most competitive schools, admissions would become more of a barrier. Based on students' current application patterns, however, application plays a larger role than admissions in shaping students' college destinations.[6]

Third, having established *when* valedictorians become funneled toward different college destinations (the application stage, and, to a lesser extent, the matriculation stage), it is important to discuss *how* and *why* students' paths diverged during these phases. Other research has suggested that differences in enrollment choice are typically explained by: (1) academic preparation, (2) family finances and difficulties covering college costs, and/or (3) informational constraints (Nagaoka, Roderick, and Coca, 2009; Pallais and Turner, 2006). This study did not find that preparation prevented high school valedictorians from entering particular college destinations. In fact, low-SES valedictorians, who had slightly lower average test scores, had their applications admitted at a higher rate to most-selective private colleges than did other SES groups. And while this study did not have heavily detailed information on families' financial situations and the aid packages they were offered, interviews did not suggest that costs learned in the matriculation stage were the major culprit for this stratification either. Instead, informational differences, broadly conceived, best explain why high school valedictorians' college destinations varied by social class.[7]

Exploring this further, HSVP data indicated that students' application and matriculation decisions were largely determined by the preferences they developed and the conclusions they made during the exploration phase. While students are certainly entitled to apply their personal likes and dislikes in making college choices, results presented in chapter 4 suggest that the preferences and conclusions students formed when exploring college options were often based on lack of information or inaccurate information.

Valedictorians from a range of SES families and communities revealed in interviews that their high schools provided insufficient guidance about the college admissions process, need-based financial aid, and college options. They reported that their guidance counselors typically did not even mention out-of-state, private, and most-selective colleges as possibilities—let alone relate the potential benefits of attending such institutions.

In the absence of clear and comprehensive college information from their high schools, valedictorians depended largely on their families for assistance. Yet parents varied by social class in their knowledge of college admissions and financial aid, their college preferences for their child, and their tangible support in helping their child through the college destination process.

Thus, leaving college guidance to parents, instead of providing it to all students in school, enables social class to have an unnecessarily strong influence on where students ultimately enroll. And because of the effect that college destination has on an individual's socioeconomic future,[8] this system of entrusting college guidance to families allows the advantages (and disadvantages) of one generation to be passed on to the next generation. In this way, the social hierarchy is recycled or reproduced rather than restructured based on the achievements of the new generation.

What Can Be Done?

Despite most-selective colleges' increased financial aid and outreach over recent decades, social stratification has gotten worse rather than better (Astin and Oseguera, 2004). The relationship between parental income and enrollment in a highly selective college has increased substantially since the 1970s, and even in the last decade (Astin and Oseguera, 2004; Bowen, Kurzweil, and Tobin, 2005). The children of parents with at least a bachelor's degree have been more likely to attend elite baccalaureate institutions for decades, and this advantage did not change from the 1970s through the 1990s (Roksa et al., 2007). Clearly, we cannot assume that patterns will improve without taking new action.

This work was not designed to provide definitive policy solutions. Nevertheless, it can highlight the five areas that appeared to contribute most to the socioeconomic stratification in valedictorians' enrollment patterns and offer suggestions of reforms that might break down these barriers. Researchers and practitioners will need to investigate and test these proposals further, preferably under experimental settings, to determine if they are successful at achieving their desired goals. Policy makers and other decision makers will then need to weigh the impact of proven strategies relative to their cost and take the most-promising ideas to scale.

Better publicize the existence of need-based financial aid

The first major factor contributing to valedictorians' socioeconomic strat-ification was lack of information about the existence of need-based fi-nancial aid and who qualifies.[9] More than half of valedictorians applying for financial aid felt they, as well as their parents, failed to have a strong understanding of the financial aid process. Yet even this underestimates the issue, for many students who likely would have qualified for aid knew so little about it that they did not explore it as a possibility or apply.[10]

While the Department of Education maintains useful websites and hotlines about financial aid, these sources are limited in their ability to reach and impact all families. First, these pieces of information require that families proactively seek them out. Relying on families to take the first step reduces the chances that they will obtain need-based aid infor-mation at the optimal time in students' paths to college.[11] In addition, some families may not have the skills or resources to obtain information through the internet or find the phone number to call. Other families may not bother going to a website or calling because they erroneously think they are ineligible for financial aid.

To have a greater impact, the federal government should mail con-cise, clear information about need-based financial aid to families when students are in middle school. This timing will positively influence the preferences that students and families develop during the predisposition stage, students' motivation to succeed during the preparation stage, and the types of colleges considered during the exploration phase.[12] In ad-dition, this method of communicating ensures that all families have access to this important information, regardless of their research skills and initiative. Its presence within the home in a digestible form may even cause those who think they know about financial aid to revisit their assumptions.[13]

The resource distributed should highlight the range of families of varying socioeconomic circumstances who can qualify for different types of aid. It should also give examples that show how families' net prices after aid are lower than the sticker prices that colleges advertise. Materials should also demonstrate that after subtracting aid from all sources, some colleges with high sticker prices may actually cost less than colleges with low sticker prices. Once families are better informed as to whether need-based aid can reduce their costs, details on when to complete the Free Application for Federal Student Aid (FAFSA) and how and where to receive help in filing it should be addressed. The existence of net price calculators should also be noted here, but the primary goal of this mailing should be to explain the existence of need-based aid and to identify who generally qualifies.[14]

This basic overview of need-based aid should be distributed to teachers who are instructing or advising high school juniors and seniors as well. It is important that teachers have a basic understanding of need-based aid because, as shown in chapters 4, 5, and 7, they sometimes advise students about college as much as, or more than, counselors do.

Encourage families to consider net price rather than sticker price

Second, valedictorians eliminated possibly good college options based on sticker price. The newly required net price calculators should help in addressing this issue. Net price calculators are designed to allow families to obtain an estimate of the price they would pay to attend a specific college after subtracting the financial aid they would receive based on their socioeconomic circumstances. The hope is that such calculators will prevent families from ruling out promising colleges due to sticker prices that do not reflect what their actual costs would be given their personal finances.

To help these calculators live up to their potential, it is critical that families know that they exist, and that they are encouraged to use them even at colleges they think would be out of financial reach. To these ends, institutions should prominently display calculators on their websites (College Board and Art & Science Group, 2010; Institute for College Access and Success, 2011). They should also make it easy for users to input key information, understand results, and compare costs across universities (Institute for College Access and Success, 2011). In addition, it is essential that families feel they can trust the estimates obtained. As Grodsky and Jackson (2009) emphasize, families are more likely to act on cost information if they feel greater certainty about it. If families come to believe that these estimates are not close to the actual net costs they will be presented with in the matriculation stage, the ability of these calculators to expand the college options considered and change application behavior will be greatly diminished.

Facilitate comparisons between colleges based on both quality and cost

Third, the valedictorians studied did not have efficient ways to compare institutions based on quality and cost. Many families relied mainly on what they had heard about various institutions from their social networks. Less-affluent HSVP families often did not recognize that student outcomes at various colleges can differ and therefore tended to focus just on cost. Others used gut impressions of prestige. Having more quantitative measures on how a college fares compared with other institutions in terms of students' average net costs, debt, and outcomes will help families become better informed consumers.

While many have offered ideas on this front (for example, Long, 2010; Morgan, 2011), the most recent proposal comes from the Obama administration. Under the administration's plan, each college would have a "scorecard" that would show how enrollees' average net price, graduation rate, loan debt, loan repayment status, and earnings potential compares to students at other universities (White House, 2012a, 2012b).[15] The exact content of the scorecard as well as the comparisons included should be tested with counselors and first-generation students and families to make sure all of the information displayed is relevant and clear (Fishman, 2012). This scorecard would also be most helpful to families if it was easily located and appeared in multiple settings. Reporting it on university website home pages, in admissions and enrollment materials, and when students select institutions on the electronic FAFSA, would be ideal (Fishman, 2012; Morgan, 2012). Seeing this information repeatedly will help college consumers pay attention to it and consider it in deciding where to apply and enroll. While some standardized information is currently available on the U.S. Department of Education's College Navigator website, unlike the proposed scorecards, this website does not allow for quick comparisons on important metrics and is not as easily digestible and reviewable when making application and matriculation decisions.

Some might argue that students are not always rational in their college decisions, limiting the scorecard's potential. Yet even if students ultimately are irrational, they deserve to have access to information that would enable them to make more-informed decisions. For example, if students decide they want to attend the college with the better football team, this preference is permissible, but they should know that they may be less likely to graduate and may pay more for their education because of this choice. Moreover, there is good reason to believe that providing better information will help students make more-optimal college decisions. Long (2010) finds that informational changes have improved health care, health insurance, and K–12 education. A more directly related study concludes that providing individuals with just college graduation rates can make them savvier college consumers (Kelly and Schneider, 2011).

Provide quality college counseling that considers students'
academic preparation

Fourth, valedictorians did not receive adequate advice from their schools about college options that matched their preparation. Therefore, this book recommends that students be given high-quality college counseling that considers their academic achievements. Federal and state governments need to recognize that investing in K–12 education but skimping on the counseling students need to successfully transition to postsecondary education puts the talent the government has spent time and money developing for more than a decade at risk of failing to reach its full potential. Better counseling will help students not to undermatch, thereby improving their likelihood of degree completion (Bowen, Chingos, and McPherson, 2009; Carnevale and Strohl, 2010; Nagaoka, Roderick, and Coca, 2009). Personalized counseling will also reduce the existing socioeconomic variation in students' college destination process because students will not be as dependent on the advice of their families and social networks, which are heavily informed by social class. Multiple scholars have found improvements in various college-going outcomes when counselors, recent college graduates, or current undergraduates provide high school students with customized counseling.[16]

To help achieve better quality college counseling, student-to-counselor ratios should be reduced.[17] Clinedinst, Hurley, and Hawkins (2011) report that at public secondary schools, the ratio of students to *counselors* was 285 to 1 and the ratio of students to *college counselors* was 338 to 1. Only 26 percent of public schools employed at least one full- or part-time counselor whose exclusive responsibility was college counseling. Just as a point of comparison, 73 percent of private schools did so. Given these figures it is not surprising that public school counselors report that only 23 percent of their time is spent on college counseling. But, according to Bridgeland and Bruce (2011), this is not because counselors view preparing students for college and careers as unimportant—72 percent say that it is. Instead, counselors are burdened with other administrative duties, many of which could be handled by other staff.[18]

Yet giving counselors more time to advise students about college is not sufficient. Counselors also need to receive training in how to prepare students for college. This instruction should occur during the credentialing process and throughout counselors' careers in the form of funded professional development (Bridgeland and Bruce, 2011; Laturno and Lemons, 2011; Lee et al., 2011). Clinedinst, Hurley, and Hawkins (2011) report that only 20 percent of public school counselors are required to participate in professional development related to postsecondary counseling. In trainings, counselors should learn how to talk to students and parents about need-based aid, net price calculators, and how to compare institutions based on both cost and student outcomes. Counselors should also be taught not just about the colleges most of their charges attend but about a range of colleges. In addition, they should practice identifying the types of institutions that students of different levels of academic preparation are eligible to attend.[19]

As schools make college advising more of a priority, schools and counselors should be evaluated in part by improvements in students' transitions to college (Laturno and Lemons, 2011). As increasing numbers of high schools gain access to postsecondary information on their alumni, it will become easier to track students' enrollment and persistence (Sagawa and Schramm, 2008).

Improve college outreach to less-affluent high achievers

Finally, this study found that less-affluent valedictorians know less than high-SES valedictorians about most-selective colleges and the possible benefits to attending. Given this finding, this book's last suggestion is directed toward elite colleges—both public and private. In recent years, these colleges have tried to enroll more low-income students by offering generous financial aid packages. While this definitely helps low-SES students who do enroll, it has not dramatically changed the proportion enrolled. Colleges have also flirted with the idea of giving greater preference to low-SES students in admissions, yet this work suggests that even an admissions advantage is likely not enough to compensate for the much lower application rates of low-SES students and ultimately produce large increases in low-SES enrollment.

Therefore, colleges must go beyond trying to ease the path of less-affluent students who manage to apply. They have to tackle their low application rates directly. While it is harder to find low-SES students with the high levels of preparation expected at elite institutions, there are low-SES high achievers in the country who are not applying to elite colleges (Hill and Winston 2006b; Pallais and Turner, 2006), and institutions need to do a better job finding them and encouraging them to submit an application.[20]

There are a couple of ways that colleges currently identify and contact students. More than 1,100 colleges and scholarship programs use the College Board's Student Search Service to find and then send written materials to students meeting specific profiles (College Board, 2012). Colleges also do some personalized outreach, but they concentrate such activities at established feeder schools, programs, and communities that are likely to net them multiple competitive applicants. Top students living in areas where elite college attendance is less common, however, may receive mailings but are less likely to have the opportunity to personally interact with staff from elite institutions (Avery et al., 2009; Golden, 2006: 58; Stevens, 2007: 77; Zemsky and Oedel, 1983: 11).

Obviously, colleges need to develop other ways of connecting with promising students. California public colleges, which had to expand their outreach efforts after affirmative action was banned by voters (Sanchez, 1996), may be able to offer insight into more- and less-effective techniques.[21] Technology may also offer new opportunities. Yale and other colleges have started using a service that allows admissions officers to identify promising students based on their grades, course taking, and academic interests, as well as on test scores. They can then reach out directly to these students early in their high school career and personally guide them through the college destination process, developing them much like a college coach might nurture an athletic recruit (Carey, 2011).

Once high-achieving students are better identified, improved recruiting needs to occur. Mailing promotional materials in the later years of high school is not enough. First of all, outreach needs to happen earlier. As this study shows, by the second half of high school students' predispositions are already formed and they have established parameters on the colleges they will consider. At this point, even the glossiest of brochures were unable to persuade students to give up their plan of attending, for example, only colleges they knew, institutions that were in state, or schools that fell below a certain sticker price, and begin considering an entirely different type of college.

Second, contact needs to be more personal. This study found that more-affluent valedictorians were more likely than less-affluent valedictorians to apply to most-selective colleges in part because of their different social networks. During the predisposition stage, high-SES students' networks awakened them to the idea of elite colleges and made them think these institutions were appropriate places to consider. These networks also introduced high-SES students to a broader number of top colleges. This was important in the exploration stage because students often only investigated colleges with which they were familiar. Knowing people who had attended most-selective institutions through their social networks also helped high-SES students feel confident that they would be able to meet the academic rigor of these institutions as well as have an enjoyable social experience. Because of their very different social networks, less-affluent students, in contrast, were less predisposed to elite colleges, knew fewer of them, and were often concerned about the academic and social environments of these institutions.

To compensate for this difference in social networks in a cost-effective way, colleges need to make better use of their students and alumni. After colleges identify promising less-affluent students, they should have current and former undergraduates reach out to these prospective students and talk with them about high school and their college plans. These "ambassadors" should share their own college experiences, highlight the existence of need-based aid, and encourage students to use net price calculators so they have a better idea of what attending a specific institution might cost their family. In addition to one-on-one contact, alumni groups should plan local events that allow high school students and their families to speak with current undergraduates and alumni, and meet other high school students and families going through the college destination process. Such outreach would help less-advantaged students learn about colleges that match their academic performance and become more comfortable with the idea of attending. More than half the respondents in a recent study indicated that they would be much more likely to apply to a more-selective four-year college if they could meet a greater number of students like themselves who were successful at this college (College Board Advocacy & Policy Center, 2011).

Final Thoughts

In this era, only about 60 percent of all public high school students in the United States have a parent who has completed college (Herrold and O'Donnell, 2008). We simply cannot rely on families to provide college guidance if we ever want to reach President Obama's goal of being first in the world in college completion rates (Lederman, 2009a). Instead, in order to prevent wasting high achievers' talent, and indeed the talent of all students, this book's findings suggest that policies should be developed and improved to: (1) better publicize the existence of need-based financial aid, (2) encourage families to consider net price rather than sticker price when making early determinations about affordable college options, (3) facilitate comparisons between colleges based on both quality and cost, (4) provide quality college counseling that considers students' academic preparation, and (5) improve college outreach to less-affluent high achievers.

This book also demonstrates a need for future research. First, as policy recommendations are developed and implemented, it is critical that they be evaluated so that students' paths to college can be continually improved. Second, the lives of the high school valedictorians who participated in this project were not decided when they made their college enrollment decisions. Where has life taken Karen, Paul, Elizabeth, and their fellow valedictorians? As the introduction to this book indicated, other research finds that the educational attainment, earnings, and occupational prestige of students at large vary by college attended. Chapter 1 also presented existing evidence suggesting that the futures of even highly accomplished students are affected by their undergraduate institution (Arnold, 2002; Arnold and Youn, 2006; Bowen and Bok, 1998; Carnevale and Strohl, 2010). Still, more research needs to be conducted to determine the extent to which college alma mater is related to valedictorians' educational attainment and careers. These questions will be explored in a planned follow-up study.

List of Most-Selective Colleges

TABLE A.1 The Seventy-Two Public and Private Colleges Rated "Most Selective" by *U.S. News & World Report*, by Control and Then Alphabetical Order

Name of Institution	Name of Institution
Public	*Private Nonprofit (Continued)*
College of William and Mary	Cornell University
Georgia Institute of Technology	Dartmouth College
University of California-Berkeley	Davidson College
University of California-Irvine	Duke University
University of California-Los Angeles	Emory University
University of California-San Diego	Georgetown University
University of California-Santa Barbara	Grinnell College
University of Florida	Hamilton College
University of Michigan-Ann Arbor	Harvard University
University of North Carolina at Chapel Hill	Harvey Mudd College
University of Virginia-Main Campus	Haverford College
	Johns Hopkins University
Private Nonprofit	Kenyon College
Amherst College	Lehigh University
Bard College	Macalester College
Barnard College	Massachusetts Institute of Technology
Bates College	Middlebury College
Boston College	New York University
Bowdoin College	Northwestern University
Brandeis University	Oberlin College
Brown University	Pomona College
Bucknell University	Princeton University
California Institute of Technology	Rice University
Carleton College	Scripps College
Carnegie Mellon University	Stanford University
Claremont McKenna College	Swarthmore College
Colby College	Tufts University
Colgate University	Tulane University
Colorado College	University of Chicago
Columbia University	University of Notre Dame
Cooper Union	University of Pennsylvania

(continued)

Name of Institution	Name of Institution
Private Nonprofit (Continued)	*Private Nonprofit (Continued)*
University of Rochester	Washington University in St. Louis
University of Southern California	Webb Institute
Vanderbilt University	Wellesley College
Vassar College	Wesleyan University
Wake Forest University	Williams College
Washington and Lee University	Yale University

Source: U.S. News & World Report (2006).

The High School Valedictorian Project Social Class Variable

In order to analyze results by students' social class background, participants in the High School Valedictorian Project (HSVP) needed to be classified by socioeconomic status (SES). For this kind of analysis, using narrower indicators of social class like parents' income and education is problematic. First, using parents' income is not ideal because the data for this study come from students' self-reports, and students are notorious for not accurately knowing their parents' income (see, for example, Massey et al., 2003: 27). Seven percent of the HSVP sample did not even try to answer the question about parents' income. While parents' education is better known and reported by students, conducting this book's analysis solely by parents' education would be remiss because income and wealth play critical roles in shaping families' ability (and the way they perceive their ability) to afford certain college options.

Therefore, HSVP students were assigned an SES category based on their responses to the following survey question: "How would you describe your family's social class or socioeconomic status during your senior year of high school? Please pick one of the answers below: (1) Lower Class; (2) Working Class; (3) Middle Class; (4) Upper-Middle Class; and (5) Upper Class."[1]

Then, because fewer than thirty respondents reported to be either lower class or upper class, the question's five social class categories were aggregated into three SES categories for analysis purposes. Low-SES students comprise those who reported lower- or working-class origins, middle-SES respondents indicated that they were middle class, and high-SES valedictorians chose upper middle class or upper class to describe their family's social class background.[2]

Table B.1 reveals the excellent correspondence between various social class indicators and the SES categories used. Other analyses also support these SES classifications. Ninety-nine percent of all valedictorians who were considered high-SES indicated having one or more of the following characteristics: a parent with a bachelor's degree or more, an annual household income of $100,000 or more, or family assets of $100,000

TABLE B.1 **The Relationship between Individual Social Class Measures and the SES Categories Used in HSVP Analyses (N=896)**

Individual Social Class Measures	Total	Low SES	Middle SES	High SES
Annual Household Income				
Less than $50,000	17.3	72.3	12.5	1.4
$50,000–$99,999	31.6	22.7	52.9	12.9
$100,000–$149,999	24.9	1.4	25.5	33.2
$150,000 or more	19.0	0.7	2.9	42.6
Unknown	7.3	2.8	6.3	10.0
Household Assets				
Less than $25,000	23.2	71.6	23.2	4.9
$25,000–$99,999	22.4	15.6	32.0	15.1
$100,000–$299,999	20.9	5.7	23.2	24.3
$300,000 or more	18.3	0.7	6.0	37.7
Unknown	15.2	6.4	15.6	18.1
First-Generation College Student				
Yes	15.0	39.0	17.5	3.2
No	84.9	61.0	82.3	96.8
Unknown	.1	.0	.3	.0
Highest Level of Parents' Education				
Neither Parent Has a BA or BS Degree	24.0	67.4	26.3	5.1
One Parent Has a BA or BS Degree	11.6	12.1	15.4	7.6
Both Parents Have a BA or BS Degree	10.9	7.1	12.5	10.8
One Parent Has a Graduate Degree	29.2	9.2	31.0	35.0
Both Parents Have a Graduate Degree	22.9	2.8	13.5	40.2
Unknown	1.3	1.4	1.3	1.4
Home Ownership				
Yes	89.1	63.1	92.5	95.4
No	9.0	35.5	6.0	2.2
Unknown	1.9	1.4	1.6	2.4

Note: Respondents were asked to answer all social class questions with regard to their families' situations during their senior year of high school. To be counted as a first-generation college student, respondents had to report that they were the first to attend a four-year college among their siblings, parents, and grandparents. The survey question indicated that household assets were not to include family home, businesses, farms, or retirement plans. Percentage distributions may not sum to 100 due to rounding. Differences by SES on each individual social class indicator are statistically significant at the .001 level.
Source: High School Valedictorian Project Person Dataset.

or more. Ninety-five percent of all low-SES valedictorians indicated having one or more of these characteristics: no parent with a bachelor's degree or more, an annual household income of less than \$50,000, or family assets of less than \$50,000. Finally, about nine-tenths of all middle-SES students indicated having at least one parent with a bachelor's degree but no parents with a graduate degree, an annual family income between \$50,000 and \$149,000, or assets between \$25,000 and \$99,000.

This SES measure has also been applied in previous studies with success. Espenshade and Radford (2009) used the same question to determine the social class of their sample of high-achieving students and found that these self-reported social class categories held up well to statistical scrutiny. Specifically, an Ordinary Least Squares (OLS) regression that included more than 240 independent predictor variables discovered only 27 cases (out of 4,291) where students' predicted social class was different from their self-reported SES (grouped as low, middle, and high). A factor analysis of twelve different measures of social class also found good correspondence between the factor scores generated and students' self-reported social class.

Table B.2 displays how HSVP students' personal,[3] high school, community, and state characteristics vary by SES.

TABLE B.2 **HSVP Survey Respondents' Personal, High School, Community, and State Characteristics, by Social Class**

Personal, High School, Community, and State Characteristics	Total	Social Class		
		Low SES	Middle SES	High SES
Gender (N = 896)				
Male	36.5	33.3	36.2	38.0
Female	63.5	66.7	63.8	62.0
Race (N = 896)				
White	62.8	41.1	63.8	70.1
Black	3.6	11.4	4.2	.0
Hispanic	8.5	24.1	8.9	2.2
Asian	25.1	23.4	23.2	27.8
Percent of Seniors at Respondent's High School Who Took the SAT I (N = 886)				
<50	26.8	46.7	29.6	16.5
50–75	39.3	39.3	44.8	33.6
>75	34.0	14.1	25.7	49.9

(*continued*)

Personal, High School, Community, and State Characteristics	Total	Social Class		
		Low SES	Middle SES	High SES
Average Combined Math and Verbal SAT I Score Earned by Seniors at Respondent's High School (N=885)				
<950	21.7	50.4	23.6	9.2
950–1100	59.3	45.9	66.0	57.3
>1100	19.0	3.7	10.5	33.4
Percent of Students at Respondent's High School Who Were Eligible for Free/ Reduced-Price Lunch (N=883)				
<20	49.9	20.6	45.7	65.2
20–50	40.7	52.9	44.9	31.8
>50	9.4	26.5	9.5	3.0
Community Type (N=893)				
Urban	29.9	37.1	27.7	29.5
Suburban	49.5	41.4	48.0	54.1
Rural	20.6	21.4	24.3	16.5
Percent of Adult Residents within High School Zip Code with BA or BS (N=816)				
<12	12.5	33.6	12.5	4.7
12–36	49.1	54.7	60.3	35.9
>36	38.4	11.7	27.3	59.5
State (N=896)				
California	16.9	11.4	14.1	21.8
Florida	21.1	37.6	21.1	14.8
Indiana	14.0	18.4	16.2	10.0
New Jersey	32.4	27.7	30.7	35.9
North Carolina	15.7	5.0	18.0	17.5

Note: See appendix C for more information on how high school and community data were collected. Percentage distributions may not sum to 100 due to rounding. Differences by social class are statistically significant at the .05 level for community type and not statistically significant for gender. Other differences by social class are statistically significant at the .001 level.
Source: High School Valedictorian Project Person Dataset.

Quantitative Data Collection

This appendix outlines how HSVP quantitative data on high school valedictorians were collected.

To begin, a search was conducted and found that five newspapers from five different states consistently reported local valedictorians' names, high schools, and college destinations. Using these newspapers to develop a sample was attractive for several reasons. First, these newspaper listings contained valedictorians from rural, suburban, and urban areas. In addition, the states were located throughout the country: the Northeast (New Jersey), the Midwest (Indiana), the South (North Carolina and Florida), and the West (California). Studying students in these states therefore provides not only geographic diversity but also racial diversity. Furthermore, data from the U.S. Department of Education's Integrated Postsecondary Education Data System (IPEDS) and the National Center for Public Policy and Higher Education (2009) reveal that these states offer varying postsecondary landscapes in terms of college participation rates, number of institutions of various types by sector within their borders, college costs, and merit aid programs.[1]

The High School Valedictorian Project (HSVP) survey was administered in the spring of 2007. In an effort to obtain the highest-quality responses possible, only the four most recent cohorts of valedictorians were sampled. In 2003, 2004, 2005, and 2006, the newspapers printed the names of 1,537 public high school valedictorians.[2] A "working" email address matching the student's name and college or a "working" mailing address matching the student's name and town or a parent's name and town was obtained for 1,369 valedictorians,[3] or 89 percent of the original newspaper list.[4] More than two-thirds of all valedictorians with some type of contact information took the twenty- to thirty-minute HSVP web survey, which is located in appendix D. This response rate is particularly high considering that students were not given any compensation for participating.

The web survey results were used to create two datasets: the High School Valedictorian Project Person Dataset, in which the unit of analysis was valedictorians, and the High School Valedictorians Project Application Dataset, in which the unit of analysis was applications submitted by valedictorians. Most of this book uses the Person Dataset, but chapter 6 on admissions incorporates findings from both datasets. While the majority of variables in these datasets come from web survey results, data from other sources on postsecondary institutions and valedictorians' high schools and communities were also incorporated to enhance analyses.

Specifically, IPEDS data were used to identify the state, control (private nonprofit or public), and level (four-year or less-than-four-year) of every U.S. postsecondary institution listed by HSVP participants in the survey. Postsecondary institutions were also coded for college selectivity using *U.S. News & World Report*'s (2006) rankings. This particular year's rankings were used in order to best reflect the colleges that were considered most selective during the time HSVP students were enrolling in college: between 2003 and 2006.

The study adopted *U.S. News* selectivity measure for several reasons. First, the magazine's ranking takes into account several factors, including college acceptance rate and enrollees' test scores and class rank (Morse and Flanigan, 2006). It is therefore a more comprehensive indicator of selectivity than freshman matriculants' average SAT I score, which is sometimes used as a proxy for selectivity by researchers. Second, this magazine appeared to best represent how students and their families tend to perceive institutions' selectivity. In HSVP interviews, students frequently cited the *U.S. News* rankings, but never mentioned Barron's or Carnegie selectivity classifications. Furthermore, Bowman and Bastedo (2009) find evidence that who applies to an institution is shaped strongly by *U.S. News* rankings, indicating that applicants are responsive and paying attention to this publication. As for the specific selectivity measure used in this book, institutions were coded as either "most selective" or "not most selective/regular" based on whether or not the institution was one of seventy-two identified by the magazine as "most selective" that year. Appendix A lists these most-selective colleges.

Next, high school and community measures were collected. First, two high school SAT measures were gathered.[5] One is the percentage of fellow seniors at the respondent's high school who took the SAT I. This variable is often used as a proxy for the percentage of students with four-year college plans since entrance to a four-year institution typically requires taking some type of college entrance examination. Classmates' four-year college plans are thought to shape students' aspirations, as well as their knowledge of colleges and the college admissions process (Perna, 2000). The second SAT variable incorporated was the average SAT I score achieved by fellow seniors at the respondent's high school. Both of these SAT measures were obtained from publicly available data on the five sample states' Department of Education websites.

Other data sources helped shed further light on valedictorians' high schools and communities. The U.S. Department of Education's National Center for Education Statistics' Common Core of Data, which compiles statistics on public primary and secondary schools, first provided the type of community (rural, suburban, or urban) in which the valedictorian attended high school.[6] Community type has been identified as an important measure of high school resources (Provasnik et al., 2007) and social capital (Perna, 2000). Common Core data also produced the percentage of students eligible for free or reduced-price lunch at each valedictorian's high school.[7] This was added as an indicator of high school socioeconomic composition, another key factor in students' academic performance (Coleman, 1966).

An additional socioeconomic status (SES) measure capturing the social class of valedictorians' communities was incorporated using the U.S. Census's 2000 Summary File 3 data. High school zip code was matched to census data to establish the percentage of adults age twenty-five or older who possessed at least a bachelor's degree within that zip code.

The High School Valedictorian Project Web Survey[1]

A comprehensive nationwide study of high school valedictorians' transition to life after secondary school

Please report your email address, first name, last name, and the high school from which you graduated. Again, any and all information you report is strictly confidential and protected.

Please use the blank space to write your answers.

Email address

First Name

Last Name

High School

You must be 18 or older to take this survey. Please indicate whether you were born 18 or more years ago today.

Please pick one of the answers below.

☐ Yes

○ No

Please rate your experience transitioning from high school to life after high school using the following scale.

Please mark the corresponding circle - only one per line.

	Very Difficult				Very Easy
	☐	☐	☐	☐	☐

At some point in your life have you considered continuing your education beyond high school?

Please pick one of the answers below.

☐ Yes

○ No

Approximately when do you first remember thinking that you would continue your education beyond high school?

Please pick one of the answers below.

- ○ Since I can remember / Always
- ○ Fifth grade or earlier
- ○ Between 6th and 8th grade
- ○ Between 9th and 11th grade
- ○ Twelfth grade
- ○ After graduating from high school

Thinking back to when you were entering high school, to what extent was it important to you, your father, and your mother that you attend COLLEGE?

Please mark the corresponding circle - only one per line.

	Not Applicable	Not at All		Somewhat		Very Much
You	○	○	○	○	○	○
Your Father	○	○	○	○	○	○
Your Mother	○	○	○	○	○	○

Thinking back to when you were entering high school, to what extent was it important to you, your father, and your mother that you attend A FOUR-YEAR COLLEGE?

Please mark the corresponding circle - only one per line.

	Not Applicable	Not at All		Somewhat		Very Much
You	○	○	○	○	○	○
Your Father	○	○	○	○	○	○
Your Mother	○	○	○	○	○	○

Thinking back to when you were entering high school, to what extent was it important to you, your father, and your mother that you attend A PRESTIGIOUS COLLEGE?

Please mark the corresponding circle - only one per line.

	Not Applicable	Not at All		Somewhat		Very Much
You	○	○	○	○	○	○
Your Father	○	○	○	○	○	○
Your Mother	○	○	○	○	○	○

During the fall of your senior year of high school, how would you rate your and your parents' understanding of the college admissions process?

Please mark the corresponding circle - only one per line.

	Poor				Excellent
Your understanding	○	○	○	○	○
Your parents' understanding	○	○	○	○	○

During the fall of your senior year of high school, how would you rate your and your parents' understanding of the college financial aid process?

Please mark the corresponding circle - only one per line.

	Poor				Excellent
Your understanding	○	○	○	○	○
Your parents' understanding	○	○	○	○	○

Have you ever APPLIED to be a student at a post-secondary school (a school you attend after high school such as a technical school, beauty school, college, etc.)?

Please pick one of the answers below.

○ Yes

○ No

I want you to think back to when you were deciding for the first time where to APPLY to post-secondary school. Did you apply for financial aid?

Please pick one of the answers below.

○ Yes

○ No

Thinking again of when you were APPLYING to post-secondary school for the first time, please check any and all sources that influenced where you decided to APPLY (but not necessarily where to enroll).

Please check all that apply.

☐   Parents

☐   Peers

☐   Boyfriend or Girlfriend

☐   High School College/Guidance Counselor

☐   Teacher(s)

☐   Private College Counselor/Consultant

☐   Alumnus/ni or current student(s) at that school

☐   College guidebooks

☐   Information provided by college itself (brochures, personnel, website)

☐   Third-party online resources

Thinking again of when you were APPLYING to post-secondary school for the first time, please check the FIVE factors that most influenced where you decided to APPLY (but not necessarily enroll). Please check only the FIVE most influential items.

Please check all that apply.

☐ Campus visit

☐ Desire to attend college while living at home

☐ Desire to attend college near hometown

☐ Desire to attend college away from hometown

☐ Geographic location of school (specific state or city/community)

☐ Type of community in which school is located (rural, suburban, urban)

☐ Desire to attend a single sex college

☐ Religious affiliation of school

☐ Size of School

☐ Academic reputation/prestige of institution

☐ School facilities

☐ Faculty attention/involvement in teaching

☐ Rankings in national magazines

☐ Presence of students who share my ethnic/racial background

☐ Presence of students who share my social class background

☐ Knowing that there would be other people I know also attending

☐ Special academic program (major, honors, joint degree, accelerated degree, etc.)

☐ Special extracurricular (study abroad program, able to play on a sports team, etc.)

☐ Good employment outcomes for graduates

☐ Graduates gain admission to top graduate/professional schools

☐ Cost of attending

☐ Opportunity to receive merit scholarship(s)

☐ Financial aid availability

Have you ever ENROLLED as a student in a post-secondary school (a school you attend after high school such as a technical school, beauty school, college, etc.)?

Please pick one of the answers below.

☐ Yes

☐ No

Thinking back to when you were deciding for the first time in which post-secondary school to ENROLL (from the schools to which you were accepted), please check any and all sources that influenced where you decided ultimately to ENROLL.

Please check all that apply.

☐ Parents

☐ Peers

☐ Boyfriend or Girlfriend

☐ High School College/Guidance Counselor

☐ Teacher(s)

☐ Private College Counselor/Consultant

☐ Alumnus/ni or current student(s) at that school

☐ College guidebooks

☐ Information provided by college itself (brochures, personnel, website)

☐ Third-party online resources

Thinking of when you were deciding for the first time in which post-secondary school to ENROLL (from the schools to which you were accepted), please check the FIVE factors that most influenced your ENROLLMENT decision. Please check only the FIVE most influential items.

Please check all that apply.

- ☐ Campus visit
- ☐ Desire to attend college while living at home
- ☐ Desire to attend college near hometown
- ☐ Desire to attend college away from hometown
- ☐ Geographic location of school (specific state or city/community)
- ☐ Type of community in which school is located (rural, suburban, urban)
- ☐ Desire to attend a single sex college
- ☐ Religious affiliation of school
- ☐ Size of School
- ☐ Academic reputation/prestige of institution
- ☐ School facilities
- ☐ Faculty attention/involvement in teaching
- ☐ Rankings in national magazines
- ☐ Presence of students who share my ethnic/racial background
- ☐ Presence of students who share my social class background
- ☐ Knowing that there would be other people I know also attending
- ☐ Special academic program (major, honors, joint degree, accelerated degree, etc.)
- ☐ Special extracurricular (study abroad program, able to play on a sports team, etc.)
- ☐ Good employment outcomes for graduates
- ☐ Graduates gain admission to top graduate/professional schools
- ☐ Cost of attending
- ☐ Opportunity to receive merit scholarship(s)
- ☐ Financial aid package

In Column A, please type in the complete names of any and all trade schools, beauty schools, technical schools, community colleges, universities, etc. to which you applied to be a student during your senior year of high school.
In Column B, please type in the names of the towns in which these schools are located.
In Column C, please type in the names of the states or countries (if not located in the United States) in which these schools are located.
In Column D, please indicate for each school whether you applied through an early admissions notification program.
In Column E, please indicate for each school whether your parents attended this college as an undergraduate.
In Column F, please indicate for each school whether you were an athletic recruit.
In Column G, please select the final outcome at each school.

Please fill in the answers in the table below (mark appropriate circles and squares and fill in the blank spaces).

Matrix: part 1 of 2

	Column A	Column B	Column C	Column D
1	....	....	....	O Applied Early Action (not required to enroll) O Applied Early Decision (required to enroll) O Did Neither
2	....	....	....	O Applied Early Action (not required to enroll) O Applied Early Decision (required to enroll) O Did Neither
3	....	....	....	O Applied Early Action (not required to enroll) O Applied Early Decision (required to enroll) O Did Neither
4	....	....	....	O Applied Early Action (not required to enroll) O Applied Early Decision (required to enroll) O Did Neither
5	....	....	....	O Applied Early Action (not required to enroll) O Applied Early Decision (required to enroll) O Did Neither
6	....	....	....	O Applied Early Action (not required to enroll) O Applied Early Decision (required to enroll) O Did Neither
7	....	....	....	O Applied Early Action (not required to enroll) O Applied Early

				Decision (required to enroll) ☐ Did Neither
8	....	....	....	☐ Applied Early Action (not required to enroll) ☐ Applied Early Decision (required to enroll) ☐ Did Neither
9	....	....	....	☐ Applied Early Action (not required to enroll) ☐ Applied Early Decision (required to enroll) ☐ Did Neither
10	....	....	....	☐ Applied Early Action (not required to enroll) ☐ Applied Early Decision (required to enroll) ☐ Did Neither

In Column A, please type in the complete names of any and all trade schools, beauty schools, technical schools, community colleges, universities, etc.
 to which you applied to be a student during your senior year of high school.
In Column B, please type in the names of the towns in which these schools are located.
In Column C, please type in the names of the states or countries (if not located in the United States) in which these schools are located.
In Column D, please indicate for each school whether you applied through an early admissions notification program.
In Column E, please indicate for each school whether your parents attended this college as an undergraduate.
In Column F, please indicate for each school whether you were an athletic recruit.
In Column G, please select the final outcome at each school.

Please fill in the answers in the table below (mark appropriate circles and squares and fill in the blank spaces).

Matrix: part 2 of 2

	Column E	Column F	Column G
1	○ Yes ○ No	○ Yes ○ No	○ Accepted and enrolled ○ Accepted but did not enroll ○ Waitlisted ○ Denied admission
2	○ Yes ○ No	○ Yes ○ No	○ Accepted and enrolled ○ Accepted but did not enroll ○ Waitlisted ○ Denied admission
3	○ Yes ○ No	○ Yes ○ No	○ Accepted and enrolled ○ Accepted but did not enroll ○ Waitlisted ○ Denied admission
4	○ Yes ○ No	○ Yes ○ No	○ Accepted and enrolled ○ Accepted but did not enroll ○ Waitlisted ○ Denied admission
5	○ Yes ○ No	○ Yes ○ No	○ Accepted and enrolled ○ Accepted but did not enroll ○ Waitlisted ○ Denied admission
6	○ Yes ○ No	○ Yes ○ No	○ Accepted and enrolled ○ Accepted but did not enroll ○ Waitlisted ○ Denied admission
7	○ Yes ○ No	○ Yes ○ No	○ Accepted and enrolled ○ Accepted but did not enroll ○ Waitlisted ○ Denied admission
8	○ Yes ○ No	○ Yes ○ No	○ Accepted and enrolled ○ Accepted but did not enroll ○ Waitlisted ○ Denied admission
9	○ Yes ○ No	○ Yes ○ No	○ Accepted and enrolled ○ Accepted but did not enroll ○ Waitlisted ○ Denied admission

10	O Yes O No	O Yes O No	O Accepted and enrolled O Accepted but did not enroll O Waitlisted O Denied admission

Would you describe the first post-secondary school in which you enrolled to be a student as your first choice, second choice, or third or lower choice?

Please pick one of the answers below.

O   First choice

O   Second choice

O   Third of lower choice

Compared to all the other U.S. high school students who graduated the same year that you did, how would you rank yourself in terms of academic ability?

Please pick one of the answers below.

O   Top one percent

O   Top two to five percent

O   Top six to ten percent

O   Top 11 to 20 percent

O   Below top 20 percent

Did you take any International Baccalaureate (IB) exams during high school?

Please pick one of the answers below.

O   Yes

O   No

Please select the number of International Baccalaureate (IB) exams on which you received a score of 4 or above.

Please pick one of the answers below.

O   0

O   1

O   2

O   3

O   4

O   5

O   6

Did you take any Advanced Placement (AP) exams during high school?

Please pick one of the answers below.

☐ Yes

○ No

Please select the number of Advanced Placement (AP) exams you took on which you received a score of 3 or above. If you took an International Baccalaureate (IB) exam in the same subject area please do not include this AP exam in your total.

Please pick one of the answers below.

☐ 0

○ 1

☐ 2

○ 3

☐ 4

○ 5

☐ 6

○ 7

☐ 8 or more

Did you take the SAT Reasoning Test (SAT I)?

Please pick one of the answers below.

☐ Yes

○ No

Please type in the highest official score you received on the mathematics and verbal/critical reading portions of the SAT Reasoning Test (SAT I).

Please use the blank space to write your answers.

SAT I: Mathematics

....

SAT I: Verbal/Critical Reading

....

Did you take the ACT Assessment Test?

Please pick one of the answers below.

☐ Yes

○ No

Please type in the highest official composite exam score you received on the ACT.

Please use the blank space to write your answers.

ACT Composite Score

....

Did you take any SAT II Subject Tests?

Please pick one of the answers below.

☐ Yes

☐ No

Please type in your three highest SAT II Subject test scores.

Please use the blank space to write your answers.

1) SAT II Test Score

....

2) SAT II Test Score

....

3) SAT II Test Score

....

What is your gender?

Please pick one of the answers below.

☐ Male

☐ Female

During your senior year of high school, with whom were you primarily living?

Please pick one of the answers below.

☐ Mother and Father

☐ Father and Stepmother

☐ Mother and Stepfather

☐ Father

☐ Mother

☐ Other

During your senior year of high school, how many people were members of your household? Include yourself and any individuals away at college.

Please pick one of the answers below.

☐ One

○ Two

☐ Three

○ Four

☐ Five

○ Six

☐ Seven

○ Eight or more

What is your race and/or ethnicity? Please check all that apply.

Please check all that apply.

☐ Black/African American

☐ Hispanic/Latino

☐ Asian/Asian American

☐ American Indian/Native American or Alaska Native

☐ Native Hawaiian or Pacific Islander

☐ White

Please choose from below what you consider to be your primary race/ethnicity. Choose only one.

Please pick one of the answers below.

○ Black/African American

○ Hispanic/Latino

○ Asian/Asian American

○ American Indian/Native American or Alaska Native

○ Native Hawaiian or Pacific Islander

○ White

Please select your, your parents', and your grandparents' country of birth from the following list of countries. If the correct country is not listed or you do not remember the precise country of birth please choose the appropriate world region of birth from the end of the list.

Please fill in the answers in the table below (mark appropriate circles and squares and fill in the blank spaces).

Matrix: part 1 of 2

	Your Country of Birth	Your Father's Country of Birth	Your Mother's Country of Birth	Your Paternal Grandfather's Country of Birth
	○ Afghanistan	○ Afghanistan	○ Afghanistan	○ Afghanistan
	○ American Samoa	○ American Samoa	○ American Samoa	○ American Samoa
	○ Argentina	○ Argentina	○ Argentina	○ Argentina
	○ Armenia	○ Armenia	○ Armenia	○ Armenia
	○ Australia	○ Australia	○ Australia	○ Australia
	○ Austria	○ Austria	○ Austria	○ Austria
	○ Azores	○ Azores	○ Azores	○ Azores
	○ Bahamas	○ Bahamas	○ Bahamas	○ Bahamas
	○ Bangladesh	○ Bangladesh	○ Bangladesh	○ Bangladesh
	○ Barbados	○ Barbados	○ Barbados	○ Barbados
	○ Belgium	○ Belgium	○ Belgium	○ Belgium
	○ Belize	○ Belize	○ Belize	○ Belize
	○ Bermuda	○ Bermuda	○ Bermuda	○ Bermuda
	○ Bolivia	○ Bolivia	○ Bolivia	○ Bolivia
	○ Brazil	○ Brazil	○ Brazil	○ Brazil
	○ Burma	○ Burma	○ Burma	○ Burma
	○ Cambodia	○ Cambodia	○ Cambodia	○ Cambodia
	○ Canada	○ Canada	○ Canada	○ Canada
	○ Chile	○ Chile	○ Chile	○ Chile
	○ China	○ China	○ China	○ China
	○ Colombia	○ Colombia	○ Colombia	○ Colombia
	○ Costa Rica	○ Costa Rica	○ Costa Rica	○ Costa Rica
	○ Cuba	○ Cuba	○ Cuba	○ Cuba
	○ Czech Republic	○ Czech Republic	○ Czech Republic	○ Czech Republic
	○ Czechoslovakia	○ Czechoslovakia	○ Czechoslovakia	○ Czechoslovakia
	○ Denmark	○ Denmark	○ Denmark	○ Denmark
	○ Dominican Republic	○ Dominican Republic	○ Dominican Republic	○ Dominican Republic
	○ Dominica	○ Dominica	○ Dominica	○ Dominica
	○ El Salvador	○ El Salvador	○ El Salvador	○ El Salvador
	○ England	○ England	○ England	○ England
	○ Ethiopia	○ Ethiopia	○ Ethiopia	○ Ethiopia
	○ Figi	○ Figi	○ Figi	○ Figi
	○ Finland	○ Finland	○ Finland	○ Finland
	○ France	○ France	○ France	○ France
	○ Germany	○ Germany	○ Germany	○ Germany
	○ Ghana	○ Ghana	○ Ghana	○ Ghana
	○ Great Britian	○ Great Britian	○ Great Britian	○ Great Britian
	○ Greece	○ Greece	○ Greece	○ Greece
	○ Grenada	○ Grenada	○ Grenada	○ Grenada
	○ Guam	○ Guam	○ Guam	○ Guam
	○ Guatemala	○ Guatemala	○ Guatemala	○ Guatemala
	○ Guyana	○ Guyana	○ Guyana	○ Guyana
	○ Haiti	○ Haiti	○ Haiti	○ Haiti
	○ Holland	○ Holland	○ Holland	○ Holland
	○ Honduras	○ Honduras	○ Honduras	○ Honduras
	○ Hong Kong	○ Hong Kong	○ Hong Kong	○ Hong Kong
	○ Hungary	○ Hungary	○ Hungary	○ Hungary
	○ India	○ India	○ India	○ India
	○ Indonesia	○ Indonesia	○ Indonesia	○ Indonesia
	○ Iran	○ Iran	○ Iran	○ Iran
	○ Iraq	○ Iraq	○ Iraq	○ Iraq

☐ Ireland	☐ Ireland	☐ Ireland	☐ Ireland
☐ Israel	☐ Israel	☐ Israel	☐ Israel
☐ Italy	☐ Italy	☐ Italy	☐ Italy
☐ Jamaica	☐ Jamaica	☐ Jamaica	☐ Jamaica
☐ Japan	☐ Japan	☐ Japan	☐ Japan
☐ Jordan	☐ Jordan	☐ Jordan	☐ Jordan
☐ Kenya	☐ Kenya	☐ Kenya	☐ Kenya
☐ Korea	☐ Korea	☐ Korea	☐ Korea
☐ Laos	☐ Laos	☐ Laos	☐ Laos
☐ Latvia	☐ Latvia	☐ Latvia	☐ Latvia
☐ Lebanon	☐ Lebanon	☐ Lebanon	☐ Lebanon
☐ Lithuania	☐ Lithuania	☐ Lithuania	☐ Lithuania
☐ Malaysia	☐ Malaysia	☐ Malaysia	☐ Malaysia
☐ Mexico	☐ Mexico	☐ Mexico	☐ Mexico
☐ Morocco	☐ Morocco	☐ Morocco	☐ Morocco
☐ Netherlands	☐ Netherlands	☐ Netherlands	☐ Netherlands
☐ New Zealand	☐ New Zealand	☐ New Zealand	☐ New Zealand
☐ Nicaragua	☐ Nicaragua	☐ Nicaragua	☐ Nicaragua
☐ Nigeria	☐ Nigeria	☐ Nigeria	☐ Nigeria
☐ North Ireland	☐ North Ireland	☐ North Ireland	☐ North Ireland
☐ Norway	☐ Norway	☐ Norway	☐ Norway
☐ Pakistan	☐ Pakistan	☐ Pakistan	☐ Pakistan
☐ Palestine	☐ Palestine	☐ Palestine	☐ Palestine
☐ Panama	☐ Panama	☐ Panama	☐ Panama
☐ Peru	☐ Peru	☐ Peru	☐ Peru
☐ Philippines	☐ Philippines	☐ Philippines	☐ Philippines
☐ Poland	☐ Poland	☐ Poland	☐ Poland
☐ Portugal	☐ Portugal	☐ Portugal	☐ Portugal
☐ Puerto Rico	☐ Puerto Rico	☐ Puerto Rico	☐ Puerto Rico
☐ Romania	☐ Romania	☐ Romania	☐ Romania
☐ Russia	☐ Russia	☐ Russia	☐ Russia
☐ Saudi Arabia	☐ Saudi Arabia	☐ Saudi Arabia	☐ Saudi Arabia
☐ Scotland	☐ Scotland	☐ Scotland	☐ Scotland
☐ Singapore	☐ Singapore	☐ Singapore	☐ Singapore
☐ Slovakia/Slovak Rep.	☐ Slovakia/Slovak Rep.	☐ Slovakia/Slovak Rep.	☐ Slovakia/Slovak Rep.
☐ South Africa	☐ South Africa	☐ South Africa	☐ South Africa
☐ Spain	☐ Spain	☐ Spain	☐ Spain
☐ Sweden	☐ Sweden	☐ Sweden	☐ Sweden
☐ Switzerland	☐ Switzerland	☐ Switzerland	☐ Switzerland
☐ Syria	☐ Syria	☐ Syria	☐ Syria
☐ Taiwan	☐ Taiwan	☐ Taiwan	☐ Taiwan
☐ Thailand	☐ Thailand	☐ Thailand	☐ Thailand
☐ Trinidad & Tobago	☐ Trinidad & Tobago	☐ Trinidad & Tobago	☐ Trinidad & Tobago
☐ Turkey	☐ Turkey	☐ Turkey	☐ Turkey
☐ United States	☐ United States	☐ United States	☐ United States
☐ U.S. Virgin Islands	☐ U.S. Virgin Islands	☐ U.S. Virgin Islands	☐ U.S. Virgin Islands
☐ USSR	☐ USSR	☐ USSR	☐ USSR
☐ Ukraine	☐ Ukraine	☐ Ukraine	☐ Ukraine
☐ Uruguay	☐ Uruguay	☐ Uruguay	☐ Uruguay
☐ Venezuela	☐ Venezuela	☐ Venezuela	☐ Venezuela
☐ Vietnam	☐ Vietnam	☐ Vietnam	☐ Vietnam
☐ Yugoslavia	☐ Yugoslavia	☐ Yugoslavia	☐ Yugoslavia
☐ Asia	☐ Asia	☐ Asia	☐ Asia
☐ North America	☐ North America	☐ North America	☐ North America
☐ Central America	☐ Central America	☐ Central America	☐ Central America
☐ South America	☐ South America	☐ South America	☐ South America
☐ Caribbean	☐ Caribbean	☐ Caribbean	☐ Caribbean
☐ Europe	☐ Europe	☐ Europe	☐ Europe
☐ Middle East	☐ Middle East	☐ Middle East	☐ Middle East
☐ North Africa	☐ North Africa	☐ North Africa	☐ North Africa
☐ Other Africa	☐ Other Africa	☐ Other Africa	☐ Other Africa
☐ Pacific Islands	☐ Pacific Islands	☐ Pacific Islands	☐ Pacific Islands
☐ Other	☐ Other	☐ Other	☐ Other
☐ Unknown	☐ Unknown	☐ Unknown	☐ Unknown

Please select your, your parents', and your grandparents' country of birth from the following list of countries. If the correct country is not listed or you do not remember the precise country of birth please choose the appropriate world region of birth from the end of the list.

Please fill in the answers in the table below (mark appropriate circles and squares and fill in the blank spaces).

Matrix: part 2 of 2

	Your Paternal Grandmother's Country of Birth	Your Maternal Grandfather's Country of Birth	Your Maternal Grandmother's Country of Birth
	○ Afghanistan	○ Afghanistan	○ Afghanistan
	○ American Samoa	○ American Samoa	○ American Samoa
	○ Argentina	○ Argentina	○ Argentina
	○ Armenia	○ Armenia	○ Armenia
	○ Australia	○ Australia	○ Australia
	○ Austria	○ Austria	○ Austria
	○ Azores	○ Azores	○ Azores
	○ Bahamas	○ Bahamas	○ Bahamas
	○ Bangladesh	○ Bangladesh	○ Bangladesh
	○ Barbados	○ Barbados	○ Barbados
	○ Belgium	○ Belgium	○ Belgium
	○ Belize	○ Belize	○ Belize
	○ Bermuda	○ Bermuda	○ Bermuda
	○ Bolivia	○ Bolivia	○ Bolivia
	○ Brazil	○ Brazil	○ Brazil
	○ Burma	○ Burma	○ Burma
	○ Cambodia	○ Cambodia	○ Cambodia
	○ Canada	○ Canada	○ Canada
	○ Chile	○ Chile	○ Chile
	○ China	○ China	○ China
	○ Colombia	○ Colombia	○ Colombia
	○ Costa Rica	○ Costa Rica	○ Costa Rica
	○ Cuba	○ Cuba	○ Cuba
	○ Czech Republic	○ Czech Republic	○ Czech Republic
	○ Czechoslovakia	○ Czechoslovakia	○ Czechoslovakia
	○ Denmark	○ Denmark	○ Denmark
	○ Dominican Republic	○ Dominican Republic	○ Dominican Republic
	○ Dominica	○ Dominica	○ Dominica
	○ El Salvador	○ El Salvador	○ El Salvador
	○ England	○ England	○ England
	○ Ethiopia	○ Ethiopia	○ Ethiopia
	○ Figi	○ Figi	○ Figi
	○ Finland	○ Finland	○ Finland
	○ France	○ France	○ France
	○ Germany	○ Germany	○ Germany
	○ Ghana	○ Ghana	○ Ghana
	○ Great Britian	○ Great Britian	○ Great Britian
	○ Greece	○ Greece	○ Greece
	○ Grenada	○ Grenada	○ Grenada
	○ Guam	○ Guam	○ Guam
	○ Guatemala	○ Guatemala	○ Guatemala
	○ Guyana	○ Guyana	○ Guyana
	○ Haiti	○ Haiti	○ Haiti
	○ Holland	○ Holland	○ Holland
	○ Honduras	○ Honduras	○ Honduras
	○ Hong Kong	○ Hong Kong	○ Hong Kong
	○ Hungary	○ Hungary	○ Hungary
	○ India	○ India	○ India
	○ Indonesia	○ Indonesia	○ Indonesia
	○ Iran	○ Iran	○ Iran
	○ Iraq	○ Iraq	○ Iraq

○ Ireland	○ Ireland	○ Ireland
○ Israel	○ Israel	○ Israel
○ Italy	○ Italy	○ Italy
○ Jamaica	○ Jamaica	○ Jamaica
○ Japan	○ Japan	○ Japan
○ Jordan	○ Jordan	○ Jordan
○ Kenya	○ Kenya	○ Kenya
○ Korea	○ Korea	○ Korea
○ Laos	○ Laos	○ Laos
○ Latvia	○ Latvia	○ Latvia
○ Lebanon	○ Lebanon	○ Lebanon
○ Lithuania	○ Lithuania	○ Lithuania
○ Malaysia	○ Malaysia	○ Malaysia
○ Mexico	○ Mexico	○ Mexico
○ Morocco	○ Morocco	○ Morocco
○ Netherlands	○ Netherlands	○ Netherlands
○ New Zealand	○ New Zealand	○ New Zealand
○ Nicaragua	○ Nicaragua	○ Nicaragua
○ Nigeria	○ Nigeria	○ Nigeria
○ North Ireland	○ North Ireland	○ North Ireland
○ Norway	○ Norway	○ Norway
○ Pakistan	○ Pakistan	○ Pakistan
○ Palestine	○ Palestine	○ Palestine
○ Panama	○ Panama	○ Panama
○ Peru	○ Peru	○ Peru
○ Philippines	○ Philippines	○ Philippines
○ Poland	○ Poland	○ Poland
○ Portugal	○ Portugal	○ Portugal
○ Puerto Rico	○ Puerto Rico	○ Puerto Rico
○ Romania	○ Romania	○ Romania
○ Russia	○ Russia	○ Russia
○ Saudi Arabia	○ Saudi Arabia	○ Saudi Arabia
○ Scotland	○ Scotland	○ Scotland
○ Singapore	○ Singapore	○ Singapore
○ Slovakia/Slovak Rep.	○ Slovakia/Slovak Rep.	○ Slovakia/Slovak Rep.
○ South Africa	○ South Africa	○ South Africa
○ Spain	○ Spain	○ Spain
○ Sweden	○ Sweden	○ Sweden
○ Switzerland	○ Switzerland	○ Switzerland
○ Syria	○ Syria	○ Syria
○ Taiwan	○ Taiwan	○ Taiwan
○ Thailand	○ Thailand	○ Thailand
○ Trinidad & Tobago	○ Trinidad & Tobago	○ Trinidad & Tobago
○ Turkey	○ Turkey	○ Turkey
○ United States	○ United States	○ United States
○ U.S. Virgin Islands	○ U.S. Virgin Islands	○ U.S. Virgin Islands
○ USSR	○ USSR	○ USSR
○ Ukraine	○ Ukraine	○ Ukraine
○ Uruguay	○ Uruguay	○ Uruguay
○ Venezuela	○ Venezuela	○ Venezuela
○ Vietnam	○ Vietnam	○ Vietnam
○ Yugoslavia	○ Yugoslavia	○ Yugoslavia
○ Asia	○ Asia	○ Asia
○ North America	○ North America	○ North America
○ Central America	○ Central America	○ Central America
○ South America	○ South America	○ South America
○ Caribbean	○ Caribbean	○ Caribbean
○ Europe	○ Europe	○ Europe
○ Middle East	○ Middle East	○ Middle East
○ North Africa	○ North Africa	○ North Africa
○ Other Africa	○ Other Africa	○ Other Africa
○ Pacific Islands	○ Pacific Islands	○ Pacific Islands
○ Other	○ Other	○ Other
○ Unknown	○ Unknown	○ Unknown

Which of the following categories best reflects your religious preference during your senior year of high school?

Please pick one of the answers below.

☐ Protestant

☐ Catholic

☐ Jewish

☐ None

☐ Buddhist

☐ Hindu

☐ Other Eastern Religion

☐ Muslim

☐ Orthodox Christian

☐ Christian

☐ Native American

☐ Inter-Nondenominational

☐ Another religion not listed here

When it comes to your religious identity, would you say you are a pentacostal, fundamentalist, evangelical, mainline, or liberal Protestant or do none of these describe you?

Please pick one of the answers below.

☐ Pentacostal

☐ Fundamentalist

☐ Evangelical

☐ Mainline

☐ Liberal

☐ None

☐ Don't Know

During your senior year of high school, approximately how often did you attend religious services?

Please pick one of the answers below.

- ○ Never
- ○ Less than once a year
- ○ About once or twice a year
- ○ Several times a year
- ○ About once a month
- ○ Two-three times a month
- ○ Nearly every Week
- ○ Every Week
- ○ Several times a week
- ○ Not Applicable

How would you describe your immediate family's social class or socioeconomic status during your senior year of high school?

Please pick one of the answers below.

- ○ Lower class
- ○ Working class
- ○ Middle class
- ○ Upper-middle class
- ○ Upper class

Are you the first among your siblings, parents, and grandparents to attend a four-year college?

Please pick one of the answers below.

- ○ Yes
- ○ No, I never attended a four-year college
- ○ No, someone else attended a four-year college before I did

Please select the highest amount of education your father and mother had obtained by the start of your senior year of high school.

Please mark the corresponding circle - only one per line.

	A	B	C	D	E	F	G	H	I
Your Father	O	O	O	O	O	O	O	O	O
Your Mother	O	O	O	O	O	O	O	O	O

Legend for Rank Grid table: Please select the highest amount of education your father and mother had obtained by the start of your senior year of high school.

Columns:

A	- Less than high school
B	- High school
C	- Some college but no degree
D	- Associate's degree
E	- Bachelor's degree
F	- Master's degree
G	- Professional degree
H	- Doctoral degree
I	- Not applicable

In Column A, please type in the names of any and all schools (trade schools, beauty schools, technical schools, community colleges, universities, etc.) in which your parents had enrolled with the intention of earning a certificate or degree (associate's, undergraduate, graduate, etc.) prior to your senior year of high school.
In Column B, please type in the names of the towns in which these schools are located.
In Column C, please type in the names of the states or countries (if not located in the United States) in which these schools are located.

Please fill in the answers in the table below (mark appropriate circles and squares and fill in the blank spaces).

	Column A	Column B	Column C
1	....	....	....
2	....	....	....
3	....	....	....
4	....	....	....
5	....	....	....
6	....	....	....
7	....	....	....
8	....	....	....
9	....	....	....
10	....	....	....

During your senior year of high school, did your family own or rent the home in which you lived?

Please pick one of the answers below.

☐   Own

○   Rent

During your senior year of high school, what is your best estimate of your household's total annual income? Consider all sources before taxes.

Please pick one of the answers below.

- ☐ Less than $24,999
- ○ $25,000-49,999
- ☐ $50,000-74,999
- ○ $75,000- 99,999
- ☐ $100,000-124,999
- ○ $125,000-149,999
- ☐ $150,000-199,999
- ○ $200,000-250,000
- ☐ More than $250,000

During your senior year of high school, what is your best estimate of your household's total assets not including family home, businesses, farms, or retirement plans?

Please pick one of the answers below.

- ☐ Less than $2,500,
- ○ $2,500-9,999
- ☐ $10,000-24,999
- ○ $25,000-49,999
- ☐ $50,000-99,999,
- ○ $100,000-199,999
- ☐ $200,00-299,999,
- ○ $3000,000-399,999
- ☐ $400,000-500,000
- ☐ More than $500,000

We may want to contact you for future phases of the High School Valedictorian Project. Please type in the following information:

Please use the blank space to write your answers.

a. Your expected city and state of residence this coming summer

....

b. Your expected city and state of residence during the next academic year

....

c. Any and all email addresses at which you can be reached (If listing more than one, please separate by semicolons.)

....

d. Any and all phone numbers at which you can be reached during the coming summer and year (If listing more than one, please separate by semicolons.)

....

e. Since you may not be permanently settled at this point in your life, please provide the name, phone number, address, and relation (i.e. parent, sibling, grandparent) of someone who is more settled and should know how to reach you if you cannot be located using the above means. (Please separate each piece of information by semicolons.)

....

The High School Valedictorian Project Interview Schedule[1]

Predisposition

1. When did you first start thinking about college? What is your earliest memory?
2. How would you describe your family's approach to education in general and higher education?
3. How did your high school classmates approach education and higher education?
4. What were most community residents' views about education and higher education?
5. Are there any other individuals in your life (relatives, siblings, teachers, other adults, etc.) who had an impact on how you approached your education and higher education?
6. If and when college was discussed by your family while you were growing up, what types of colleges were discussed?
7. If and when college was discussed in your community while you were growing up, what types of colleges were discussed?
8. Which schools, if any, did the adults you knew attend?

Preparation

9. Is there anything you did to prepare for the college admissions process? Academic programs, test preparation, extracurricular involvement, summer programs?

Exploration

10. Tell me about how you explored college options. When did you start looking? How did you gather information? Who did you talk to?
11. What were the primary sources of information you had about college admissions and financial aid? Was any particular source (individual, book, website, etc.) especially helpful to you in this endeavor?
12. How much guidance did your school provide? What kinds of things did they do?
13. How involved was your family in this process? What kinds of things did they do?
14. Did your family have in mind a type or quality of college to which you should apply or attend? What were their suggestions?
15. What characteristics were you looking for in a college?
16. Did you visit any of the colleges to which you applied before applying? How did you come to visit those schools?
17. How did you first find out about the colleges to which you applied? Did you know someone attending or who attended? Did you receive direct contact from the university, a mailing for example?
18. Are there any schools you applied to that you wouldn't have, were it not for receiving something in the mail from that school?

Application

19. Where did you apply?
20. (Depending on earlier answer), did you consider applying to a four-year college? A college out of state? A college in state? A public college? A private college? Why or why not?
21. Tell me about any people who helped you decide where to apply. Who were they? What did they do?
22. I now want to understand what shaped your application decisions. Did college location shape where you applied? How so and how much?

23. Did you have a preferred distance and a maximum distance that you were willing to be away from home? Did your family have a preferred or maximum distance from home in mind for you?

24. Had you visited the states of the colleges to which you applied before submitting your application? Did you know anyone currently living in the states in which you applied to schools?

25. Did college cost shape where you applied? How so and how much?

Matriculation

26. How did you choose the college you decided to attend or what made you choose this school over another school?

27. Was this your first-choice school? If you did not enroll in your first-choice school, please explain.

28. Tell me about any people who helped you decide where to attend. Who were they? What did they do?

29. How big of a factor was location in your college choice?

30. How big of a factor was cost in your college choice? Were there less-expensive options that you decided not to choose? Why or why not?

31. Did you have a limit to the amount that you were willing to pay or go into debt to pay for college?

32. Did your family? Did you or your family have different limits on what you or they would pay depending on the college?

College Purpose

33. Did you have any life goals when you graduated from high school? What were they? What did you see yourself doing?

34. What impact do you think attending your particular college will have on your life? How much of a difference do you think attending another college would have?

35. Is there anything else you think I should know? Do you have any questions for me?

Regression Tables

TABLE F.2.1 Odds Ratio Results from Logistic Regression Testing HSVP Students' Odds of Thinking about Continuing Their Education beyond High School Prior to Sixth Grade (N=896)

Variables	Odds Ratio
Personal Characteristics	
Social Class	
Low SES	.41**
(Middle SES)	—
High SES	3.10**
Gender	
(Male)	—
Female	2.08**
Race	
(White)	—
Black	1.20
Hispanic	1.51
Asian	1.95
High School and Community Characteristics	
Average Combined Math and Verbal SAT I Score Earned by Fellow Seniors	
<950	1.30
(950–1100)	—
>1100	.25*
Percentage of Fellow Seniors Taking the SAT I	
<50	1.00
50–75	—
>75	2.84*
Percentage of Neighbors with a BA or BS	
<12	1.62
12–36	—
>36	4.05*

(continued)

Variables	Odds Ratio
Log Likelihood	−220.8064
LR chi-squared	(29) 88.22
Pseudo R-squared	.1665

Note: Students who began thinking about attending college prior to sixth grade were coded as "yes" (1) and students who did not were coded as "no" (0). Reference groups are in parentheses. The following variables were included but are not presented because they are not statistically significant or are not substantive: personal SAT I score, parent attended a most selective college; foreign-born parent status; percentage of high school class-mates eligible for free or reduced-price lunch; community type; state; and missing variables for personal SAT I score, parent attended a most selective college, foreign-born parent status, high school data, and percentage of college-educated community residents within high school zip code. *$p < .05$; **$p < .01$; ***$p < .001$

Source: High School Valedictorian Project Person Dataset.

TABLE F.2.2 Odds Ratio Results from Logistic Regressions Testing the Odds That HSVP Students' Attending College, a Four-Year College, or a Prestigious College Was Very Important to Their Fathers or Mothers When They Entered High School (N=896)

Variables	College		Four-Year College		Prestigious College	
	Father	Mother	Father	Mother	Father	Mother
Personal Characteristics						
Social Class						
Low SES	.35***	—	.42***	.70	.78	1.05
(Middle SES)	—	—	—	—	—	—
High SES	1.78*	1.61	1.90**	1.55*	2.34***	2.28***
Gender						
(Male)	—	—	—	—	—	—
Female	1.19	1.33	.85	.94	.97	.87
Race						
(White)	—	—	—	—	—	—
Black	.97	1.42	1.44	2.44*	.84	.45
Hispanic	1.99	1.57	1.41	1.37	1.31	1.07
Asian	2.56*	3.41**	2.94***	3.27***	1.96*	1.80*
Foreign-Born Parent						
Yes	1.53	1.53	1.20	1.31	2.59**	2.54**
(No)	—	—	—	—	—	—
A Parent Attended a Most-Selective College						
Yes	1.42	1.44	1.57	1.94**	2.08**	1.54
(No)	—	—	—	—	—	—

(continued)

TABLE F.2.2 *continued*

Variables	College		Four-Year College		Prestigious College	
	Father	Mother	Father	Mother	Father	Mother
High School and Community Characteristics						
Average Combined Math and Verbal SAT I Score Earned by Fellow Seniors						
<950	.80	.50*	.80	.57	1.55	1.38
(950–1100)	—	—	—	—	—	—
>1100	1.26	1.66	1.07	1.17	1.15	0.88
Community Type						
Rural	.72	.94	.87	1.05	1.01	0.88
(Suburban)	—	—	—	—	—	—
Urban	1.89*	2.09*	1.41	1.24	1.14	1.15
Log Likelihood	−375.3290	−337.3268	−497.5423	−493.4284	−381.6591	−386.5813
LR chi-squared	(29) 134.29	(29) 84.92	(29) 163.15	(29) 150.04	(29) 146.55	(29) 133.99
Pseudo R-squared	.1518	.1118	.1409	.1320	.1611	.1477

Note: These results are based on students' appraisals of their parents' attitudes. See notes of table 2.1 for more details on the outcome measures used. Reference groups are in parentheses. The following variables were included but are not presented because they are not statistically significant or are not substantive: personal SAT I score; percentage of fellow seniors who took the SAT I; percentage of high school classmates eligible for free or reduced-price lunch; percentage of college-educated residents within high school zip code; state; and missing variables for personal SAT I score, parent attended a most-selective college, foreign-born parent status, high school data, and percentage of college-educated community residents within high school zip code. *p < .05; **p < .01; ***p < .001
Source: High School Valedictorian Project Person Dataset.

TABLE F.2.3 **Odds Ratio Results from Logistic Regressions Testing the Odds That Attending College, a Four-Year College, or a Prestigious College Was Very Important to HSVP Students When They Entered High School (N=896)**

Variables	College	Four-Year College	Prestigious College
Personal Characteristics			
Social Class			
Low SES	.61	.62	1.32
(Middle SES)	—	—	—
High SES	1.32	1.53	1.75**
Gender			
(Male)	—	—	—
Female	3.03***	1.59*	.95
Race			
(White)	—	—	—
Black	1.28	2.20	.77
Hispanic	6.07**	2.98*	1.27
Asian	2.51*	2.54**	1.21
A Parent Attended a Most-Selective College			
Yes	1.54	1.33	1.63*
(No)	—	—	—
Log Likelihood	−246.3942	−355.5586	−548.3325
LR chi-squared	(29) 60.20	(29) 58.75	(29) 106.56
Pseudo R-squared	.1089	.0763	.0886

Note: Reference groups are in parentheses. The following variables were included but are not presented because they are not statistically significant or are not substantive: personal SAT I score; foreign-born parent status; percentage of fellow seniors who took the SAT I; average SAT I score earned by fellow seniors; percentage of high school classmates eligible for free or reduced-price lunch; community type; percentage of college-educated residents within high school zip code; state; and missing variables for personal SAT I score, parent attended a most-selective college, foreign-born parent status, high school data, and percentage of college-educated residents within high school zip code. *$p < .05$; **$p < .01$; ***$p < .001$
Source: High School Valedictorian Project Person Dataset.

TABLE F.4.1 **Odds Ratio Results from Logistic Regressions Testing HSVP Students' Odds of Having a Strong Understanding of the College Admissions Process (N=896)**

Characteristics	Model I	Model II	Model III
Social Class			
Low SES	.67	.75	.90
(Middle SES)	—	—	—
High SES	1.63**	1.34	1.15
Gender			
(Male)	—	—	—
Female	1.18	1.18	1.16
Race			
(White)	—	—	—
Black	2.27	2.42	2.47
Hispanic	1.52	1.60	1.12
Asian	1.47	1.49	0.91
First-Generation College Student			
Yes	—	.61*	.61*
(No)	—	—	—
A Parent Attended a			
Most-Selective College			
Yes	—	1.92*	1.48
(No)	—	—	—
Percentage of High School			
Students Eligible for			
Free/Reduced-Price			
Lunch			
<20	—	—	.60*
(20–50)	—	—	—
>50	—	—	0.62
Log Likelihood	−452.3769	−444.7220	−418.8233
LR chi-squared	18.48 (6)	33.79 (9)	85.58 (40)
Pseudo R-squared	.0200	.0366	.0927

Note: Students' knowledge of the college admissions process is considered strong if they gave themselves a 4 or 5 on a scale of 1 to 5, in which a 1 reflects a poor and a 5 represents an excellent understanding. Reference groups are in parentheses. All Model I variables are presented in the table. The following variable was included in Model II but is not presented because it is not substantive: missing parents' selective college attendance status. The following variables were included in Model III but are not presented because they are not statistically significant or are not substantive: foreign-born parent status; personal SAT I score; percentage of fellow seniors who took the SAT I; average SAT I score earned by fellow seniors; percentage of college-educated residents within high school zip code; community type; state; whether respondent (R) started thinking about continuing R's education beyond high school prior to entering high school, the importance R, R's mother, and R's father attached to R attending college, a four-year college, and a prestigious college; and missing variables for parents' selective college attendance status, foreign-born parent status, high school data. $*p<.05$; $**p<.01$; $***p<.001$

Source: High School Valedictorian Project Person Dataset.

TABLE F.4.2 **Odds Ratio Results from Logistic Regressions Testing the Odds That Parents of HSVP Students Have a Strong Understanding of the College Admissions Process (N=896)**

Variables	Model I	Model II	Model III
Social Class			
Low SES	.39***	.41***	.48**
(Middle SES)	—	—	—
High SES	2.04***	2.06***	1.64**
Gender			
(Male)	—	—	—
Female	1.22	1.24	1.31
Race			
(White)	—	—	—
Black	.98	1.30	1.56
Hispanic	.51*	0.98	1.21
Asian	.72*	1.42	1.31
Foreign-Born Parent			
Yes	—	.43***	.47**
(No)	—	—	—
First-Generation College Student			
Yes	—	—	.57*
(No)	—	—	—
Community Type			
Rural	—	—	1.22
(Suburban)	—	—	—
Urban	—	—	2.02**
Log Likelihood	−574.0833	−566.6581	−540.1832
LR chi-squared	85.69 (6)	100.54 (8)	153.49 (36)
Pseudo R-squared	.0694	.0815	.1244

Note: Parents' knowledge of the college admissions process is considered strong if students gave them a 4 or 5 on a scale of 1 to 5, in which a 5 represents an excellent understanding. Reference groups are in parentheses. All Model I variables are presented in the table. The following variable was included in Model II but is not presented because it is not substantive: missing foreign-born parent status. The following variables were included in Model III but are not presented because they are not statistically significant or are not substantive: parents' selective college attendance status; respondent's SAT I score; percentage of fellow seniors who took the SAT I; average SAT I score earned by fellow seniors; percentage of students in high school who qualified for free or reduced-price lunch; percentage of college-educated residents within high school zip code; state; the importance respondent's (R's) mother and R's father attached to R attending college, a four-year college, and a prestigious college; and missing variables for parents' selective college attendance status, foreign-born parent status, and high school data. *$p < .05$; **$p < .01$; ***$p < .001$
Source: High School Valedictorian Project Person Dataset.

TABLE F.4.3 **Odds Ratio Results from Logistic Regressions Testing HSVP Financial Aid Applicants' Odds of Having a Strong Understanding of the Financial Aid Process (N=521)**

Characteristics	Model I	Model II	Model III
Social Class			
Low SES	1.46	1.42	1.27
(Middle SES)	—	—	—
High SES	1.00	1.00	.98
Gender			
(Male)	—	—	—
Female	1.28	1.27	1.33
Race			
(White)	—	—	—
Black	2.62*	2.40	1.50
Hispanic	2.38**	1.60	1.30
Asian	2.19**	1.48	1.61
Foreign-Born Parent			
Yes	—	1.64	1.04
(No)	—	—	—
Percentage of High School Students Eligible for Free/Reduced-Price Lunch			
<20	—	—	.66
(20–50)	—	—	—
>50	—	—	.36*
Log Likelihood	−339.44052	−337.76431	−318.68465
LR chi-squared	27.40 (6)	30.75 (8)	68.91 (31)
Pseudo R-squared	.0388	.0435	.0976

Note: Students' knowledge of the financial aid process is considered strong if they gave themselves a 4 or a 5 on a scale of 1 to 5, in which a 1 reflects a poor and a 5 represents an excellent understanding. Reference groups are in parentheses. All Model I variables are presented in the table. The following variable was included in Model II but is not presented because it is not substantive: missing foreign-born parent status. The following variables were included in Model III but are not presented because they are not statistically significant or are not substantive: first-generation college student status; parents' selective college attendance status; personal SAT I score; percentage of fellow seniors who took the SAT I; average SAT I score earned by fellow seniors; percentage of college-educated residents within high school zip code; community type; state; the importance respondent's (R's) mother attached to R attending a prestigious college (the only significant predisposition result when tested descriptively); and missing variables for foreign-born parent status, parents' selective college attendance status, and high school data. *$p < .05$; **$p < .01$; ***$p < .001$
Source: High School Valedictorian Project Person Dataset.

TABLE F.4.4 **Odds Ratio Results from Logistic Regressions Testing the Odds That Parents of HSVP Financial Aid Applicants Have a Strong Understanding of the Financial Aid Process (N=896)**

Characteristics	Model I	Model II	Model III
Social Class			
Low SES	.44**	.49*	.54*
(Middle SES)	—	—	—
High SES	1.53*	1.40	1.24
Gender			
(Male)	—	—	—
Female	1.05	1.08	1.16
Race			
(White)	—	—	
Black	1.22	1.28	1.62
Hispanic	.80	.88	1.49
Asian	.81	.83	1.57
First-Generation College Student			
Yes		.63	.62
(No)		—	—
A Parent Attended a Most-Selective College			
Yes		.82	.88
(No)		—	—
Foreign-Born Parent			
Yes			.50*
(No)			—
Community Type			
Rural			1.07
(Suburban)			—
Urban			2.21*
Log Likelihood	−347.6791	−334.4678	−325.3968
LR chi-squared	24.27 (6)	30.69 (9)	68.84 (33)
Pseudo R-squared	.0337	.0427	.0957

Note: Parents' knowledge of the financial aid process is considered strong if students gave their parents a 4 or 5 on a scale of 1 to 5, in which a 1 reflects a poor and a 5 represents an excellent understanding. Reference groups are in parentheses. All Model I variables are presented in the table. The following variable was included in Model II but is not presented because it is not substantive: missing parents' selective college attendance status. The following variables were included in Model III but are not presented because they are not statistically significant or are not substantive: respondent's SAT I score; percentage of fellow seniors who took the SAT I; average SAT I score earned by fellow seniors; percentage of students in high school who qualified for free or reduced-price lunch; percentage of college-educated residents within high school zip code; state; the predisposition variables found to be statistically significant when tested descriptively, whether respondent (R) started thinking about continuing their education beyond high school prior to entering high school, and the importance R's mother and father attached to R attending college; and missing variables for foreign-born parent status, parents' selective college attendance status, and high school data. *$p<.05$; **$p<.01$; ***$p<.001$
Source: High School Valedictorian Project Person Dataset.

TABLE F.5.1 **Coefficients from Ordinary Least Squares (OLS) Regressions Analyzing the Number of Applications HSVP Students Submit (N=715)**

Characteristics	Model I	Model II	Model III
Social Class			
Low SES	−.21	1.04	.01
(Middle SES)	—	—	—
High SES	.83**	.52*	.26
Gender			
(Male)	—	—	—
Female	−.09	−.01	−.13
Race			
(White)	—	—	—
Black	−.06	.12	−.43
Hispanic	.18	.39	−.51
Asian	1.18***	.43	−.04
Foreign-Born Parent			
Yes	—	1.02**	.74*
(No)	—	—	—
Percentage of Neighbors with a BA or BS			
<12	—	—	.72
(12–36)	—	—	—
>36	—	—	.71*
Constant	4.33***	4.19***	3.31***
R-squared	.0518	.0863	.1678

Note: Reference groups are in parentheses. All variables included in Model I are presented in the table. The following variables are included in Models II and III but not presented because they are not statistically significant or are not substantive: first-generation college student status; parents' selective college attendance status; personal SAT I score; and missing variables for personal SAT I score, parents' selective college attendance status, and foreign-born parent status. The variables included but not presented in Model III for the same reasons are: percentage of fellow seniors who took the SAT I; average SAT I score earned by fellow seniors; percentage of students in high school who qualified for free or reduced-price lunch; community type; state; and missing variables for the percentage of college-educated residents within high school zip code and high school data. $*p < .05$; $**p < .01$; $***p < .001$
Source: High School Valedictorian Project Person Dataset.

TABLE F.5.2 **Odds Ratio Results from Logistic Regressions Testing HSVP Students' Odds of Applying to at Least One Regular Public Institution (N=715)**

Characteristics	Model I	Model II	Model III	Model IV
Social Class				
Low SES	.97	.82	.84	.90
(Middle SES)	—	—	—	—
High SES	.46***	.64*	.67*	.61*
Gender				
(Male)	—	—	—	—
Female	1.20	1.08	1.00	1.02
Race				
(White)	—	—	—	—
Black	1.34	.83	.93	1.05
Hispanic	.38**	.42*	.52	.54
Asian	.92	1.36	.86	.86
A Parent Attended a Most-Selective College				
Yes	—	.54**	.59*	.53*
(No)	—	—	—	—
Personal Combined Math and Verbal SAT I Score				
1200 or Less	—	2.62*	2.41	2.57
(1210–1390)	—	—	—	—
1400 or More	—	.49***	.47**	.43***
Percentage of Fellow Seniors Taking the SAT I				
<50	—	—	1.38	1.53
(50–75)	—	—	—	—
>75	—	—	.56*	.53*
Average Combined Math and Verbal SAT I Score Earned by Fellow Seniors				
<950	—	—	.51*	.45*
(950–1100)	—	—	—	—
>1100	—	—	.62	.67
Total Number of Applications Submitted	—	—	—	1.23***
Log Likelihood	−462.3394	−440.1039	−387.2203	−367.7999
LR chi-squared	(6) 32.65	(14) 77.12	(30) 182.89	(31) 221.73
Pseudo R-squared	.0341	.0806	.1910	.2316

Note: Reference groups are in parentheses. All variables included in Model I are presented in the table. The following variables are included in Models II, III, and IV but not presented because they are not statistically significant or are not substantive: first-generation college student status; foreign-born parent status; and missing variables for personal SAT I score, parent attended a most-selective college, and foreign-born parent. The variables included but not presented in Models III and IV for the same reasons are: percentage of students in high school who were eligible for free or reduced-price lunch; community type; percentage of college-educated residents within high school zip code; state; and missing variables for the percentage of college-educated residents within high school zip code and high school data. *$p < .05$; **$p < .01$; ***$p < .001$
Source: High School Valedictorian Project Person Dataset.

TABLE F.5.3 **Odds Ratio Results from Logistic Regressions Testing HSVP Students' Odds of Applying to at Least One Regular Private Institution (N = 715)**

Characteristics	Model I	Model II	Model III	Model IV
Social Class				
Low SES	1.50	1.19	.78	.77
(Middle SES)	—	—	—	—
High SES	.56**	.77	.84	0.72
Gender				
(Male)	—	—	—	—
Female	1.63**	1.47*	1.72**	1.85**
Race				
(White)	—	—	—	—
Black	1.45	1.12	.84	1.00
Hispanic	.70	.67	.53	.55
Asian	.50**	.60	.71	.66
A Parent Attended a Most-				
Selective College				
Yes	—	.62*	1.10	.97
(No)	—	—	—	—
Personal Combined Math				
and Verbal SAT I Score				
1200 or Less	—	1.18	1.08	1.16
(1210–1390)	—	—	—	—
1400 or More	—	.44***	.47***	.43***
Total Number of	—	—	—	1.34***
Applications Submitted				
Log Likelihood	−466.5193	−442.0680	−393.0616	−357.1762
LR chi-squared	(6) 49.85	(14) 98.76	(30) 196.77	(31) 268.54
Pseudo R-squared	.0507	.1005	.2002	.2732

Note: Reference groups are in parentheses. All variables included in Model I are presented in the table. The following variables are included in Models II, III, and IV but not presented because they are not statistically significant or are not substantive: first-generation college student status; foreign-born parent status; and missing variables for personal SAT I score, parent attended a most-selective college, and foreign-born parent status. Though they were included in both Models III and IV, none of the substantive high school or community variables were significant. The variables included but not presented in Models III and IV are: percentage of fellow seniors who took the SAT I; average SAT I score earned by fellow seniors; percentage of students in high school who qualified for free or reduced-price lunch; percentage of college-educated residents within high school zip code; community type; state; and missing variables for the percentage of college-educated residents within high school zip code and high school data. $*p < .05$; $**p < .01$; $***p < .001$
Source: High School Valedictorian Project Person Dataset.

TABLE F.5.4 **Odds Ratio Results from Logistic Regressions Testing HSVP Students' Odds of Applying to at Least One Most-Selective Public Institution (N = 715)**

Characteristics	Model I	Model II	Model III	Model IV
Social Class				
Low SES	.66	.86	.95	1.08
(Middle SES)	—	—	—	—
High SES	1.66**	1.34	1.60	1.73
Gender				
(Male)	—	—	—	—
Female	1.19	1.20	1.18	1.33
Race				
(White)	—	—	—	—
Black	1.11	1.23	1.70	2.15
Hispanic	1.87*	1.43	1.02	1.55
Asian	1.75**	1.46	2.14	3.08*
A Parent Attended a Most-Selective College				
Yes	—	2.75***	1.76	1.56
(No)	—	—	—	—
Foreign-Born Parent				
Yes	—	1.88*	.81	.49
(No)	—	—	—	—
Average Combined Math and Verbal SAT I Score Earned by Fellow Seniors				
<950	—	—	.96	.75
(950–1100)	—	—	—	—
>1100	—	—	.45*	.40*
Percentage of Students at High School Eligible for Free/Reduced-Price Lunch				
<20	—	—	3.28**	3.48**
(21–49)	—	—	—	—
>50	—	—	1.54	1.61
Total Number of Applications Submitted	—	—	—	1.44***
Log Likelihood	−477.9951	−457.2700	−268.5430	−236.9883
LR chi-squared	(6) 27.74	(14) 69.19	(30) 446.65	(31) 509.76
Pseudo R-squared	.0282	.0703	.4540	.5182

Note: Reference groups are in parentheses. All variables included in Model I are presented in the table. The following variables were included in Models II, III, and IV but are not presented because they are not statistically significant or are not substantive: first-generation college student status and missing variables for personal SAT I score and parent attended a most-selective college. The variables included but not presented in Models III and IV for the same reasons are: percentage of fellow seniors who took the SAT I; percentage of college-educated residents within high school zip code; community type; state; and missing variables for high school data and percentage of college-educated residents within high school zip code. *p < .05; **p < .01; ***p < .001
Source: High School Valedictorian Project Person Dataset.

TABLE F.5.5 **Odds Ratio Results from Logistic Regressions Testing HSVP Students' Odds of Applying to at Least One Most-Selective Private Institution (N=715)**

Characteristics	Model I	Model II	Model III	Model IV
Social Class				
Low SES	.69	.84	.89	.78
(Middle SES)	—	—	—	—
High SES	2.88***	1.77**	1.51	1.43
Gender				
(Male)	—	—	—	—
Female	.57**	.71	.57*	.54*
Race				
(White)	—	—	—	—
Black	.46	1.03	.44	.45
Hispanic	2.53**	2.72*	2.35	3.24*
Asian	2.87***	1.76	1.53	1.79
A Parent Attended a Most-Selective College				
Yes	—	2.13**	1.67	1.54
(No)	—	—	—	—
Personal Combined Math and Verbal SAT I Score				
1200 or Less	—	.26**	.24**	.24**
(1210–1390)	—	—	—	—
1400 or More	—	3.83***	3.16***	4.13***
Percentage of Fellow Seniors Taking the SAT I				
<50	—	—	.64	.77
(50–75)	—	—	—	—
>75	—	—	1.97*	1.97
Percentage of Neighbors with a BA or BS				
<12	—	—	2.08*	1.59
(12–36)	—	—	—	—
>36	—	—	2.36*	2.43*
Community Type				
Rural	—	—	.44*	.65
(Suburban)	—	—	—	—
Urban	—	—	.58	.51
Total Number of Applications Submitted	—	—	—	1.75***
Log Likelihood	−410.3129	−357.6478	−313.3413	−254.7044
LR chi-squared	(6) 94.59	(14) 199.92	(30) 288.53	(31) 405.81
Pseudo R-squared	.1034	.2184	.3153	.4434

Note: Reference groups are in parentheses. All variables included in Model I are presented in the table. The following variables are included in Models II, III, and IV, but not presented because they are not statistically significant or are not substantive: first-generation college student status; foreign-born parent status; and missing variable for personal SAT I score. The variables included but not presented in Models III and IV for the same reasons are: average SAT I score earned by fellow seniors; percentage of students in high school who qualified for free or reduced-price lunch; state; and missing variables for the percentage of college-educated residents within high school zip code and high school data. $*p < .05$; $**p < .01$; $***p < .001$

Source: High School Valedictorian Project Person Dataset.

TABLE F.6.1 **Odds Ratio Results from Logistic Regressions Testing HSVP Applications' Odds of Acceptance at Most-Selective Private Universities (N=1,436)**

Variables	Model I	Model II	Model III
Personal Characteristics			
Social Class			
Low SES	1.68[#]	2.10*	2.14*
(Middle SES)	—	—	—
High SES	1.59*	1.32	1.27
Gender			
Female	.78	.98	.97
(Male)	—	—	—
Race			
(White)	—	—	—
Black	7.63*	20.28***	29.20***
Hispanic	3.37***	5.68***	6.62***
Asian	1.22	.91	1.01
Academic Achievement			
Combined Math and Verbal SAT I Score			
(<1300)	—	—	—
1300–1390	—	2.63*	2.53#
1400–1500	—	2.83*	2.58*
>1500	—	8.56***	8.57***
Number of AP or IB Exams Passed			
(Zero to Two)	—	—	—
Three to Four	—	.83	.99
Five to Six	—	1.40	1.50
Seven or More	—	2.15*	2.31*
Application Status			
Early Action			
Yes	—	—	2.36***
(No)	—	—	—
Early Decision			
Yes	—	—	3.50*
(No)	—	—	—
Legacy			
Yes	—	—	6.93**
(No)	—	—	—
Athletic Recruit			
Yes	—	—	3.72**
(No)	—	—	—
Log Pseudo Likelihood	−778.4875	−718.8589	−692.0970
Wald chi-squared	(52) 300.21	(59) 408.48	(63) 474.20
Pseudo R-squared	.2146	.2747	.3017

Note: Reference groups are in parentheses. Standard errors have been adjusted for the clustering that occurs when multiple applications are submitted by the same applicant. Though not presented in the table, Models II and III control for missing personal SAT I score, and all models include individual state dummy variables and most-selective institution dummy variables. Some institutions' dummy variables predicted success or failure of acceptance perfectly and were thus dropped from the models in order to retain a full sample. [#]$p<.1$; *$p<.05$; **$p<.01$; ***$p<.001$
Source: High School Valedictorian Project Survey Application Dataset.

TABLE F.7.1 **Odds Ratio Results from Logistic Regressions Testing HSVP Students' Odds of Enrolling in a Regular Public Institution If Admitted to at Least One Regular Public Institution (N = 380)**

Characteristics	Model I	Model II	Model III	Model IV
Social Class				
Low SES	1.03	.69	.59	.61
(Middle SES)	—	—	—	—
High SES	.52**	.69	.88	1.17
Gender				
(Male)	—	—	—	—
Female	.88	.76	.87	.75
Race				
(White)	—	—	—	—
Black	2.46	1.74	1.98	1.41
Hispanic	.85	.69	.70	.65
Asian	.63	.52	.60	.62
A Parent Attended a Most-Selective College				
Yes	—	.34**	.40*	.52
(No)	—	—	—	—
Personal Combined Math and Verbal SAT I Score				
1200 or Less	—	2.32*	1.81	1.34
(1210–1390)	—	—	—	—
1400 or More	—	.86	.94	1.70
Percentage of Fellow Seniors Taking the SAT I				
<50	—	—	2.26*	2.64*
(50–75)	—	—	—	—
>75	—	—	.55	.71
Number of Offers of Admission from:				
Regular Public Colleges	—	—	—	1.81***
Regular Private Colleges	—	—	—	.72*
Most-Selective Public Colleges	—	—	—	.37***
Most-Selective Private Colleges	—	—	—	.36***
Log Likelihood	−249.0881	−238.3253	−214.86236	−169.52657
LR chi-squared	(6) 18.45	(14) 39.98	(30) 86.91	(34) 177.58
Pseudo R-squared	.0357	.0774	.1682	.3437

Note: Reference groups are in parentheses. All variables included in Model I are presented in the table. The following variables included in Models II, III, and IV are not presented because they are not statistically significant or are not substantive: first-generation college student status; foreign-born parent status; and missing variables for personal SAT I score, parents' selective college attendance status, and foreign-born parent status. The variables included but not presented in Models III and IV for the same reasons are: average SAT I score earned by fellow seniors, percentage of students in high school who qualified for free or reduced-price lunch, community type, percentage of college-educated residents within high school zip code, state, and missing variables for high school data and the percentage of college-educated residents within high school zip code.
*p < .05; **p < .01; ***p < .001
Source: High School Valedictorian Project Person Dataset.

TABLE F.7.2 **Odds Ratio Results from Logistic Regressions Testing HSVP Students' Odds of Enrolling in a Most-Selective Private Institution If Admitted to at Least One Most-Selective Private Institution (N=344)**

Characteristics	Model I	Model II	Model III	Model IV
Social Class				
Low SES	1.96	2.86*	1.98	1.48
(Middle SES)	—	—	—	—
High SES	2.36**	2.20**	1.91*	1.55
Gender				
(Male)	—	—	—	—
Female	.63	.76	.82	.78
Race				
(White)	—	—	—	—
Black	.57	.65	.36	.64
Hispanic	1.56	1.79	1.02	.37
Asian	1.47	.94	.77	.61
Personal Combined Math and Verbal SAT I Score				
1200 or Less		.05*	.05*	.02*
(1210–1390)		—	—	—
1400 or More		2.53**	2.86**	1.27
Average Combined Math and Verbal SAT I Score Earned by Fellow Seniors				
<950			.71	.60
(950–1100)			—	—
>1100			3.48*	2.50
Percentage of Neighbors with a BA or BS				
<12			1.17	2.24
(12–36)			—	—
>36			2.48*	2.29
Number of Offers of Admission from:				
Most-Selective Private Colleges				2.36***
Most-Selective Public Colleges				.35***
Regular Private Colleges				.38***
Regular Public Colleges				.36***
Log Likelihood	−197.3854	−185.2246	−163.5993	−122.8793
LR chi-squared	(6) 18.14	(13) 42.46	(28) 85.71	(32) 167.15
Pseudo R-squared	.0439	.1028	.2076	.4048

Note: Reference groups are in parentheses. Because this sample of students admitted to at least one most-selective private college contained just three observations missing data on foreign-born parent status and this variable predicted success perfectly, it was dropped from this set of regressions. Likewise, because this sample contained just three observations missing data on high school measures and this variable predicted failure perfectly, it was dropped from this set of regressions. All variables included in Model I are presented in the table. The following variables are included in Models II, III, and IV, but not presented because they are not statistically significant or are not substantive: first-generation college student status; parents' selective college attendance status; foreign-born parent status; and missing variables for personal SAT I score and parents' selective college attendance status. The variables included but not presented in Models III and IV for the same reasons are: percentage of fellow seniors who took the SAT I, percentage of students at high school who are eligible for free or reduced-price lunch, community type, state, and missing percentage of college-educated residents within high school zip code. *p < .05; **p < .01; ***p < .001
Source: High School Valedictorian Project Person Dataset.

Notes

Chapter One

1. Names have been changed to protect the identities of these actual students.

2. This work uses college, university, and institution interchangeably.

3. Throughout this work, colleges are categorized as "most selective" if they were rated as such by *U.S. News & World Report* (2006) and "not most selective" or "regular" if they were not. The *U.S. News* rankings were adopted as the selectivity measure in this study for a couple of reasons. First, the magazine's selectivity measure takes into account several factors, including college acceptance rate and enrollees' test scores and class rank (Morse and Flanigan 2006). Second, *U.S. News* was the main source students in the study referred to in determining colleges' selectivity. Other sources of institutional selectivity, such as Barron's, were not mentioned by students. Using the *U.S. News* definitions therefore helps ensure that the study's analyses reflect what study participants meant when asked about selective colleges. Appendix A lists the seventy-two public and private colleges *U.S. News* rated as most selective.

4. COFHE is a voluntary group of thirty-one highly selective, private liberal arts colleges and universities (COFHE, 2012).

5. Given this, it is not surprising that during America's postsecondary expansion, socioeconomic stratification within higher education has continued (Astin and Oseguera, 2004; Carnevale and Strohl, 2010; Roksa et al., 2007). In fact, parents' income has become increasingly related to enrollment at elite schools over time (Astin and Oseguera, 2004; Bowen, Kurzweil, and Tobin, 2005: 291).

6. Research also suggests that these students tend to learn more while in college (Arum and Roksa, 2010), which may facilitate their more-positive transitions to life after college (Arum et al., 2012).

7. Studies of twins indicate that each year of school completed increases a worker's wage rate by as little as 9 percent to as much as 16 percent (Ashenfelter and Krueger, 1994).

8. Of course, major and career field will shape the size of the income benefit students accrue from attending a more selective institution (Andrews, Li, and Lovenheim, 2012). That being said, 30 percent of all 2007–2008 bachelor's degree recipients officially changed their declared major at least once (author's quick analysis of the U.S. Department of Education's Baccalaureate and Beyond (B&B:08/09) data using PowerStats at http://nces.ed.gov/datalab/). It also stands to reason that even more students likely alter their major choice between enrolling and declaring. It therefore may not be in the best interests of top students (who have the ability and potential to pursue a wide range of careers) to forego attending an elite college based on what they, at age eighteen, think their major and career will be. Bowen and Bok (1998) suggest that disadvantaged students, who have less information about career opportunities, may be particularly likely to change career plans during college.

9. Studying a broader group of high achievers (students in the top quartile of test performance), Light and Strayer (2000) and Mattern, Shaw, and Kobrin (2010) observe a similar pattern in which higher-performing students' graduation rates increase as institutional selectivity rises.

10. This study excludes students from private high schools as well as those from vocational and alternative public high schools for several reasons. First, valedictorians from traditional public high schools were more consistently reported in the newspapers across all five states than were valedictorians from other types of high schools. Second, more data is publicly available on regular public high schools than on private and other types of public high schools and it was important to have measures of high school characteristics in order to control for the role of high school context on college destinations. Third, students from vocational and alternative public high schools are likely to experience a different college choice process (if they have one at all) given the unique nature of their secondary schools. The college choice process is also very different for students attending private high schools (Clinedinst, Hurley, and Hawkins, 2011; Cookson and Persell, 1985; McDonough, 1997). Focusing on the process at public high schools also makes much more sense from a policy perspective, given that about 92 percent of all high school students are enrolled in public schools (Aud et al., 2012).

11. The sample occasionally includes more than one valedictorian from the same school in the same year. While some schools name multiple valedictorians only when top students' grade point averages (GPAs) really are the same, other schools make a regular practice of bestowing the honor on multiple students by implementing policies in which, for example, all students with a weighted GPA of 4.0 or above or all students who have received A's in all of their classes earn the title. An examination of the original newspaper reports used to develop the HSVP sample reveals several schools that listed up to fifteen valedictorians in a single year. Others who have explored this phenomenon note that schools with

liberal valedictorian policies generally defend the practice by claiming that it helps reduce students' stress and competitiveness with one another (Demerath, 2009; Hu, 2010). The HSVP sample includes students from high schools with multiple valedictorians because even if a student was one of several valedictorians, he or she still demonstrated high achievement.

12. Consider that even with vast resources it would be difficult to study valedictorians while they were in each stage of the college choice process because their valedictorian status would not be confirmed until the end of their senior year. One would have to study several top contenders for the valedictorian honor in each school in order to ensure that ultimately the valedictorian's experience was captured.

13. While valedictorians who just graduated from high school could have been studied, doing so would have decreased sample size dramatically. In the end, it was deemed better to include more valedictorians, even though some would be recalling events across a slightly longer period of time.

14. As Hernández (1997) explains, class rank is a much better indicator than GPA in assessing students' performance. Grade inflation at the high school level has increased over time (Nord et al., 2011). The nationally-representative Education Longitudinal Study (ELS) indicates that 42 percent of all high school seniors earn GPAs of 3.0 or higher (Chen, Wu, and Tasoff, 2010a). Among valedictorians, the difference between those with a 4.0 and those with a 4.5 is more likely to reflect variation in how high schools treat advanced courses in GPA calculations than any real distinction in students' preparation. Comparing valedictorians' unweighted GPAs is similarly unlikely to reveal meaningful differences in achievement. Even if in this age of grade inflation a student could become valedictorian with a 3.85, it would be problematic to assume that this student is less of a high achiever than another valedictorian with a 4.0 GPA. The grading standards at the first valedictorian's school could simply be more stringent.

15. Admissions officers respond favorably to AP and IB classes for at least two reasons. First, in deciding who to accept, admissions officers consider how applicants are likely to perform as undergraduates. AP and IB scores are thought to be particularly good predictors since they are specifically designed to assess students' ability to do college-level work (College Board, 2006a; Hernández, 1997: 92; International Baccalaureate Organization, 2008). Second, elite universities want undergraduates who possess a sincere interest in learning for learning's sake. Since taking these courses can put students' GPAs and class ranks at risk, students who enroll are perceived as wanting to expand their knowledge, regardless of the cost (Hernández, 1997: 17). Several valedictorians pointed out, however, that in schools that weight GPA, performing well in AP and IB classes can help students increase their GPAs, class ranks, and their chances of becoming valedictorian. Demerath (2009) also observed high achievers taking AP courses to boost class rank.

16. The SAT I is the most common standardized test used, though it receives criticisms of bias (Freedle, 2003; Gerald and Haycock, 2006; Soares, 2007, 2011) and experiences controversy over whether it is critical to predicting potential enrollees' college academic performance (Bowen and Bok, 1998; Espenshade and Chung, 2009; Geiser and Santelices, 2007; Kobrin et al., 2008; Mattern et al., 2008; Vars and Bowen, 1998; Zwick, 2002). Recently, sections of the ACT have also come under criticism for their ability to help predict college outcomes (Bettinger, Evans, and Pope, 2011). Nevertheless, these exams are still commonly used by admissions officers to compare applicants.

17. Hernández (1997: 62) reports that Ivy League and other selective schools construct an academic index (AI) score for athletes and use the same or comparable formula in judging the academic merits of all applicants. Under the AI, the average math and verbal SAT I score represents a third of an applicant's academic rating, the average of three SAT II subject test scores counts for another third, and class rank derived from performance in all high school courses makes up the final third. Stevens (2007: 191–194) describes another scoring system at a small, elite, private liberal arts college. At this institution, students are rated on a nine-point scale that includes both academic and personal factors. Three of the points are based on SAT performance and one point each is based on the applicant's grades, rank in high school class, curriculum rigor, and high school quality measured by the percentage of high school graduates who attend four-year colleges. The final two points are based on how students rate on nonacademic criteria.

18. This study does not investigate SAT II performance to examine students' knowledge of various content areas. Because SAT II tests are not easily converted into college credit like AP and IB exams, students not interested in attending colleges that require SAT II scores have little reason to take these tests. Thus, taking the SAT II has more to do with the colleges students aspire to attend than with actual academic preparation. This difference is reflected in the fact that 68 percent of HSVP students took an SAT II exam, but, as noted, 97 percent took an AP or IB exam.

19. College Board personnel recently reported that only 80 percent of students enrolled in an AP course ultimately took the AP exam (Adams, 2012).

20. Typically, colleges award credit if students receive a score of 3 or above on an AP exam or 4 or above in an IB subject. This study considers such scores to represent passing.

21. As appendix B, table B.2 indicates, low-SES valedictorians' classmates tended to score lower on the SAT than classmates of more-affluent valedictorians.

22. If students took both an AP and an IB exam on the same subject, they were asked to count this as only one exam.

23. The ACT is the other common college entrance exam used in the United States. In the states from which the HSVP sample is drawn, however, students

at large more frequently take the SAT I (see Wainer, 2000: 9). HSVP students were also more likely to take the SAT I: 99 percent did so, while just 28 percent took the ACT. For these reasons, this study analyzes SAT I and not ACT performance.

24. Fourteen students did not report an SAT I score, but reported an ACT score. These students' ACT scores were converted into SAT I scores using the College Board's "SAT–ACT Score Comparisons" (College Board, 2007c). While HSVP students' test scores are self-reported, as noted earlier, Cole and Gonyea's (2008) analysis and literature review indicate that high test scorers, like the vast majority of students in the HSVP sample, report their scores with greater accuracy and less upward bias than lower test scorers. The authors also find that asking students for their combined score, as the HSVP survey did, increases the accuracy of self-reported scores. In sum, there is good reason to be confident in HSVP students' self-reported scores.

25. Studies show that test scores are linked to parental social class (Chaplin and Hannaway, 1998; College Board, 2006d; Rothstein, 2004). Freedle (2003) suggests that more-affluent students may do better because they share the culture of test writers and thus may be more apt to interpret the meaning of certain words used in test questions in the same way. More-affluent students may also find it easier to score more highly because there is more verbal interaction in their homes (Lareau, 2003) and their parents are more likely to place them in stronger schools (Espenshade and Radford, 2009).

26. Grodsky and Jackson (2009) also find it helpful to discuss application and matriculation choice sets separately.

27. Ideally, financial aid packages offered by universities should also be included in an analysis of this stage. Unfortunately, HSVP data do not allow for such an analysis. HSVP data come from students and focus on student decisions, which account for the majority of decisions affecting college destinations. The High School Valedictorians Project did not seek to obtain data from institutions. While institutions' admissions decisions were easily enough obtained from students in a web survey because the options are few (accepted, rejected, waitlisted) and typically well remembered, securing institutional financial aid decisions from students was deemed unfeasible for several reasons. First, students would need to report not just their financial aid package at the school in which they enrolled, but their financial aid package from every school that offered them admission. Second, it is unlikely that students would know this information. Goldrick-Rab et al. (2011) find that students do not know what grant aid they have, even from the institution they are attending, making it even less likely that they would know the aid they would have had from institutions they chose not to attend. Third, even if students had easy access to all of the financial aid packages they were offered, entering it would be quite time-consuming and thus a particularly onerous task for respondents not receiving any compensation for

completing the survey. For research on the role that financial aid packages can play in students' college choice, see Avery and Hoxby (2004), Kim (2012), and Kim, DesJardins, and McCall (2009).

28. Astin (1965) and MacAllum et al. (2007) also highlight the importance of admission in shaping students' college destinations.

29. The average acceptance rate at four-year colleges nationwide is about 66 percent (Clinedinst, Hurley, and Hawkins, 2011), and less than 150 colleges have acceptance rates of less than 50 percent (Carnevale and Rose, 2004).

Chapter Two

1. Hossler, Schmit, and Vesper (1999: 20) also find that older siblings' college attendance triggered the development of college aspirations in younger brothers and sisters.

2. More-affluent students in Mullen's (2010) and Reay's (1998) qualitative studies also talked about college being assumed and expected. Similarly, Grodsky and Riegle-Crumb's (2010) quantitative analysis of survey data from Texas shows that students with more educated parents were more likely to indicate that they had always wanted to go to college. Hossler, Schmit, and Vesper (1999) also note this phenomenon.

3. For example, to be eligible to attend an institution in the competitive public University of California system, students must take four years of English, three years of math, two years of history or social science, two years of laboratory science, two years of a foreign language, and one year of visual or performing arts. Moreover, all of these courses must be UC-certified (University of California, 2010). At private and elite universities, the requirements may be less specific, but they are similarly demanding (Hernández, 1997).

4. For the descriptive statistics reported throughout this book, Pearson's chi-squared tests were used. These tests analyze how likely it is that percentages are equal in frequency. For example, if a test assessing whether the percentage of low-, middle-, and high-SES students who planned to pursue higher education prior to sixth grade were equal resulted in a chi-squared statistic that was less than .05, that would indicate that differences by SES are statistically significant.

5. Logistic regressions produce odds ratios. The "odds" of a particular event happening is the probability of that event divided by one minus the probability of that event. An odds ratio indicates how much higher or lower the odds are of a particular event happening if a variable takes on the value of a particular category instead of the value in the reference category. Though from a strictly statistical perspective logistic regressions speak to differences in odds and not likelihood, it is common to refer to results using likelihood terminology. For variety, this work sometimes employs likelihood terminology in discussing logistic regression results.

All regression results discussed in the text of this book are held to the .05 level of statistical significance. See appendices B and C for more on control variables.

6. Others scholars also find that less-affluent parents underscore enrolling in college near home (McDonough, 1997) and are more likely to want their child to attend college while living at home (Turley, 2006).

7. It is important to note that the HSVP data on parents' attitudes came from students, and thus may not represent precisely how parents felt. Nevertheless, the way that students perceive their parents' aspirations for them may actually influence their predispositions more than their parents' actual aspirations for them.

8. This result cannot be explained by a greater absence of low-SES fathers. Even limiting the sample to just low-SES fathers and mothers whose aspirations for their children were rated and not given a "not applicable" response, low-SES fathers were 11 percentage points less likely than low-SES mothers to have conveyed to their valedictorian child that attending college was very important and 8 percentage points less likely to have indicated that attending a four-year college was very important.

9. Parents' aspirations could also have been analyzed using an Ordinary Least Squares (OLS) regression, as students rated their parents' aspirations for them on a five-point scale. That being said, students' ratings of their parents were not evenly distributed. Also, Conklin and Dailey's (1981) findings indicate that parents who provided even mixed or inconsistent messages (not just negative messages) had a negative effect. For this reason, it makes sense to combine parents who gave anything other than a strong, clear emphasis (a rating of less than 5 or not applicable) into one "no" (did not view such attendance as very important) category.

10. It is possible that HSVP students' definition of a prestigious college may vary widely. Yet, the fact that 79 percent of HSVP students applied to at least one most selective college as rated by *U.S. News & World Report* (2006) and 89 percent viewed prestigious college attendance as at least somewhat important provides support for the idea that students' conception of a prestigious college may be similar to that of this widespread publication. Still, this comparison should be viewed with some caution, as applying to a certain type of school is not exactly the same as viewing attendance as very important.

Chapter Three

1. The third prerequisite is applying to college.

2. As mentioned in chapter 2, note 3, to be eligible to attend an institution in the competitive public University of California system, students must take four years of English, three years of math, two years of history or social science, two years of laboratory science, two years of a foreign language, and one year of

visual or performing arts. Moreover, all of these courses must be UC-certified. Applicants also are required to take the American College Test (ACT) Assessment plus Writing or the SAT Reasoning Test in addition to two SAT II exams (University of California, 2010).

3. Several disclosed that they were not actively seeking to become valedictorian, but did want to "do well" in school, which sometimes meant earning a 4.0 grade point average (GPA). For example, one student expressed that earning a 4.0 for all four years of high school was a goal he had set for himself, but that "it wasn't like freshman year . . . [I decided] 'I'm going to be valedictorian. That's the person I want to be.'"

4. Yale students also suggested that a desire to attend a prestigious college motivated their high school academic accomplishments (Mullen, 2010).

5. Demerath (2009: 89) also finds that high-achieving, high-SES students made a connection between high school performance, prestigious college attendance, and better career opportunities.

6. Valedictorians from lower socioeconomic backgrounds may have been less apt to take such steps because they were less likely to be as fixated on prestigious college attendance and thus did not feel the need to reach the top of their class by gaming the system. Less-affluent valedictorians were also less likely to have an older sibling who had been a top student and knew how to guide them through this process.

7. Mullen (2010), who studied top students enrolled at Yale, reached a similar conclusion.

8. Mullen (2010) reports that Yale students also indicated that family expectations motivated them to do well in high school.

9. See Institute for Higher Education Policy (2012) for more on ways that schools can keep students and families apprised of students' academic talents.

10. To earn an IB Diploma, students participate in a two-year program that requires college-level final examinations in six subject areas.

11. HSVP survey respondents were not asked about participation in summer programs.

12. Many articles have been written about how high-SES families spend large amounts of money on SAT tutoring and courses (Gross, 1999; Lewin, 2004; Lombardi, 2004; Tugend, 2009).

13. Socioeconomic status differences in private test preparation may be more common in nonvaledictorian samples. More-affluent families in which children have lower class ranks may be more willing to pay for test prep in the hopes that classes will raise their children's scores and help compensate for their lower class rank. Parents of valedictorians may feel less pressure to raise scores because valedictorians generally score highly already, and even if they do not score at the very top of the chart, valedictorians can present their class ranks to admissions officers as evidence of high achievement.

14. It is worth highlighting that despite the emphasis on private test prep in the media, most students nationally also prepare independently. National Education Longitudinal Study (NELS) data indicate that books, videos, or computer software were the most common ways students at large and students from each SES group prepared for these exams (Buchmann, Condron, and Roscigno, 2010).

15. HSVP students were not asked about extracurricular activities in the survey. They were asked whether they were an athletic recruit, however, because that status offers a more specific admissions advantage. This is discussed further in chapter 6, which concerns admissions.

16. Students who do not have the excellent academic credentials that HSVP students enjoy may be more likely to concentrate on extracurricular involvement as a way to gain college admission.

17. Some HSVP valedictorians reported participating in extracurriculars in order to improve their chances of earning scholarships rather than gaining college admission. They did not feel they would need to stand out in extracurriculars in order to be admitted to the colleges they hoped to attend, and they generally were correct in that assumption. These students tended to be interested in either less-selective, religiously affiliated colleges, where their academic credentials already placed them in a good position to be accepted, or in large public institutions that would not consider their extracurriculars given their high grades and test scores. Though students who participated in extracurriculars for scholarship purposes had a slightly different goal than those who joined for college admissions purposes, their behavior was still influenced by the college destination process. This fact, and the fact that their numbers were very small, suggested that they were best placed in this category for analysis purposes.

18. Need-based aid information and the importance of extracurriculars are very different messages to convey. Aid information is more complicated and socially sensitive. Answers to need-based aid questions also depend on financial circumstances. Nevertheless, it is perhaps worth examining how information about extracurriculars was dispersed and absorbed so readily by the public so that these lessons can be applied in distributing need-based aid information. Such an investigation should review work by Perna and Steele (2011), which finds that merit-based aid systems are easier for students to grasp than need-based aid systems.

Chapter Four

1. For instance, private colleges may require letters of recommendation while public colleges generally do not.

2. More-selective universities may, for example, ask for SAT II scores, which less-selective institutions do not typically require.

3. Past valedictorians and other high-achieving students from this high school may have had the ability to attend top colleges but did not aspire to attend. Because prior students lacked interest, counselors had little reason to learn about the admissions policies at these institutions.

4. Counselors may not just be uninformed but also misinformed. In one study a counselor in a high school without a history of students attending selective colleges told a low-SES high achiever that early applications are "for impatient kids who can't wait for a decision" (Avery, 2009: 15), when, in fact, applying early can greatly improve odds of acceptance (Avery, Fairbanks, and Zeckhauser, 2003).

5. Reay (1998) also notes that while low-SES parents were encouraging, they lacked an understanding of the elements of the admissions process.

6. Lareau (2011) similarly finds that basic aspects of the process—like the existence of application fees and how students are notified of their acceptance—eluded less-affluent families.

7. Lareau (2011) also views parents' personal college experience or lack thereof as strongly shaping how much support they were able to provide during the college admissions process.

8. Other research has also found that students look to peers (Cabrera and La Nasa, 2001; Galotti and Mark, 1994; Litten, 1982; McDonough, 1997) and college guidebooks (Hossler and Foley, 1995; Shank and Beasley, 1998) for information about college admissions.

9. Researchers interested in exploring students' understanding of the college admissions process in greater detail should look at Avery, Fairbanks, and Zeckhauser's (2003) research and consider asking a series of questions that actually test students' knowledge. Doing so in this project was simply out of scope.

10. Although respondents rated understanding on a scale of 1 to 5, this chapter uses logistic regressions that test whether or not understanding was rated as a 4 or a 5. This was done in order to better compare regression results with the descriptive results. Adopting logistic regression also makes sense because as table 4.1 indicates, respondents' ratings do not suggest linearity.

11. It was not within the scope of this project to survey parents, so the knowledge of parents is based on their children's assessments. While not ideal, it is important to have some sense of parents' understanding and this question is a useful starting point for future, more-comprehensive investigations into this topic.

12. While merit aid is also important, particularly in states with large merit aid programs, need-based aid represents a larger proportion of aid dollars available. Furthermore, the ways in which students receive merit aid differs substantially. Some organizations give merit aid to students based on a competitive and sometimes lengthy application process, while institutions and states may offer merit aid to students who did not apply for it in an effort to incentivize their en-

rollment at their institution or within their state, respectively. In sum, the process for receiving merit aid differs much more than the process for receiving need-based aid, which is more standardized.

13. The high school experiences of these valedictorians are not atypical. Based on their review of existing research, McDonough and Calderone (2006) also conclude that school counselors are relatively unavailable to help with any college task, let alone the financial aid process, and are often uninformed about costs and financial aid.

14. More-affluent parents may also take charge of the financial aid process because they are more likely to view their high school senior as a child. See Lareau (2011).

15. This analysis of financial aid knowledge is limited to just those who applied for aid in order to avoid developing a skewed sense of the financial aid information problem. Students who do not need aid have little reason to become well versed in its many nuances, and so it is important that their understanding (or lack thereof) not be lumped with the understanding of students who do need aid. Since HSVP data cannot sufficiently distinguish students who did not apply for aid who would have qualified from those who would not have qualified, this analysis uses those who applied for aid as a proxy for those who needed aid. That being said, it is important to recognize that some students who fail to apply for aid are from low- and middle-SES backgrounds. As noted, the American Council on Education (2004) reported that 1.7 million low- and moderate-income students attending college at least part-time in 1999–2000 did not file a FAFSA. Similarly, Sallie Mae and Ipsos (2011) estimated that 13 percent of students with family incomes that are generally Pell Grant eligible do not apply for financial aid. In the HSVP sample, 6 percent of low-SES, 10 percent of middle-SES, and 41 percent of high-SES students did not apply for financial aid.

16. While students' financial aid knowledge may improve by later in the senior year, this chapter seeks to investigate students' financial aid knowledge during the exploration stage because knowledge held at that time tends to shape the types of colleges explored. Later chapters discuss the role financial aid plays in where students apply and matriculate.

17. The distribution of HSVP financial aid applicants' understanding of the college admissions process is almost identical to that of all HSVP students. The percentage of students in each 1–5 rating category do not differ by more than a percentage point.

18. The understanding of middle- and high-SES parents may be better because they are more likely than low-SES parents to have gone to college and experienced the financial aid process personally. Compared with low-SES parents, they are also more likely to have contacts in their social network who have been through this process themselves or with their children. See Lareau (2003) for

more on this idea that more- and less-affluent parents have different social networks and thus different access to certain types of knowledge.

19. This pattern also occurs when analyzing just financial aid applicants' personal and parental knowledge of the college admissions process.

20. Valedictorians also sometimes learned of more-distant colleges through sports, but most often sports called attention to local and state institutions because the local media and community members were more likely to talk about nearby teams. Other research has also noted that colleges' performance in athletics can generate interest in attending (Roderick et al., 2009).

21. The fact that local colleges tended to be well represented among students' contacts should not be surprising. Planty et al. (2008) found that three-fourths of all traditional students enrolled in a four-year college attended an institution in their home state.

22. To this point, Avery (2009) discovered that one of the major outcomes of providing personalized college counseling to high-achieving low-SES students from schools without a history of elite college admission was that it made students aware of slightly less-famous but still very prominent institutions outside of the Ivy League. This counseling caused students to be more likely than similar students who did not receive this counseling to apply to a greater number of most-competitive colleges and ultimately to enroll in one as well.

23. According to the College Board (2006b), the average college application fee around the time that HSVP students were applying was $25, though some institutions charged up to $60.

24. It should be noted that high achievers have been found to care more about a university's selectivity than other students (Cook and Frank, 1993; Frank and Cook, 1995; Manski and Wise, 1983). Students at large may not have as negative a reaction.

25. It is important to underscore that institutions following this policy may not be entirely concerned about whether the high achievers who apply to their school enroll. Fallows (2001) explains that when Tulane sent high-scoring students partially completed applications that cost nothing to submit, the number of applications received expanded by 30 percent and the credentials of the applicant pool improved as well. Both of these changes increased Tulane's selectivity and thus ranking, revealing that just altering who applies, regardless of who enrolls, can strengthen an institution's reputation.

26. Chau (2012) also reports that top students receive little support from their schools in making the transition to college—even when they are the first in their families to go to college.

27. Only 14 percent of all 2003–2004 first-time postsecondary students started at a private, nonprofit four-year institution (Skomsvold, Radford, and Berkner, 2011).

28. McDonough and Calderone (2006) find that some counselors alter their recommendations depending on their perception of a student's social class. For example, counselors would be more likely to recommend community colleges to students they perceive to be less affluent. In doing so, they fail to take into consideration the merit and need-based aid these students could receive at institutions with higher initial sticker prices. Similarly, Linneham, Weer, and Stonely (2011) find that counselors were more likely to recommend community colleges to lower-SES students and more likely to recommend four-year colleges to higher-SES students.

29. Others also find that teachers can be an important source of college information (Johnson and Rochkind, 2010; Mullen, 2010; Sagawa and Schramm, 2008; Venezia, Kirst, and Antonio, 2003).

30. Such encouragement can have a big impact on students. Yale students told Mullen (2010) that their high school teachers' great confidence in their abilities motivated them to seek out colleges that would live up to the expectations of those teachers.

31. This type of involvement by more-affluent parents has also been documented by Lareau (2003), who explains that higher-SES parents engage in "concerted cultivation," in which they actively work to develop their children's talents in "a concerted fashion." She also finds that higher-SES parents instruct their children to communicate with adults as relative equals in order to obtain what they want (5, 23, 111, 129). Reay (1998) also observes this in the college search process. She notes that more-affluent parents taught their children to use their social network to gather information about various colleges. Mullen (2010) also indicates that Yale matriculants drew upon their social network to gather information about different colleges. She reports that the generally more-affluent students attending Yale were more likely than the generally less-affluent students attending Southern Connecticut State University to find members in their social network interested in offering college guidance.

32. Lareau (2011) also reports that more-affluent parents, especially mothers, were heavily involved in gathering information about colleges for their children. A study by the College Board Advocacy & Policy Center (2011) found that 80 percent of higher-income students reported receiving help from their parents with researching colleges.

33. In their sample of elite college applicants, Espenshade and Radford (2009) also observe that low-SES students were less likely than high-SES students to make multiple visits to a campus before applying. Avery, Fairbanks, and Zeckhauser (2003: 60) suggest that low-SES students are less likely to visit campuses before applying because if they are not admitted, the financial outlay involved is of little value.

34. A recent study found that lower-income students were 19 percentage points less likely than higher-income students to indicate that their parents helped them

with college visits (College Board Advocacy & Policy Center, 2011). The lack of involvement by low-SES parents in exploring college options with their children has also been documented elsewhere (McDonough, 1997; Rowan-Kenyon, Bell, and Perna, 2008) and is consistent with Lareau's (2003) contention that low-SES parents adopt a more laissez-faire approach to child rearing and her (2011) assessment that low-SES parents perceived their involvement in the transition to college as nonessential.

35. Espenshade and Radford (2009) obtained similar results in their study of elite college applicants.

36. As noted previously, at the time HSVP students were applying and enrolling, many most selective colleges did not require parents making less than $60,000 to contribute anything toward college costs (Pallais and Turner, 2006, 2007). Specifically, Stanford and Yale no longer required families making less than $45,000 a year to contribute any money toward their child's education, while the University of Pennsylvania and Harvard made the same offer to families earning less than $50,000 and $60,000 a year, respectively (Hill and Winston, 2006a; Tomsho, 2006; Wasley, 2006; Winter, 2005). At some institutions, students can qualify for aid even if their parents earn up to $200,000 a year (Jaschik, 2011).

37. Mullen's (2010) interviews with students also suggest that low-SES parents valued location over selectivity.

38. Rowan-Kenyon, Bell, and Perna (2008) also report that Latino and immigrant families prefer to keep their children, particularly daughters, at colleges close to home. See also Turley (2006).

39. McDonough (1997) also observes that low-SES students expected to take primary responsibility for their college costs.

40. To get to the top of their high school class, students typically need to be highly responsible and self-directed. Having these traits as well as strong credentials may make securing the services of a private college consultant seem less necessary to valedictorians and their families than it might to other students and families.

41. When HSVP students were applying to colleges, many elite private universities had recently expanded their financial aid programs to cover the full cost of attendance for less-affluent students. See note 36 of this chapter.

42. These low-SES female students' concerns about partying may have been warranted. See Armstrong and Hamilton (forthcoming) for more on how attending a large public but not most selective flagship public university with a dominant party culture can be particularly alienating or distracting to less-affluent female students, ultimately impeding their upward mobility.

43. Perhaps the new federal requirement that all Title IV institutions have a net price calculator on their websites will change this behavior.

44. UCs are colleges in the University of California system, the top tier of a three-tier system that also includes California State colleges and community colleges.

45. Espenshade and Radford (2009) find that only 11 percent of the students at the elite private and public colleges in their sample were from lower or working-class backgrounds. Leonhardt (2004) notes that "at the most selective private universities across the country, more fathers of freshmen are doctors than are hourly workers, teachers, clergy members, farmers or members of the military—combined."

46. See chapter 1 for a detailed discussion of the advantages researchers have documented.

Chapter Five

1. HSVP students are compared to 2003 freshmen for both simplicity and comparability, as HSVP students were college freshmen between 2003 and 2006. These national freshmen results come from UCLA's Higher Education Research Institute's Cooperative Institutional Research Program's annual Freshman Survey. For more details about this survey, see Sax et al. (2003).

2. This suggested number of applications is based in part on the application strategy students are urged to pursue. Students are generally advised by numerous entities, including the College Board's (2009) website, to apply to three different categories of colleges: (1) where they have an extremely good chance of being admitted (also known as safeties); (2) where they should be very competitive for admission (in range/match/target colleges); and (3) where they might find admission to be a more difficult prospect given that admitted students generally have higher test scores and grades (reach colleges).

3. As noted in chapter 4, the average college application fee was around $25 in 2006, though some colleges charged up to $60 (College Board, 2006b).

4. That being said, some interviewed students who lived in milder climates indicated that they were reluctant to apply to institutions that had colder weather. A few others mentioned not wanting to apply to a "party school." These factors, however, did not reflect students' primary considerations.

5. A student's interest in a college's academic characteristics often becomes indistinguishable from an interest in a college's reputation. As Krukowski (1985) explains, students have shifted from perceiving academic quality in terms of school characteristics (quality of the faculty and student body) to perceptions about graduates' outcomes (their admission to desirable graduate schools and employment in desirable jobs). Since applicants "do not have figures available to them indicating how the graduating class of one college fared compared to

the graduating class of another . . . to judge the merits of competing schools they establish a hierarchy of institutions based on their sense of each college's relative 'prestige'" (Krukowski, 1985: 23). Thus, rightly or wrongly, reputation often comes to be viewed as a proxy for academic quality (Flanagan, 2001). To avoid confusion, this study categorizes factors like special academic program (major, honors, joint degree) and faculty attention/involvement in teaching as purely academic factors, and considers factors that sometimes straddle both academic and reputation considerations to be reputation factors. The precise categorizations used are shown in table 5.1.

6. Scholars often identify location as a factor that influences students (Choy and Ottinger, 1998; Sax et al., 2003; Warwick and Mansfield, 2003). Yet location can mean a lot of different things, as Choy and Ottinger (1998: 26) detail:

> Location-related reasons can include proximity or distance. Some students who cite location as a factor in their choice of institution may be looking for an institution close to their home or job because family or work responsibilities make convenient access to a campus crucial. Others may want to remain close to home to maintain close ties with their family and friends or to be assured that they could get home quickly and inexpensively for vacations or in case of emergency. Other students focusing on location might be looking for an institution far away from home for the experience of living on campus or on their own. Some students may have very specific location criteria and want to be in a particular part of the country or in a location that affords them ready access to desired amenities such as recreational opportunities or cultural activities.

Because of these multiple meanings, the degree to which location is observed as an important factor depends of how questions in a given study are phrased. For example, two different nationally representative datasets from the U.S. Department of Education (the 2004–2009 Beginning Postsecondary Longitudinal Study and the Education Longitudinal Study of 2002) indicate that around 70 to 79 percent of recent high school graduates who enroll in four-year institutions feel location was a factor in where they enrolled (Bozick and Lauff, 2007; Radford and Tasoff, 2009). In contrast, other research suggests that only 10 percent of baccalaureate-bound students agree that "being able to *live at home* was very important to them" (Sanderson et al., 1996, emphasis mine; see also Gardner, 1987). To cut through this confusion, this study does not use the term "location" in defining aspects that influence students' application decisions. Instead, location items related to distance from home are placed in a distance from home category, and location items related to attending college in a particular community or setting are placed in the campus environment category. See table 5.1 for more detail on these categorizations.

7. Warwick and Mansfield (2003: 117) report that reputation of the degree is one of their ten most important factors to students in general in appraising colleges. High achievers may give particular weight to reputation-related factors (Litten, Sullivan, and Brodigan, 1983: 89). In fact, according to Chapman and Jackson (1987), high-ability applicants are motivated *primarily* by an institution's academic reputation.

8. Academic reputation/prestige of institution and campus visit may have received more votes because these options are broader than others. Academic reputation/prestige of institution could encompass the other reputation items listed, just as campus visit could comprise many of the individual campus environment factors presented.

9. See Bowman and Bastedo (2009) for more on the relationship between *U.S. News* rankings and applications.

10. Data from the Education Longitudinal Study (ELS) similarly indicate that the importance students place on financial aid and low expenses decreases as social class increases. See Ingels, Planty, and Bozick (2005).

11. Ways to prevent more students and families from eliminating good college options based on reactions to sticker price are discussed more in the conclusion.

12. Other research also suggests that less-affluent students are more likely to value attending college near home (Avery and Turner, 2008; Choy and Ottinger, 1998; McDonough, 1997; Sanderson et al., 1996).

13. ELS data exhibit the same pattern by social class among students at large (Ingels, Planty, and Bozick, 2005).

14. Other research also indicates that Americans who are more educated and wealthier are more likely to move (Taylor et al., 2008).

15. For more on use of private consultants, see chapter 4.

16. See chapter 4 for a discussion of why most HSVP students did not consider two-year colleges. Note that Hossler, Schmit, and Vesper (1999) also found two-year college attendance to be rare among high achievers; 91 percent of the "A" students in their sample enrolled in four-year colleges.

17. Private for-profit institutions were not analyzed because less than 1 percent of HSVP students applied to this type of college and this percentage did not vary by social class.

18. Only eleven public institutions were rated most selective by *U.S. News* in 2006 compared with sixty-one private institutions. Soares (2007: 14–15) explains that it is more difficult for public than private colleges to become prestigious nationally because they have to cater to state residents, which means they have a smaller number of top students from which they can draw. Private colleges, in contrast, can pull top students from any and all states.

19. Others have also found that high-SES students are more likely to submit applications to more-selective colleges (Chen, Wu, and Tasoff, 2010b; Soares, 2007: 184; Turley, Santos, and Ceja, 2007). Even among just high achievers, those

with higher family incomes are more likely than others to apply to an elite college (Avery and Turner, 2008; Pallais and Turner, 2006; McPherson and Schapiro, 1991).

Chapter Six

1. In 2012, Harvard admitted less than 6 percent of applicants. Yale, Columbia, and Princeton also each admitted less than 8 percent (Ellis, 2012).

2. In 2009, Harvard received applications from nearly 3,700 valedictorians, but had just 1,655 seats available for the whole class (Jan, 2009). In 2001, Harvard rejected 80 percent of valedictorians (Shea and Marcus, 2001).

3. Ideally, financial aid packages offered by universities would also be included in an examination of the admissions stage. Unfortunately, HSVP data do not allow for such an analysis. As noted in chapter 1, HSVP data focus on students, as they are the primary actors in most of the stages of the college destination process. While institutions' *admissions* decisions were easily enough obtained from students in a web survey because the options are few (accepted, rejected, waitlisted) and typically well remembered, securing institutions' much more complex *financial aid* awards from students in a web survey was deemed unfeasible for several reasons. First, students would need to report not just their financial aid package at the school in which they enrolled, but their financial aid package from every school that offered them admission. Second, it is unlikely that students would know this information. Goldrick-Rab et al. (2011) find that students do not know what grant aid they have from the institution they are attending, making it even less likely that they would know the aid they would have had from institutions they chose not to attend. Third, even if students had easy access to all of the financial aid packages they were offered, entering all of the details would be quite time-consuming, and thus a particularly onerous task for respondents not receiving any monetary compensation for completing the survey. For research on the role financial aid packages can play in students' college choice, see Avery and Hoxby (2004), Kim (2012), and Kim, DesJardins, and McCall (2009).

4. Because this book uses HSVP data, which was collected from students, this chapter focuses on what students can report about their admissions experience: final admissions outcomes. For more on the inner workings of college admissions offices, consult works by Fetter (1995), Hernández (1997), Steinberg (2002), Stevens (2007), and Toor (2001).

5. As chapter 1 notes, research indicates that selectivity of undergraduate institution attended is related to educational attainment, income, and occupational prestige and power (Alexander and Eckland, 1977; Arnold, 2002; Arnold and Youn, 2006; Behrman, Rosenzweig, and Taubman, 1996; Black and Smith, 2006; Bowen and Bok, 1998; Bowen, Chingos, and McPherson, 2009; Brand Halaby,

2006; Brewer, Eide, and Ehrenberg, 1999; Carnevale and Strohl, 2010; Cohodes and Goodman, 2012; Daniel, Black, and Smith, 1997; Fitzgerald, 2000; Hershbein, 2011; Kane, 1998; Long, 2008; Loury and Garman, 1995; Melguizo, 2008, 2010; Monks, 2000; Smart, 1986; Solmon, 1975; Thomas and Zhang, 2005; Zhang, 2005a, 2005b).

6. For example, during the 2011–2012 admissions cycle, Princeton received 26,664 applications for 1,300 seats (Mbugua, 2012).

7. Espenshade has used a similar technique in a series of college admission analyses (Espenshade and Chung, 2009; Espenshade, Chung, and Walling, 2004; Espenshade, Hale, and Chung, 2005; Espenshade and Radford, 2009).

8. Still, some try to maintain a geographically diverse student body and thus give students from states that send few applicants extra consideration (Hernández, 1997).

9. Out-of-state public colleges tend to be less attractive to students and their families not just because of their often greater distance from home, but because they generally cost more to attend than in-state public colleges. Though private colleges tend to be even more expensive, out-of-state public colleges may not be viewed as different enough from in-state public colleges to be worth the additional expense. During the 2006–2007 academic year, when HSVP students would have been enrolled, the College Board (2006e) estimated that average total cost for a resident student was \$16,357 at an in-state four-year public college, \$26,304 at an out-of-state four-year public college, and \$33,301 at a four-year private college.

10. At the time of this examination, most schools' acceptance rates were for students entering in the fall of 2010, but some schools reported only fall 2009 rates.

11. Though meeting enrollment targets and convincing high achievers to matriculate is not difficult at elite private colleges, adopting an early admissions system makes it easier for institutions to secure top candidates without having to compete with other universities and have a sense of the student characteristics that will be present in their freshman class earlier in the process (Avery, Fairbanks, and Zeckhauser, 2003; Stevens, 2007: 203). Given these benefits to the university, colleges have been willing to reward early applicants with higher admit rates. One analysis found early applicants' admit rate was four times as great at Princeton, three times as great at Harvard, more than two times as great at Stanford and the University of Pennsylvania, and about two times as great at Dartmouth (Avery, Fairbanks, and Zeckhauser, 2003: 66). Put another way, the advantage to applying early was roughly equivalent to scoring an extra 100 points on the combined math and verbal SAT I, with early decision programs offering a slightly larger advantage than early action programs (137).

12. Numerous studies reveal that universities offer legacies increased chances of admission (Argetsinger, 2003; Bowen and Bok, 1998; Espenshade, Chung, and

Walling, 2004; Karen, 1990, 1991; Shulman and Bowen, 2001; Steinberg, 2003), even controlling for other factors that also improve chances of admission like SAT scores, minority status, and athletic ability (Bowen and Bok, 1998; Espenshade, Chung, and Walling, 2004). In fact, the advantage given to legacies often rivals or even exceeds that given to black students (Bowen and Bok, 1998; Espenshade, Chung, and Walling, 2004; Hurwitz, 2011) and may be worth about 160 additional points on the SAT I at elite private colleges (Espenshade, Chung, and Walling, 2004).

Colleges give preferences to legacy applicants first because they are believed to have greater institutional loyalty and better gift-giving potential in adulthood (Bowen and Bok, 1998). That being said, others argue that legacy preferences are not in fact critical in securing alumni donations (Kahlenberg, 2010b). Legacies may also be given preferential treatment because they are perceived to be more likely than other applicants to enroll, which helps increase the institution's yield rate and improve its rank (Toor, 2001: 211–212), which in turn advances the university's prestige and strengthens its applicant pool (Bowman and Bastedo, 2009).

13. Applicants who catch a college coach's eye are put in an admissions category all their own. It is argued that athletes not only add to the student body's extracurricular diversity but also help the university maintain its prestige and rally its alumni base (Stevens, 2007). In return for these perceived contributions, athletic recruits are admitted at higher rates than other students. Sometimes their admissions rate is two to four times the rate of nonathletes (Bowen and Levin, 2003; Espenshade, Chung, and Walling, 2004; Espenshade and Radford, 2009; Shulman and Bowen, 2001; Soares, 2007). While some argue that athletic recruits are admitted at higher rates because coaches prescreen potential recruits and only put those on their recruit list whom they feel can be admitted (Toor, 2001), even controlling for other factors, Espenshade, Chung, and Walling (2004) report that the admissions bonus of being an athletic recruit at highly elite private colleges is roughly equal to scoring 200 points higher on the combined math and verbal SAT.

14. For example, their acceptance rate may be higher because their SAT I scores tended to be slightly higher. HSVP students who applied to at least one most selective private college had an average SAT I score of 1456, while those who applied to two or more, three or more, four or more, or five or more had average SAT scores of 1464, 1476, 1490, and 1494, respectively.

Chapter Seven

1. As noted in chapter 5 on application, academic reputation/prestige of institution and campus visit may have received more votes because these options are

broader than others. Academic reputation/prestige of institution could encompass the other reputation items listed, just as campus visit could comprise many of the individual campus environment factors presented.

2. Krukowski (1985) summarizes that students have shifted from perceiving academic quality in terms of school characteristics (quality of the faculty and student body) to perceptions about graduates' outcomes (their admission to desirable graduate schools and employment in desirable jobs). Since applicants "do not have figures available to them indicating how the graduating class of one college fared compared to the graduating class of another . . . to judge the merits of competing schools[,] they establish a hierarchy of institutions based on their sense of each college's relative 'prestige'" (23). Thus, rightly or wrongly, reputation often comes to be viewed as a proxy for academic quality (Flanagan, 2001).

3. See Chapman (1993), Choy and Ottinger (1998), Gardner (1987), Litten and Hall (1989), Manski and Wise (1983), McDonough and Antonio (1996: 15), Pryor et al. (2006), Sanderson et al. (1996), and Shank and Beasley (1998).

4. See Archer and Bailey (2000), Litten, Sullivan, and Brodigan (1983: 97), Randall (1999), and Sanderson et al. (1996).

5. This difference and other differences between the application and matriculation results noted in this section cannot be attributed to the variation in the application and matriculation samples. Running the application analysis again using the sample that produced these matriculation results produces the same pattern.

6. McDonough and Antonio (1996) also find that graduate school aspirations can lead students toward different types of college destinations. Students who indicated that preparing or receiving training for graduate school was important in their college choice were more likely to enroll in a less-selective college. In contrast, students who reported that graduates getting into top graduate and professional schools was a factor in their enrollment decision were more likely to matriculate at a more-selective college.

7. Note that the survey question about factors that influenced application choice referred to merit aid opportunities and financial aid availability while the survey question about factors that influenced matriculation choice referred to merit aid and financial aid package.

8. Low-SES students have been observed to be more likely to report that level of college expenses is a very important consideration in their college choice (McDonough, 1997: 146–147; Sanderson et al., 1996), and more likely to eliminate colleges from consideration during the matriculation phase due to cost (Sallie Mae and Gallup, 2008). Low-SES students have also been shown to be more sensitive than other students to tuition and aid (Heller, 1997) and overall expenses (Avery and Turner, 2008) in selecting a college. In one study, more than 74 percent of low-income students reported choosing a college because of low tuition, student

aid, or both, compared with 25 percent of upper-income students (Paulsen and St. John, 2002: 207–209).

9. Another study similarly found that even low-SES students who score in the highest test quartile were more likely than their high-SES equivalents to report that "financial aid was an important consideration" in their enrollment decisions (Sanderson et al., 1996: 22).

10. This idea that higher education is an investment is also encouraged by highly educated education policy experts like Baum and Schwartz (2012). While their piece focuses on investing in higher education at large and not on paying more for particular institutions, they discuss how families' willingness to invest in education is related to their faith that this investment will pay off well in the long term. Parents' willingness to invest in more-selective institutions may similarly depend on their faith that doing so will provide additional financial benefits. In thinking about this idea it is important to recognize that, as one reviewer of this work suggested, the personal consumption preferences of high-SES parents could also be behind parents' desire to have their child attend a more-selective college. Interviews with valedictorians, however, indicate that parents professed investment rather than status motivations to their children. A study conducted directly with parents would be better able to investigate what motives are at play.

11. As noted in chapter 1, the "Big Three" is composed of Harvard, Princeton, and Yale.

12. The College Board and Art & Science Group (2010) also report that high percentages of respondents would stretch financially for a college with really strong academics in their field of interest, a prestigious academic reputation, or excellent graduate school or job placement success.

13. College visits mainly occurred prior to applying, after being admitted, or at both times. Students occasionally visited schools in between the application and matriculation stages if doing so happened to be particularly convenient, but this was less common for a couple of reasons. First, visits in between these phases cannot shape application decisions since application deadlines have passed. Second, students do not know whether they will be admitted to the institutions visited during this period. Thus, making a special trip to campus at this point might not be the best use of funds. For more on this, see Avery, Fairbanks, and Zeckhauser (2003).

14. See Gardner (1987), Pryor et al. (2006), and Warwick and Mansfield (2003).

15. These results cannot be attributed to the variation in the application and matriculation samples. Rerunning the application analysis based on the sample of individuals used to obtain these matriculation results produces the same pattern.

16. These four college categories are used because they best reflect the way HSVP students distinguish between institutions, and students make the decisions in this phase. In chapter 6, where admissions officers are the decision makers, public colleges were divided along one additional line, state residency, because of the role it plays in public institutions' admissions decisions.

Chapter Eight

1. All results presented in this chapter are based on HSVP students with enrollment data. Therefore, the percentages shown here may differ slightly from those reported in earlier chapters.

2. Cost, distance, admissions, and institutional capacity barriers that can limit classmates and community members' enrollment at most-selective private colleges are less of an issue at regular public colleges.

3. The evidence does not suggest that low- and middle-SES students were more attracted to this type of institution because of greater interest in attending a religiously affiliated college. Less than 5 percent of all students indicated that this shaped their application decision and there were no statistically significant differences in the selection of this factor by SES.

4. Note that while valedictorians as *individuals* did not differ by SES in their likelihood of having an acceptance letter from a most selective college if they applied to one or more, chapter 6 did find that individual *applications'* admit rates did differ by SES, with applications filed by low-SES valedictorians receiving an admissions advantage even with controls.

5. See chapter 7 for more detail on why merit aid is more enticing to middle- than to high- or low-SES students.

6. Bowen, Chingos, and McPherson (2009: 105) also find that undermatching occurs mainly during the application stage and that admissions contributes little to this phenomenon.

7. See Berguson (2009) for more on the movement within the college choice literature to recognize that students' access to college information and resources differs by social class and shapes ultimate enrollment.

8. As discussed in the introduction to this book, educational attainment, income, and status and power have all been found to be related to undergraduate alma mater (Alexander and Eckland, 1977; Andrews, Li, and Lovenheim, 2012; Arnold, 2002; Arnold and Youn, 2006; Behrman, Rosenzweig, and Taubman, 1996; Black and Smith, 2006; Bowen and Bok, 1998; Bowen, Chingos, and McPherson, 2009; Brand and Halaby, 2006; Brewer, Eide, and Ehrenberg, 1999; Carnevale and Strohl, 2010; Cohodes and Goodman, 2012; Daniel, Black, and Smith, 1997; Fitzgerald, 2000; Hershbein, 2011; Kane, 1998; Long, 2008; Loury and Garman,

1995; Melguizo, 2008, 2010; Monks, 2000; Smart, 1986; Solmon, 1975; Thomas and Zhang, 2005; Zhang, 2005a, 2005b).

9. A study by the College Board Advocacy & Policy Center (2011) found that about half of students indicated that they would be much more likely to apply to a more selective four-year college if someone helped them understand the actual cost of college and options for paying it. Avery et al. (2009) also argue that improved information about financial aid is a potential point of leverage in getting high-achieving, low-income students to apply to institutions at or above their level of achievement. Perna and Steele (2011) also report that few students have accurate or complete knowledge of financial aid and emphasize that need-based aid systems are harder for students to grasp and plan on than more-straightforward, merit-based aid systems. Grodsky and Jackson (2009) and Hahn and Price (2008) also stress the importance of clearer need-based financial aid information.

10. Sallie Mae and Ipsos (2011) found that 13 percent of families with college students that had annual incomes of less than $35,000 and 18 percent of families making between $35,000 and $100,000 each year did not apply for financial aid.

11. The latest data from the U.S. Department of Education's High School Longitudinal Study of 2009 indicate that one-third of all families who expect their ninth grader to pursue postsecondary education—and even plan to help pay—have not yet started financially preparing (Jones and Radford, 2012).

12. Research suggests that when low-income middle school students are confident that they will be able to afford college, they are more likely to prepare academically and to enroll in institutions with higher graduation rates (Lumina Foundation, 2008).

13. Although students often disregard college brochures received in the mail, there is good reason to believe that financial aid information mailed by the U.S. Department of Education will be received differently. First, need-based aid information will be distributed when students are in middle school, before families are bombarded with college brochures. Second, some students ignore college brochures because they see them as sales materials designed to get them to pay an application fee, and eventually, tuition. Information from the Department of Education about grants and subsidized loans should not be viewed in the same way because the department does not stand to financially benefit by providing this information.

14. Work by college access programs like the ACCESS College Foundation can likely provide helpful insight into what should be included in such materials (see Institute for Higher Education Policy, 2010).

15. While such measures cannot capture the quality of the education that colleges provide or even how much students learn, the metrics suggested are obtainable and of great importance to families. These measures may not be exhaustive,

capturing the entire undergraduate experience, but even this limited information is better than families relying on gut impressions or what they have heard about various institutions from their social network.

16. See, for example, Avery (2009), Avery and Kane (2004), Bryan et al. (2011), Carrell and Sacerdote (2012), McDonough (2005), McDonough and Calderone (2006), and Sherwin (2012).

17. See Bryan et al. (2011) and Pham and Keenan (2011) for more on the impact of student-to-counselor ratios.

18. For more on what high schools are doing (or not doing) to prepare students for the transition to college and the impact counselors can have on ninth-grade students' college attitudes and plans see Radford and Ifill's (2013) study that uses new data from the High School Longitudinal Study of 2009 conducted by the U.S. Department of Education's National Center for Education Statistics.

19. The Institute for Higher Education Policy (2012) provides a list of counselor-recommended college planning resources that may prove useful in preparing trainings and teaching materials.

20. As Hill and Winston (2010) show, parts of the Midwest and America's mountain states have particularly high numbers of high-achieving, low-SES students.

21. Unfortunately, however, even with expanded outreach, California colleges lost shares of underrepresented minorities (Colburn, Young, and Yellen, 2008).

Appendix B

1. Jackman and Jackman's (1983) work on self-reported social class advises that it is best to allow participants to select from five social class categories. When given five options, 86 percent of respondents were perceived by their interviewers not to have any difficulty answering this social class question. Moreover, 80 percent of respondents reported feeling at least somewhat confident that the class they selected was their class. Indeed, respondents' perceptions of their class were well grounded in their nuclear family's actual socioeconomic standing, with education, occupation, and income the most influential. This research suggests that the social class reported by HSVP students is a good measure of their socioeconomic background.

2. Four out of 896 HSVP students did not answer this survey question and were given an SES category based on their answers to parents' education and other socioeconomic questions. Specifically, a student who had one parent with a bachelor's degree and the other with some college but no degree and a student who had one parent with a bachelor's degree and the other with an associate's degree were both designated as middle SES. Another student who indicated

having one parent with a professional degree and the other with a college degree was placed in the high-SES category. A final valedictorian whose parents both had less than a high school degree was assigned to the low-SES category. These categorizations are consistent with the SES distribution by parents' education displayed in table B-1.

3. One of these personal variables is race. The survey asked two race questions. To allow students the opportunity to indicate any multiracial heritage, the first question (hereafter referred to as the "all race" question) read: "What is your race or ethnicity? Please check all that apply: (1) Black/African American; (2) Hispanic/Latino; (3) Asian/Asian American; (4) American Indian, Native American, or Alaska Native; (5) Native Hawaiian or Pacific Islander; (6) White." For analysis purposes, a second question (hereafter referred to as the "primary race" question) asked: "Please choose from below what you consider to be your primary race or ethnicity. Choose only one: (1) Black/African American; (2) Hispanic/Latino; (3) Asian/Asian American; (4) American Indian, Native American, or Alaska Native; (5) Native Hawaiian or Pacific Islander; (6) White." A total of 886 students provided a primary race or ethnicity. No students reported being American Indian, Native American, or Alaska Native and only four reported being Native Hawaiian or Pacific Islander. Because Asians and Native Hawaiians and Pacific Islanders were grouped together in the 1980 and 1990 U.S. censuses and the number of Native Hawaiians and Pacific Islanders in this sample was too small to analyze independently, these four Native Hawaiian and Pacific Islanders were added to the Asian category.

The "all race" question in the HSVP survey was then used to try to establish a racial category for those who did not answer the "primary race" question. Three students missing a "primary race" response had only checked one box in the "all race" question. They were allocated to the "primary race" category that corresponded with the box that they checked in the "all race" question. Three other students who did not complete the "primary race" question had checked two race boxes. These students were assigned a single race category as follows: the respondent who indicated being Hispanic and Asian was classified as Hispanic, another who reported being Asian and white was placed in the Asian category, and finally, the third student with Hispanic and Native Hawaiian and Pacific Islander heritage was put into the Hispanic group.

To create a "primary race" category for others still missing on this measure, nativity reports were used. Eight individuals missing a "primary race" completed the nativity question. Three individuals' parents and grandparents were all born in South Asian or East Asian countries. These students' "primary race" was thus categorized as Asian. One individual listed his parents' and grandparents' birthplaces as in the Middle East. Following the Office of Management and Budget's (1997) *Revisions to the Standards for the Classifica-*

tion of Federal Data on Race and Ethnicity Guidelines, this person was coded as white. Finally, again following the Office of Management and Budget's instructions, four individuals with roots in Guyana were placed in the Hispanic category.

Appendix C

1. For some examples, the college participation rates of eighteen- to twenty-four-year-olds in the sample states range from 29 to 40 percent. Not surprisingly given its size, California has many more public and private not-for-profit colleges than other states. New Jersey has a particularly small number of private institutions. It is also worth noting that some of these states have most-selective public colleges within their borders (California, North Carolina, and Florida), while others do not. College costs vary by state as well. Public four-year colleges are most affordable in Florida and North Carolina and least affordable in New Jersey. That being said, in-state private college costs represent a smaller percentage of New Jersey residents' average income than California, North Carolina, or Florida residents' average income. Florida's inclusion in the sample also helps ensure that a state with a generous merit aid program is represented.

2. All students included in the sample were listed in the newspapers as either valedictorian (although some schools had more than one valedictorian) or as "top of their class." All students listed as valedictorians were included, whether they shared the title with classmates or not.

3. Two of the newspapers listed the names of valedictorians' parents as well.

4. An email or mailing address was deemed to be "working" if the invitation to the survey was delivered to the email or home address and not returned. It is very possible that some students who did not respond to the survey never received their invitation to participate.

5. SAT I data were obtained rather than ACT data because students in the HSVP sample states all take the SAT I at much higher rates than they take the ACT (Wainer, 2000: 9).

6. The original high school locale data obtained contained seven categories. For analysis purposes, these categories were collapsed as follows. Students' community was categorized as urban if high school locale was either "Large Central City" or "Mid-Size Central City;" rural if identified as "Rural, inside CBSA," "Rural, outside CBSA," or "Small Town;" and suburban if indicated as "Urban Fringe of Large City" or "Urban Fringe of Mid-Size City."

7. Students eligible for free or reduced-price lunch are at 185 percent of the U.S. poverty line or below (U.S. Department of Agriculture, 2008).

Appendix D

1. Approved by Princeton University's Institutional Review Panel for Human Subjects.

Appendix E

1. Approved by Princeton University's Institutional Review Panel for Human Subjects.

References

Ad Council. 2006. "College Access: Results from a Survey of Low-Income Parents and Low-Income Teens." February, www.collegeaccessmarketing.org /WorkArea/downloadasset.aspx?id=2070 (accessed May 11, 2010).

Adams, Caralee. 2012. "More Students Could Likely Excel in AP." *Education Week*, February 8, http://blogs.edweek.org/edweek/college_bound/2012 /02/today_the_college_board_came.html (accessed February 9, 2012).

Ainsworth, James W. 2002. "Why Does It Take a Village? The Mediation of Neighborhood Effects on Educational Achievement." *Social Forces* 81 (1): 117–152.

Alexander, Karl L., and Bruce K. Eckland. 1977. "High School Context and College Selectivity: Institutional Constraints in Educational Stratification." *Social Forces* 56 (1): 166–188.

American Council on Education. 2004. "Missed Opportunities: Students Who Do Not Apply for Financial Aid." October, http://www.cherrycommission.org/docs /Resources/Participation/Student_FinancialAidArticle.pdf (accessed March 2, 2009).

Andrews, Rodney J., Jing Li, and Michael F. Lovenheim. 2012. "Quantile Treatment Effects of College Quality on Earnings: Evidence from Administrative Data in Texas." Working Paper 18068, National Bureau of Economic Research, Cambridge, MA.

Archer, Billie D. A., and Jerry D. Bailey. 2000. "Kansas 1999 National Merit Semifinalists: A Profile and College/University Enrollment Choices." Report, Jones Institute for Educational Excellence, Emporia State University.

Argetsinger, Amy. 2003. "Legacy Students: A Counterpoint to Affirmative Action." *Washington Post*, March 12, p. A6.

Armstrong, Elizabeth A., and Laura Hamilton. Forthcoming. *Paying for the Party: How College Maintains Inequality.* Cambridge, MA: Harvard University Press.

Arnold, Karen D. 1995. *Lives of Promise: What Becomes of High School Vale-dictorians: A Fourteen-Year Study of Achievement and Life Choices.* San Francisco, CA: Jossey-Bass.

———. 2002. "Getting to the Top—What Role Do Elite Colleges Play?" *About Campus* 7 (5): 4–12.

Arnold, Karen D., and Ted I. K. Youn. 2006. "Generating Leaders in an Age of Diversity: Fifty Years of U.S. Rhodes Scholars." Final Report to the Andrew W. Mellon Foundation, http://oxcheps.new.ox.ac.uk/MainSite%20pages/Resources/OxCHEPS_OP26.pdf (accessed June 24, 2012).

Arum, Richard, Esther Cho, Jeannie Kim, and Josipa Roksa. 2012. "Documenting Uncertain Times: Post-graduate Transitions of the *Academically Adrift* Cohort." Social Science Research Council, New York, http://highered.ssrc.org/wp-content/uploads/2012/01/Documenting-Uncertain-Times-2012.pdf (accessed March 2, 2012).

Arum, Richard, and Josipa Roksa. 2010. *Academically Adrift: Limited Learning on College Campuses.* Chicago: University of Chicago Press.

Ashenfelter, Orley, and Alan Krueger. 1994. "Estimates of the Economic Return to Schooling from a New Sample of Twins." *American Economic Review* 84 (5): 1157–1173.

Astin, Alexander W. 1965. *Who Goes Where to College?* Chicago: Science Research Associates.

Astin, Alexander W., and Leticia Oseguera. 2004. "The Declining 'Equity' of American Higher Education." *Review of Higher Education* 27 (3): 321–341.

Aud, Susan, William Hussar, Frank Johnson, Grace Kena, Erin Roth, Eileen Manning, Xiaolei Wang, and Jijun Zhang. 2012. "The Condition of Education, 2012." *NCES 2012-045*, National Center for Education Statistics, U.S. Department of Education, Washington, DC.

Aud, Susan, Angelina KewalRamani, and Lauren Frohlich. 2011. "America's Youth: Transitions to Adulthood." *NCES 2012-026*, National Center for Education Statistics, U.S. Department of Education, Washington, DC.

Avery, Christopher. 2009. "The Effects of College Counseling on High-Achieving, Low-Income Students." Working Paper, September, Harvard University, Harvard Kennedy School of Government, Cambridge, MA.

Avery, Christopher, Eric Bettinger, Caroline Hoxby, and Sarah Turner. 2009. "Reaching the Underrepresented: What the Evidence Reveals." Presentation given at the College Board Forum, New York, October 21–23.

Avery, Christopher, Andrew Fairbanks, and Richard Zeckhauser. 2003. *The Early Admissions Game: Joining the Elite.* Cambridge, MA: Harvard University Press.

Avery, Christopher, and Caroline M. Hoxby. 2004. "Do and Should Financial Aid Packages Affect Students' College Choices?" In *College Choices: The Economics of Where to Go, When to Go, and How to Pay for It*, ed. Caroline

M. Hoxby, 239–299. Chicago: University of Chicago Press and National Bureau of Economic Research.

Avery, Christopher, and Tomas J. Kane. 2004. "Student Perceptions of College Opportunities: The Boston COACH Program." In *College Choices: The Economics of Where to Go, When to Go, and How to Pay for It*, ed. Caroline M. Hoxby, 355–391. Chicago: University of Chicago Press and National Bureau of Economic Research.

Avery, Christopher, and Sarah Turner. 2008. "Playing the College Application Game: Critical Moves and the Link to Socio-Economic Circumstances." Preliminary Draft, December 29, Harvard University, National Bureau of Economic Research, and University of Virginia.

Baum, Sandy, and Jennifer Ma. 2007. "Education Pays: The Benefits of Higher Education for Individuals and Society." New York: College Board.

Baum, Sandy and Saul Schwartz. 2012. "Is College Affordable? In Search of a Meaningful Definition." Institute for Higher Education Policy, http://www.ihep.org/publications/publications-detail.cfm?id=156, (accessed August 28, 2012).

Behrman, Jere R., Mark R. Rosenzweig, and Paul Taubman. 1996. "College Choice and Wages: Estimates Using Data on Female Twins." *Review of Economics and Statistics* 78 (4): 672–685.

Berguson, Amy Aldous. 2009. "College Choice and Access to College: Moving Policy, Research, and Practice to the 21st Century." *ASHE Higher Education Report* 35 (4): 1–140.

Berkner, Lutz, and Lisa Chavez. 1997. "Access to Postsecondary Education for the 1992 High School Graduates." *NCES 98-105*, National Center for Education Statistics, U.S. Department of Education, Washington, DC.

Bernstein, Elizabeth. 2003. "Want to Go to Harvard Law?" *Wall Street Journal*, September 26, p. W1.

Bettinger, Eric P., Brent J, Evans, and Devin G. Pope. 2011. "Improving College Performance and Retention the Easy Way: Unpacking the ACT Exam." Working Paper 17119, National Bureau of Economic Research, Cambridge, MA.

Black, Dan A., and Jeffrey Smith. 2006. "Estimating the Returns to College Quality with Multiple Proxies for Quality." *Journal of Labor Economics* 24: 701–728.

Bloom, Janice L. 2007. "(Mis)reading Social Class in the Journey toward College: Youth Development in Urban America." *Teachers College Record* 109 (2): 343–368.

Boas, Katherine. 2002. "The Latest Essential for College Applicants: A Summer Already Spent on Campus." *New York Times*, August 21, p. B8.

Bordua, David J. 1960. "Educational Aspirations and Parental Stress on College." *Social Forces* 38 (3): 262–269.

Bourdieu, Pierre. 1977. *Outline of a Theory of Practice*. Cambridge and New York: Cambridge University Press.

Bowen, Howard Rothmann. 1997. *Investment in Learning: The Individual and Social Value of American Higher Education*. Baltimore, MD: Johns Hopkins University Press.

Bowen, William G., and Derek Bok. 1998. *The Shape of the River: Long-Term Consequences of Considering Race in College and University Admissions*. Princeton, NJ: Princeton University Press.

Bowen, William G., Matthew M. Chingos, and Michael S. McPherson. 2009. *Crossing the Finish Line: Completing College at America's Public Universities*. Princeton, NJ: Princeton University Press.

Bowen, William G., Martin A. Kurzweil, and Eugene M. Tobin. 2005. *Equity and Excellence in American Higher Education*. Charlottesville: University of Virginia Press.

Bowen, William G., and Sarah A. Levin. 2003. *Reclaiming the Game: College Sports and Educational Values*. Princeton, NJ: Princeton University Press.

Bowman, Nicholas A., and Michael N. Bastedo. 2009. "Getting on the Front Page: Organizational Reputation, Status Signals, and the Impact of *U.S. News & World Report* on Student Decisions." *Research in Higher Education* 50: 415–436.

Bozick, Robert, and Erich Lauff. 2007. "Education Longitudinal Study of 2002 (ELS:2002): A First Look at the Initial Postsecondary Experiences of the High School Sophomore Class of 2002." *NCES 2008-309*, National Center for Education Statistics, U.S. Department of Education, Washington, DC.

Brand, Jennie E., and Charles N. Halaby. 2006. "Regression and Matching Estimates of the Effects of Elite College Attendance on Educational and Career Achievement." *Social Science Research* 35 (3): 749–770.

Brewer, Dominic J., Eric R. Eide, and Ronald G. Ehrenberg. 1999. "Does It Pay to Attend an Elite Private College? Cross-Cohort Evidence on the Effects of College Type on Earnings." *Journal of Human Resources* 34 (1): 104–123.

Bridgeland, John, and Mary Bruce. 2011. "2011 National Survey of School Counselors: Counseling at a Crossroads." November, College Board Advocacy & Policy Center, New York.

Briggs, Derek C. 2001. "The Effect of Admissions Test Preparation: Evidence from NELS:88." *Chance* 14 (1): 10–18.

———. 2004. "Evaluating SAT Coaching: Gains, Effects and Self-Selection." In *Rethinking the SAT: The Future of Standardized Tests in University Admissions*, ed. Rebecca Zwick, 217–233. New York: RoutledgeFalmer.

———. 2009. "Preparation for College Admissions Exams." Report, National Association for College Admission Counseling, Arlington, VA.

Bryan, Julia, Cheryl Moore-Thomas, Norma L. Day-Vines, and Cheryl Holcomb-McCoy. 2011. "School Counselors as Social Capital: The Effects of High School College Counseling on College Application Rates." *Journal of Counseling and Development* 89 (2): 190–199.

Buchmann, Claudia, Dennis J. Condron, and Vincent J. Roscigno. 2010. "Shadow Education, American Style: Test Preparation, the SAT and College Enrollment." *Social Forces* 89 (2): 435–461.

Cabrera, Alberto F., and Steven M. La Nasa. 2001. "On the Path to College: Three Critical Tasks Facing America's Disadvantaged." *Research in Higher Education* 42 (2): 119–149.

Carey, Kevin. 2011. "The End of College Admissions as We Know It: Everything You've Heard about Getting In Is about to Go Out the Window." *Washington Monthly* 43 (9/10): 22–30.

Carnevale, Anthony P., and Stephen J. Rose. 2004. "Socioeconomic Status, Race/Ethnicity, and Selective College Admissions." In *America's Untapped Resource: Low-Income Students in Higher Education*, ed. Richard D. Kahlenberg, 101–156. New York: Century Foundation Press.

Carnevale, Anthony P., and Jeff Strohl. 2010. "How Increasing College Access Is Increasing Inequality, and What to Do about It." In *Rewarding Strivers: Helping Low-Income Students Succeed in College*, ed. Richard D. Kahlenberg, 71–190. New York: Century Foundation Press.

Carrell, Scott, and Bruce Sacerdote. 2012. "Do Late Interventions Matter Too? An Experiment to Raise College Going among NH High School Seniors." Presentation provided to author, March 8.

Chaker, Anne Marie. 2005. "Your Money Matters (A Special Report): Family Money; Early Remittance: We All Know about the High Cost of Tuition; But the Bills Can Start Piling Up Well before Your Child Applies." *Wall Street Journal*, November 28, p. R8.

Chaplin, Duncan, and Jane Hannaway. 1998. "Course Taking, Student Activities, School Performance, and SAT Performance." African American High Scorers Project, Technical Report No. 3, November. Washington, DC: Urban Institute.

Chapman, Randall G. 1993. "Non-Simultaneous Relative Importance-Performance Analysis: Meta-results from 80 College Choice Surveys with 55,276 Respondents." *Journal of Marketing for Higher Education* 4 (1/2): 405–422.

Chapman, Randall G., and Rex Jackson. 1987. *College Choices of Academically Able Students: The Influence of No-Need Financial Aid and Other Factors*." Research Monograph No. 10. New York: College Entrance Examination Board. http://www.eric.ed.gov/PDFS/ED282467.pdf (accessed September 1, 2011).

Chau, Joanna. 2012. "The Biggest Obstacle for First-Generation College Students." *Chronicle of Higher Education*, April 25, http://chronicle.com/blogs/headcount/the-biggest-obstacle-for-first-generation-college-students/30126 (accessed June 16, 2012).

Chen, Xianglei, Joanna Wu, and Shayna Tasoff. 2010a. "Academic Preparation for College in the High School Senior Class of 2003–04." *NCES 2010-169,*

National Center for Education Statistics, U.S. Department of Education, Washington, DC.

———. 2010b. "The High School Senior Class of 2003–04: Steps toward Postsecondary Enrollment." *NCES 2010-203*, National Center for Education Statistics, U.S. Department of Education, Washington, DC.

Chinni, Dante. 2006. "Heaven's Gate: Will Gaining Admission to One of the Nation's Elite Colleges Guarantee a Prosperous Future—Or Just a Mountain of Debt?" *Washington Post*, April 2, p. W10.

Choy, Susan, 2001. "Students Whose Parents Did Not Go to College: Postsecondary Access, Persistence, and Attainment." *NCES 2001-126*, National Center for Education Statistics, U.S. Department of Education, Washington, DC.

Choy, Susan P., and Cecilia Ottinger. 1998. "Choosing a Postsecondary Institution." *NCES 98-080*, National Center for Education Statistics, U.S. Department of Education, Washington, DC.

Clinedinst, Melissa E., Sarah F. Hurley, and David A. Hawkins. 2011. "2011 State of College Admission." National Association for College Admission Counseling, Arlington, VA.

COFHE. 2012. "Consortium on Financing Higher Education." http://web.mit.edu /cofhe/ (accessed February 6, 2012).

Cohen, Katherine. 2002. *The Truth about Getting In: A Top College Advisor Tells You Everything You Need to Know.* New York: Hyperion.

Cohodes, Sarah and Joshua Goodman. 2012. "First Degree Earns: The Impact of College Quality of College Completion Rates." Research Working Paper RWP12-033, August, Harvard Kennedy School, Harvard University, Cambridge, MA.

Colburn, David R., Charles E. Young, and Victor M. Yellen. 2008. "Admissions and Public Higher Education in California, Texas, and Florida: The Post-Affirmative Action Era." *UCLA Journal of Education and Information Studies* 4 (1).

Cole, Diane. 2006. "Dear Computer: Help Me Pick a School." *U.S. News & World Report* 141 (7): 92.

Cole, James S., and Robert M. Gonyea. 2008. "Accuracy of Self-Reported SAT and ACT Test Scores: Implications for Research." Paper presented at the Association for the Study of Higher Education Annual Convention, Jacksonville, FL, November 5–8.

Coleman, James S. 1966. *Equality of Educational Opportunity (Coleman) Study.* Office of Education/National Center for Education Statistics, U.S. Department of Health, Education, and Welfare, Washington, DC.

College Board. 2005a. "Advanced Placement Report to the Nation, 2005." http:// www.collegeboard.com/prod_downloads/about/news_info/ap/2005/ap-report -nation.pdf (accessed January 21, 2012).

———. 2005b. "High School GPAs of A+, A, and A– Rise with Family Income and Parental Education." http://www.collegeboard.com/prod_downloads/about /news_info/cbsenior/yr2005/graph16-high-school-gpas.pdf (accessed December 2, 2005).

———. 2006a. "Advanced Placement Report to the Nation, 2006." http://www .collegeboard.com/prod_downloads/about/news_info/ap/2006/2006_ap-report -nation.pdf (accessed September 1, 2011).

———. 2006b. "College Application Requirements: Application Fee." http://www .collegeboard.com/student/apply/the-application/115.html (accessed June 8, 2006).

———. 2006c. "2006 College-Bound Seniors: Total Group Profile Report." http:// www.collegeboard.com/prod_downloads/about/news_info/cbsenior/yr2006 /national-report.pdf (accessed February 2, 2009).

———. 2006d. "Graph 15: SAT Scores Rise with Higher Levels of Parental Education." http://www.collegeboard.com/prod_downloads/about/news_info/cb senior/yr2006/graph15-SAT-scores-rise.pdf (accessed February 2, 2009).

———. 2006e. "Trends in College Pricing." *Trends in Higher Education Series, Report Number 060342009,* http://www.collegeboard.com/prod_downloads /press/cost06/trends_college_pricing_06.pdf (accessed July 17, 2009).

———. 2007a. "Number of AP Examinations per Student." http://apcentral.college board.com/apc/public/repository/2007_Number_of_Exams_per_Student.pdf (accessed January, 22, 2012).

———. 2007b. "SAT Percentile Ranks, 2006 College-Bound Seniors—Critical Reading+Mathematics." http://www.collegeboard.com/prod_downloads/high ered/ra/sat/SATPercentileRanksCompositeCR_M.pdf (accessed December 13, 2007).

———. 2007c. "SAT–ACT Score Comparisons." http://www.collegeboard.com /prod_downloads/highered/ra/sat/satACT_concordance.pdf (accessed December 13, 2007).

———. 2009. "How Many Applications Are Enough?" http://professionals.college board.com/guidance/applications/how-many (accessed April 5, 2009).

———. 2011. "Cracking the Student Aid Code: Parent and Student Perspectives on Paying for College." http://advocacy.collegeboard.org/sites/default/files /11b_3172_Cracking_Code_Update_WEB_110112.pdf (accessed January 29, 2011).

———. 2012. "Student Search Service (SSS)." http://professionals.collegeboard .com/k-12/prepare/sss (accessed January 3, 2012).

College Board Advocacy & Policy Center. 2011. "Complexity in College Admission: The Barriers between Aspiration and Enrollment for Lower-Income Students." http://advocacy.collegeboard.org/sites/default/files/11b-4062_ AdmissComplex_web.pdf (accessed January 9, 2012).

College Board and Art & Science Group. 2010. "Students and Parents Making
    Judgments about College Costs without Complete Information." *Student Poll*
    8 (1), http://www.artsci.com/studentpoll/v8n1/ (accessed June 30, 2011).

College Savings Foundation. 2010. "How Youth Plan to Fund College: A Survey by
    the College Savings Foundation of over 500 16- and 17-Year Olds from Across
    the Country." http://www.collegesavingsfoundation.org/pdf/YouthSurvey.pdf
    (accessed September 1, 2011).

Collison, Michele N-K. 1993. "Black Students Become More Savvy in Making
    Their College Choices." *Chronicle of Higher Education* 39 (30): A28.

Conklin, Mary E., and Ann Ricks Dailey. 1981. "Does Consistency of Parental
    Educational Encouragement Matter for Secondary School Students?" *Sociol-
    ogy of Education* 54 (4): 254–262.

Cook, Philip J., and Robert H. Frank. 1993. "The Growing Concentration of Top
    Students at Elite Schools." In *Studies of Supply and Demand in Higher Edu-
    cation*, ed. Charles T. Clotfelter and Michael Rothschild, 121–144. Chicago:
    University of Chicago Press.

Cookson, Peter W., Jr., and Caroline Hodges Persell. 1985. *Preparing for Power:
    America's Elite Boarding Schools*. New York: Basic Books.

Dale, Stacy Berg, and Alan B. Krueger. 2002. "Estimating the Payoff to Attend-
    ing a More Selective College: An Application of Selection on Observables and
    Unobservables." *Quarterly Journal of Economics* 117 (4): 1491–1527.

———. 2011. "Estimating the Return to College Selectivity over the Career Using
    Administrative Earning Data." Working Paper 563, February, Industrial Re-
    lations Section, Princeton University, Princeton, NJ.

Daniel, Kermit, Dan Black, and Jeffrey Smith. 1997. "College Quality and the
    Wages of Young Men." Working Paper, June, Wharton School of Public Policy
    and Management, University of Pennsylvania, Philadelphia.

Demerath, Peter. 2009. *Producing Success: The Culture of Personal Advance-
    ment in an American High School*. Chicago: University of Chicago Press.

Duffy, Elizabeth A., and Idana Goldberg. 1998. *Crafting a Class: College Ad-
    missions and Financial Aid, 1955–1994*. Princeton, NJ: Princeton University
    Press.

Dumais, Susan A. 2002. "Cultural Capital, Gender, and School Success: The Role
    of Habitus." *Sociology of Education* 75 (1): 44–68.

Dynarski, Susan, and Mark Wiederspan. 2012. "Student Aid Simplification:
    Looking Back and Looking Ahead," Working Paper 17834, National Bureau
    of Economic Research, Cambridge, MA.

Dynarski, Susan M., and Judith E. Scott-Clayton. 2006. "The Cost of Complex-
    ity in Federal Student Aid: Lessons from Optimal Tax Theory and Behav-
    ioral Economics." *National Tax Journal* 59 (2): 319–356.

Easterbrook, Gregg. 2004. "Who Needs Harvard?" *Atlantic Monthly* 294 (3):
    128–130, 132–133.

Eide, Eric, Dominic J. Brewer, and Ronald G. Ehrenberg. 1998. "Does It Pay to Attend an Elite Private College? Evidence on Effects of Undergraduate College Quality on Graduate School Attendance." *Economics of Education Review* 17 (4): 371–376.

Ellis, Blake. 2012. "Harvard, Princeton Post Record Low Acceptance Rates." *CNN Money*, March 30, http://money.cnn.com/2012/03/30/pf/college/acceptance_rates_ivy_league/index.htm (accessed June 16, 2012).

Espenshade, Thomas J., and Chang Y. Chung. 2009. "Diversity Implications of SAT-Optional Admission Policies at Selective Colleges." Paper prepared for the Conference on Rethinking College Admissions, Wake Forest University, April 15–16.

Espenshade, Thomas J., Chang Y. Chung, and Joan L. Walling. 2004. "Admission Preferences for Minority Students, Athletes, and Legacies at Elite Universities." *Social Science Quarterly* 85 (5): 1422–1446.

Espenshade, Thomas J., Lauren E. Hale, and Chang Y. Chung. 2005. "The Frog Pond Revisited: High School Academic Context, Class Rank, and Elite College Admission." *Sociology of Education* 78 (4): 269–293.

Espenshade, Thomas J., and Alexandria Walton Radford. 2009. *No Longer Separate, Not Yet Equal: Race and Class in Elite College Admission and Campus Life.* Princeton, NJ: Princeton University Press.

Ewers, Justin. 2004. "Drowning in Applications." *U.S. News & World Report* 137 (22): 64.

———. 2005. "Class Conscious; Low-Income Students Have Long Been a Rare and Invisible Minority at Elite Colleges. That May Be About to Change." *U.S. News & World Report* 138 (16): 42.

Fallows, James. 2001. "The Early-Decision Racket." *Atlantic Monthly* 288 (2): 37–52.

Farrell, Elizabeth. 2007. "Consultants Help Families Pay Less for College." *Chronicle of Higher Education* 54 (9): A1.

Fetter, Jean H. 1995. *Questions and Admissions: Reflections on 100,000 Admissions Decisions at Stanford University.* Stanford, CA: Stanford University Press.

Finder, Alan. 2007. "Ivy League Admissions Crunch Brings New Cachet to Next Tier." *New York Times*, May 16, p. A1.

———. 2008. "Elite Colleges Reporting Record Lows in Admission." *New York Times*, April 1, p. A16.

Fishman, Rachel. 2012. "Higher Education Needs a Flashlight." *The Quick and the Ed*, February 2, Education Sector, Washington, DC, http://www.quickanded.com/2012/02/higher-education-needs-a-flashlight.html (accessed February 7, 2012).

Fitzgerald, Robert A. 2000. "College Quality and the Earnings of Recent College Graduates." *NCES 2000-043*, National Center for Education Statistics, U.S. Department of Education, Washington, DC.

Flanagan, Caitlin. 2001. "Confessions of a Prep School College Counselor." *Atlantic Monthly* 288 (2): 53–61.

Flint, Thomas A. 1992. "Parental and Planning Influences on the Formation of Student College Choice Sets." *Research in Higher Education* 33 (6): 689–708.

Frank, Robert H., and Philip J. Cook. 1995. *The Winner-Take-All Society*. New York: Free Press.

Freedle, Roy O. 2003. "Correcting the SAT's Ethnic and Social-Class Bias: A Method for Reestimating SAT Scores." *Harvard Educational Review* 73 (1): 1–43.

Galotti, Kathleen, and Melissa C. Mark. 1994. "How Do High School Students Structure an Important Life Decision? A Short-Term Longitudinal Study of the College Decision-Making Process." *Research in Higher Education* 35 (5): 589–607.

Gardner, John A. 1987. "Transition from High School to Postsecondary Education: Analytical Studies." *CS-87-C093*, Center for Education Statistics, Office of Educational Research and Improvement, U.S. Department of Education, Washington, DC.

Geiser, Saul, and Maria Veronica Santelices. 2007. "Validity of High-School Grades in Predicting Student Success beyond the Freshman Year: High-School Record vs. Standardized Tests as Indicators of Four-Year College Outcomes." *Research & Occasional Paper Series: CSHE.6.07*, http://cshe .berkeley.edu/publications/publications.php?id=265 (accessed October 2, 2007).

Gerald, Danette, and Kati Haycock. 2006. "Engines of Inequality: Diminishing Equity in the Nation's Premier Public Universities." January, Education Trust, Washington, DC, http://www.edtrust.org/dc/publication/engines-of -inequality-diminishing-equity-in-the-nation%E2%80%99s-premier-public -universities (accessed September 1, 2011).

Gerber, Theodore P., and Sin Yi Cheung. 2008. "Horizontal Stratification in Postsecondary Education: Forms, Explanations, and Implications." *Annual Review of Sociology* 34: 299–318.

Glater, Jonathan D. 2006. "Some Parents Letting Children Choose College, and Pay for It." *New York Times Magazine*, June 11, pp. 60–68.

Golden, Daniel. 2006. *The Price of Admission: How America's Ruling Class Buys Its Way into Elite Colleges—And Who Gets Left Outside the Gates*. New York: Crown Publishers.

Goldrick-Rab, Sara, Douglas N. Harris, James Benson, and Robert Kelchen. 2011. "Conditional Cash Transfers and College Persistence: Evidence from a Randomized Need-Based Grant Program." Discussion Paper 1393-11, July, Institute for Research on Poverty, University of Wisconsin-Madison.

Gose, Ben. 1998. "Recent Shifts on Aid by Elite Colleges Signal New Push to Help the Middle Class." *Chronicle of Higher Education* 44 (26): A43–A44.

Grodsky, Eric, and Erika Jackson. 2009. "Social Stratification in Higher Education." *Teachers College Record* 111 (10): 2347–2384.

Grodsky, Eric, and Melanie Jones. 2007. "Real and Imagined Barriers to College Entry: Perceptions of Cost." *Social Science Research* 36 (2): 745–766.

Grodsky, Eric, and Catherine Riegle-Crumb. 2010. "Those Who Choose and Those Who Don't: Social Background and College Orientation." *ANNALS of the American Academy of Political and Social Science* 627 (1): 14–35.

Groen, Jeffrey A., and Michelle J. White. 2003. "In-State versus Out-of-State Students: The Divergence of Interest between Public Universities and State Governments." Working Paper W9603, April, National Bureau of Economic Research, Cambridge, MA.

Gross, Jane. 1999. "Basking in the Hamptons to Coach Students for S.A.T.'s." *New York Times*, August 9, p. B1.

Hahn, Ryan C., and Derek Price. 2008. "Promise Lost: College Qualified Students Who Don't Enroll in College." Institute for Higher Education Policy, Washington, DC, http://www.ihep.org/assets/files/publications/m-r/PromiseLostCollege Qualrpt.pdf (accessed March 18, 2012).

Handwerk, Philip, Namrata Tognatta, Richard J. Coley, and Drew H. Gitomer. 2008. "Access to Success: Patterns of Advanced Placement Participation in U.S. High Schools." Educational Testing Service, Princeton, NJ, http://www .ets.org/Media/Research/pdf/PIC-ACCESS.pdf (accessed September 1, 2010).

Hansen, Fay. 2006. "Employee Referral Programs, Selective Campus Recruitment Could Touch Off Bias Charges." *Workforce Management* 85 (12): 59–60.

Haycock, Kati, Mary Lynch, and Jennifer Engle. 2010. "Opportunity Adrift: Our Flagship Universities Are Straying from Their Public Mission." January, Education Trust, Washington, DC, http://www.edtrust.org/dc/publication /opportunity-adrift-our-flagship-universities-are-straying-from-their-public -mission (accessed June 24, 2012).

Hearn, James C. 1984. "The Relative Roles of Academic, Ascribed, and Socioeconomic Characteristics in College Destinations." *Sociology of Education* 57: 22–30.

———. 1991. "Academic and Nonacademic Influences on the College Destinations of 1980 High School Graduates." *Sociology of Education* 64: 158–171.

Heller, Donald E. 1997. "Student Price Response in Higher Education: An Update to Leslie and Brinkman." *Journal of Higher Education* 68 (6): 624–659.

———. 2004. "Pell Grant Recipients in Selective Colleges and Universities." In *America's Untapped Resource: Low-Income Students in Higher Education*, ed. Richard D. Kahlenberg, 157–166. New York: Century Foundation Press.

Hernández, Michele A. 1997. *A Is for Admission: The Insider's Guide to Getting into the Ivy League and Other Top Colleges*. New York: Warner Books.

Herring, Hubert B. 2005. "Your Child Got into an Ivy. Do You Have to Say Yes?" *New York Times*, April 17, p. 3.8.

Herrold, Kathleen, and Kevin O'Donnell. 2008. "Parent and Family Involvement in Education, 2006–07 School Year, from the National Household Education Surveys Program of 2007." *NCES 2008-050*, National Center for Education Statistics, U.S. Department of Education, Washington, DC.

Hershbein, Brad. 2011. "Worker Signals among New College Graduates: The Role of Selectivity and GPA." Job Market Paper, University of Michigan, Ann Arbor.

Heuchert, Dan. 2009. "U. Va. Releases Admissions Decisions Today to a Record 21,839 Applicants." *UVA Today*, March 26, http://www.virginia.edu/uvatoday /newsRelease.php?id=8099 (accessed April 15, 2009)

Hill, Catharine B., and Gordon C. Winston. 2006a. "A 'Free' Harvard? Now That's Rich." *Los Angeles Times*, April 2, p. M2.

———. 2006b. "How Scarce Are High-Ability, Low-Income Students?" In *College Access: Opportunity or Privilege?* ed. Michael S. McPherson and Morton Owen Schapiro, 75–102. New York: College Board.

———. 2010. "Low-Income Students and Highly Selective Private Colleges: Geography, Searching, and Recruiting." *Economics of Education Review* 29: 495–503.

Hollinshead, Byron S. 1952. *Who Should Go to College*. New York: Columbia University Press.

Hoover, Eric. 2008. "Admissions Angst Doesn't Afflict as Many as It May Seem." *Chronicle of Higher Education*, March 7, http://chronicle.com/daily/2008/03 /1971n.htm (accessed April 23, 2009).

Horn, Laura, and Anne-Marie Nuñez. 2000. "Mapping the Road to College: First-Generation Students' Math Track, Planning Strategies, and Context of Support." *NCES 2000-153*, National Center for Education Statistics, U.S. Department of Education, Washington, DC.

Horn, Laura J., Xianglei Chen, and Chris Chapman. 2003. "Getting Ready to Pay for College: What Students and Their Parents Know about the Cost of College Tuition and What They Are Doing to Find Out." *NCES 2003-030*, National Center for Education Statistics, U.S. Department of Education, Washington, DC.

Hossler, Don, and Erin M. Foley. 1995. "Reducing the Noise in the College Choice Process: The Use of College Guidebooks and Ratings." In *Evaluating and Responding to College Guidebooks and Rankings*, ed. R. Dan Walleri and Marsha K. Moss, 21–30. San Francisco, CA: Jossey-Bass.

Hossler, Don, and Karen S. Gallagher. 1987. "Studying College Choices: A Three-Phase Model and the Implication for Policy Makers." *College and University* 2: 207–221.

Hossler, Don, Jack Schmit, and Nick Vesper. 1999. *Going to College: How Social, Economic and Educational Factors Influence the Decisions Students Make*. Baltimore, MD: Johns Hopkins University Press.

Hoxby, Caroline M. 2001. "The Returns to Attending a More Selective College: 1960 to the Present." In *Forum Futures: Exploring the Future of Higher Education, 200 Papers, Forum Strategy Series, Vol. 3*, ed. Maureen Devlin and Joel Myerson, 13–42. San Francisco, CA: Jossey-Bass.

Hu, Shouping, and Don Hossler. 2000. "Willingness to Pay and Preference for Private Institutions." *Research in Higher Education* 41 (6): 685–701.

Hu, Winnie. 2010. "How Many Graduates Does It Take to Be No. 1?" *New York Times*, June 27, p. A1.

Hurwitz, Michael. 2011. "The Impact of Legacy Status on Undergraduate Admissions at Elite Colleges and Universities." *Economics of Education Review* 30 (3): 480–492.

Ikenberry, Stanley O., and Terry W. Hartle. 1998. *Too Little Knowledge Is a Dangerous Thing: What the Public Thinks and Knows about Paying for College.* Washington, DC: American Council on Education.

Ingels, Steven J., Michael Planty, and Robert Bozick. 2005. "A Profile of the American High School Senior in 2004: A First Look—Initial Results from the First Follow-Up of the Education Longitudinal Study of 2002 (ELS: 2002)." *NCES 2006-348*, National Center for Education Statistics, U.S. Department of Education, Washington, DC.

Institute for College Access and Success. 2011. "Adding It All Up: An Early Look at Net Price Calculators." March, http://www.ticas.org/files/pub/adding _it_all_up.pdf (accessed June 30, 2011).

Institute for Higher Education Policy. 2010. "Cost Perceptions and College-Going for Low-Income Students." Spring, http://pathwaystocollege.net/pdf /COST%20PERCEPTIONS%20AND%20COLLEGE-GOING%20FOR %20LOW-INCOME%20STUDENTS.pdf (accessed March 18, 2012).

———. 2012. "Maximizing the College Choice Process to Increase Fit and Match of Underserved Students." Winter, http://www.pathwaystocollege.net /pdf/Pathways%20College%20Choice%20Fit%20and%20Match%20Winter %202012%20Final[3].pdf (accessed March 18, 2012).

International Baccalaureate Organization. 2008. "What Is the Diploma Programme?" http://www.ibo.org/diploma/ (accessed October 27, 2008).

Jackman, Mary R., and Robert W. Jackman. 1983. *Class Awareness in the United States.* Berkeley: University of California Press.

Jackson, Gregory A. 1982. "Public Efficiency and Private Choice in Higher Education." *Educational Evaluation and Policy Analysis* 4 (2): 237–247.

Jan, Tracy. 2009. "Harvard Admission Rate Dips to 7 Percent." *Boston Globe*, March 30, http://www.boston.com/news/local/breaking_news/2009/03/harvard _admissi.html (accessed May 6, 2010).

Jaschik, Scott. 2010. "Mid-Market for Private Admissions Help." *Inside Higher Ed*, July 29, http://www.insidehighered.com/news/2010/07/29/princeton_review (accessed January 29, 2011).

———. 2011. "Generous, But Not So Generous." *Inside Higher Ed*, February 21, http://www.insidehighered.com/news/2011/02/21/yale_scales_back_financial _commitment_to_upper_income_aid_recipients (accessed June 29, 2011).

Jesse, David. 2011. "For Many Middle-Income Families, Elite Colleges Are No Longer Within Reach." *Detroit Free Press*, November 6, http://www.freep .com/article/20111106/NEWS06/111060474/For-many-middle-income-fami lies-college-no-longer-within-reach?odyssey=tab|topnews|text|FRONT PAGE (accessed January 9, 2011).

Johnson, Jean, and Jon Rochkind. 2010. "Can I Get a Little Advice Here? How an Overstretched High School Guidance System Is Undermining Students' College Aspirations." New York and Washington, DC: Public Agenda.

Jones, Gigi, and Alexandria Walton Radford. 2012. "Preparing to Fund College: Ninth Graders' and Parents' Planning and Saving." Presented at the Annual Student Financial Aid Research Network Conference, June 13–15, Memphis, TN.

Kahlenberg, Richard D., ed. 2004. *America's Untapped Resource: Low-Income Students in Higher Education*. New York: Century Foundation Press.

———. 2006. "Cost Remains a Key Obstacle to College Access." *Chronicle of Higher Education* 52 (27): B51.

———. 2010a. *Rewarding Strivers: Helping Low-Income Students Succeed in College*. New York: Century Foundation Press.

———. 2010b. "Ten Myths about Legacy Preferences in College Admissions." *Chronicle of Higher Education*, September 22, http://chronicle.com/article/10 -Myths-About-Legacy/124561/ (accessed June 29, 2011).

Kane, Thomas J. 1998. "Racial and Ethnic Preferences in College Admissions." In *The Black-White Test Score Gap*, ed. Christopher Jencks and Meredith Phillips, 431–456. Washington, DC: Brookings Institution Press.

Karen, David. 1990. "Toward a Political-Organizational Model of Gatekeeping: The Case of Elite Colleges." *Sociology of Education* 63 (4): 227–240.

———. 1991. "'Achievement' and 'Ascription' in Admission to an Elite College: A Political-Organizational Analysis." *Sociological Forum* 6 (2): 349–380.

Kaufman, Jonathan. 2001. "Campus Currency: At Elite Universities, a Culture of Money Highlights Class Divide—Stock Trades and Cellphones for Some Duke Students—But Not for Ms. Byrd—'I Have 2 Groups of Friends.'" *Wall Street Journal*, June 8, p. A1.

Kelly, Andrew P., and Mark Schneider. 2011. "Filling in the Blanks: How Information Can Affect Choice in Higher Education." January, American Enterprise Institute for Public Policy Research, Washington, DC, http://www.aei .org/files/2011/01/12/fillingintheblanks.pdf (accessed June 24, 2012).

Kim, Jiyun. 2012. "Exploring the Relationship between State Financial Aid Policy and Postsecondary Enrollment Choices: A Focus on Income and Race Differences." *Research in Higher Education* 53 (2): 123–151.

Kim, Jiyun, Stephen L. DesJardins, and Brian P. McCall. 2009. "Exploring the Effects of Student Expectations about Financial Aid on Postsecondary Choice: A Focus on Income and Racial/Ethnic Differences." *Research in Higher Education* 50 (8): 741–774.

Kirp, David L. 2003. *Shakespeare, Einstein, and the Bottom Line: The Marketing of Higher Education.* Cambridge, MA: Harvard University Press.

Kobrin, Jennifer L., Brian F. Patterson, Emily J. Shaw, Krista D. Mattern, and Sandra M. Barbuti. 2008. "Validity of the SAT for Predicting First-Year College Grade Point Average." *Research Report No. 2008-5.* New York: College Board.

Kotler, Phillip. 1976. "Applying Marketing Theory to College Admissions." In *A Role for Marketing in College Admissions,* 54–72. New York: College Entrance Examination Board.

Krukowski, Jan. 1985. "What Do Students Want? Status." *Change* 17: 13–29.

Lareau, Annette. 2003. *Unequal Childhoods: Class, Race, and Family Life.* Berkeley: University of California Press.

———. 2011. *Unequal Childhoods: Class, Race, and Family Life, Second Edition with an Update a Decade Later.* Berkeley: University of California Press.

Laturno, Peggy Hines, and Richard W. Lemons. 2011. "Poised to Lead: How School Counselors Can Drive College and Career Readiness." Education Trust, Washington, DC, http://www.edtrust.org/dc/publication/poised-to-lead (accessed January 2, 2012).

Lederman, Doug. 2009a. "College for All." *Inside Higher Ed,* February 25, http://www.insidehighered.com/news/2009/02/25/obama (accessed May 11, 2010).

———. 2009b. "De-hyping College Admissions (or Trying to, Anyway)." *Inside Higher Ed,* January 13, http://insidehighered.com/news/2009/01/13/admissions (accessed April 21, 2009).

Lee, John Michael, Jr., Kelcey Edwards, Rozanna Menson, and Anita Rawls. 2011. "The College Completion Agenda: 2011 Progress Report." College Board Advocacy & Policy Center, New York.

Leonhardt, David. 2004. "As Wealthy Fill Top Colleges, Concerns Grow over Fairness." *New York Times,* April 22, p. A1.

———. 2011. "Top Colleges, Largely for the Elite." *New York Times,* May 25, p. B1.

Lewin, Tamar. 2004. "How I Spent Summer Vacation: Going to Get-into-College Camp." *New York Times,* April 18, p. 1.1.

———. 2009. "Easing a College Financial Aid Headache." *New York Times,* June 24, p. A12.

Lewis, Gordon H., and Sue Morrison. 1975. "A Longitudinal Study of College Selection." Technical Report No. 2, February, School of Urban and Public Affairs, Carnegie-Mellon University, Pittsburgh, PA.

Light, Audrey, and Wayne Strayer. 2000. "Determinants of College Completion: School Quality or Student Ability? *Journal of Human Resources* 35 (2): 299–332.

Linneham, Frank, Christy H. Weer, and Paul Stonely. 2011. "High School Guidance Counselor Recommendations: The Role of Student Race, Socioeconomic Status, and Academic Performance." *Journal of Applied Social Psychology* 41 (3): 536–558.

Litten, Larry H. 1982. "Different Strokes in the Applicant Pool: Some Refinements in a Model of Student College Choice." *Journal of Higher Education* 53 (4): 383–402.

Litten, Larry H., and Alfred E. Hall. 1989. "In the Eyes of Our Beholders: Some Evidence on How High-School Students and Their Parents View Quality in Colleges." *Journal of Higher Education* 60 (3): 302–324.

Litten, Larry H., Daniel Sullivan, and David L. Brodigan. 1983. *Applying Market Research in College Admissions.* New York: College Entrance Examination Board.

Lombardi, Kate Stone. 2004. "Tutoring for the Already Brainy." *New York Times,* May 23, p. 14WC1.

Long, Bridget Terry. 2010. "Grading Higher Education: Giving Consumers the Information They Need." December, Brookings Institution, Washington, DC, http://www.brookings.edu/papers/2010/12_higher_ed_long.aspx (accessed September 1, 2011).

Long, Mark C. 2008. "College Quality and Early Adult Outcomes." *Economics of Education Review* 27 (5): 588–602.

Loury, Linda Datcher, and David Garman. 1995. "College Selectivity and Earnings." *Journal of Labor Economics* 13 (2): 289–308.

Lumina Foundation. 2008. "Results and Reflections: An Evaluation Report." http://www.luminafoundation.org/publications/Results_and_Reflections-21st_Century_Scholars.pdf (accessed June 17, 2012).

Luna De La Rosa, Maria. 2006. "Is Opportunity Knowing? Low-Income Students' Perceptions of College and Financial Aid." *American Behavioral Scientist* 49 (12): 1670–1686.

Lynch, Mamie, Jennifer Engle, and José L. Cruz. 2011. "Priced Out: How the Wrong Financial-Aid Policies Hurt Low-Income Students." June, Education Trust, Washington, DC, http://www.edtrust.org/dc/publication/priced-out (accessed September 1, 2011).

MacAllum, Keith, Denise M. Glover, Barbara Queen, and Angela Riggs. 2007. "Deciding on Postsecondary Education: Final Report." *NPEC 2008-850,* National Postsecondary Education Cooperative, U.S. Department of Education, Washington, DC.

Maguire Associates. 2009. "Students' Application Choices and College Preferences in the 2009 Admissions Cycle: Results from the 2009 College Decision Impact Survey." May, http://www.maguireassoc.com/resource/documents/StudentsApplicationChoicesandCollegePreferences2009.pdf (accessed January 29, 2011).

Manski, Charles, and David Wise. 1983. *College Choice in America*. Cambridge, MA: Harvard University Press.

Marklein, Mary Beth. 2010. "New FAFSA Makes It Easier for Students to Apply for Aid." *USA Today*, http://www.usatoday.com/news/education/2010-01-06 -fafsa06_ST_N.htm (accessed February 10, 2012).

Massey, Douglas S., Camille Z. Charles, Garvey F. Lundy, and Mary J. Fischer. 2003. *The Source of the River: The Social Origins of Freshmen at America's Selective Colleges and Universities*. Princeton, NJ: Princeton University Press.

Mattern, Krista D., Brian F. Patterson, Emily J. Shaw, Jennifer L. Kobrin, and Sandra M. Barbuti. 2008. "Differential Validity and Prediction of the SAT." *Research Report No. 2008-4*. College Board, New York, http://professionals .collegeboard.com/profdownload/Differential_Validity_and_Prediction_of _the_SAT.pdf (accessed July 4, 2008).

Mattern, Krista D., Emily J. Shaw, and Jennifer L. Kobrin. 2010. "Academic Fit: Is the *Right* School the Best School or Is the *Best* School the Right School?" *Journal of Advanced Academics* 21 (3): 368–391.

Mayher, Bill. 1998. *The College Admissions Mystique*. New York: Farrar, Straus and Giroux.

Mbugua, Martin. 2012. "Princeton Offers Admission to 7.86 Percent of Applicants." Princeton University News Release, March 29, http://www.princeton .edu/main/news/archive/S33/30/35K46/index.xml?section=newsreleases (accessed June 24, 2012).

McDill, Edward L., and James Coleman. 1965. "Family and Peer Influences in College Plans of High School Students." *Sociology of Education* 38 (2): 112–126.

McDonough, Patricia M. 1997. *Choosing Colleges: How Social Class and Schools Structure Opportunity*. Albany: State University of New York Press.

——. 2004. "Counseling Matters: Knowledge, Assistance, and Organizational Commitment in College Preparation." In *Preparing for College: Nine Elements of Effective Outreach,* ed. William G. Tierney, Zoe B. Corwin, & Julia E. Colyar, 69–87. Albany: State University of New York Press.

——. 2005. "Counseling and College Counseling in America's High Schools." In *The 2004-05 State of College Admission,* ed., David Hawkins, 107–127. Washington, DC: National Association for College Admissions Counseling.

McDonough, Patricia M., and Anthony Lising Antonio. 1996. "Ethnic and Racial Differences in Selectivity of College Choice." Paper presented at the Annual Meeting of the American Educational Research Association, New York, April 8–13.

McDonough, Patricia M., Anthony Lising Antonio, MaryBeth Walpole, and Leonor Xochitl Perez. 1998. "College Rankings: Democratized Knowledge for Whom?" *Research in Higher Education* 39 (5): 513–537.

McDonough, Patricia M., and Shannon Calderone. 2006. "The Meaning of Money: Perceptual Differences between College Counselors and Low-Income Families about College Costs and Financial Aid." *American Behavioral Scientist* 49 (12): 1703–1718.

McGinn, Daniel. 2005. "Holding Less Sway." *Newsweek* 145 (18): 12.

McPherson, Michael S., and Morton Owen Schapiro. 1991. *Keeping College Affordable: Government and Educational Opportunity.* Washington, DC: Brookings Institution.

Melguizo, Tatiana. 2008. "Quality Matters: Assessing the Impact of Attending More Selective Institutions on College Completion Rates of Minorities." *Research in Higher Education* 49 (3): 214–236.

——. 2010. "Are Students of Color More Likely to Graduate from College If They Attend More Selective Institutions? Evidence from the First Cohort of Recipients and Non-recipients of the Gates Millennium Scholarship (GMS) Program." *Education Evaluation and Policy Analysis* 32 (2): 230–248.

Menand, Louis. 2003. "The Thin Envelope." *New Yorker* 79 (7): 88–92.

Miller, Elizabeth I. 1997. "Parents' Views on the Value of a College Education and How They Will Pay for It." *Journal of Student Financial Aid* 27 (1): 7–20.

Monks, James. 2000. "The Returns of Individual and College Characteristics: Evidence from the National Longitudinal Survey of Youth." *Economics of Education Review* 19: 279–289.

Morgan, Julie Margetta. 2011. "Buying College: What Consumers Need to Know." March, Center for American Progress, Washington, DC, http://www.americanprogress.org/issues/2011/03/pdf/buying_college.pdf (accessed September 1, 2011).

——. 2012. "Making College More Affordable: The President's Plan to Lower College Tuition Is a Good First Step But More Can Be Done." February, Center for American Progress, Washington, DC, http://www.americanprogress.org/issues/2012/02/pdf/morgancollegecost.pdf (accessed February 4, 2012).

Morgan, Stephen L. 2005. *On the Edge of Commitment: Educational Attainment and Race in the United States.* Stanford, CA: Stanford University Press.

Morse, Robert J., and Samuel Flanigan. 2006. "How the Ratings Work." *U.S. News & World Report* 141 (7): 109.

Mullen, Ann L. 2010. *Degrees of Inequality: Culture, Class, and Gender in American Higher Education.* Baltimore, MD: Johns Hopkins University Press.

Nagaoka, Jenny, Melissa Roderick, and Vanessa Coca. 2009. *Barriers to College Attainment: Lessons from Chicago.* Washington, DC, and Chicago: Center for American Progress and the Consortium on Chicago School Research at the University of Chicago.

National Center for Public Policy and Higher Education. 2009. "Measuring Up: The National Report Card on Higher Education, Compare States: Graded

Performance, 2006." http://measuringup.highereducation.org/compare/state _comparison.cfm (accessed June 16, 2009).

Nord, Christine, Shep Roey, Robert Perkins, Marsha Lyons, Nita Lemanski, and Jason Schuknecht. 2011. "America's High School Graduates: Results of the 2009 NAEP High School Transcript Study." *NCES 2011-462*, National Center for Education Statistics, U.S. Department of Education, Washington, DC.

Office of Management and Budget. 1997. "Federal Register Notice: Revisions to the Standards for the Classification of Federal Data on Race and Ethnicity." October 30, http://www.whitehouse.gov/omb/fedreg/1997standards.html (accessed January 11, 2009).

Pallais, Amanda, and Sarah Turner. 2006. "Opportunities for Low-Income Students at Top Colleges and Universities: Policy Initiatives and the Distribution of Students." *National Tax Journal* 59 (2): 357–386.

———. 2007. "Access to Elites." In *Economic Inequality and Higher Education: Access, Persistence and Success*, ed. Stacy Dickert-Conlin and Ross Rubenstein, 128–156. New York: Russell Sage Foundation.

Paulsen, Michael B., and Edward P. St. John. 2002. "Social Class and College Costs: Examining the Financial Nexus between College Choice and Persistence." *Journal of Higher Education* 73 (2): 189–236.

Pearson, Robert W., Michael Ross, and Robyn M. Dawes. 1992. "Personal Recall and the Limits of Retrospective Questions." In *Questions about Questions: Inquiries into the Cognitive Bases of Surveys*, ed. Judith M. Tanur, 65–94. New York: Russell Sage Foundation.

Perna, Laura W. 2000. "Racial and Ethnic Group Differences in College Enrollment Decisions." In *Understanding the College Choice of Disadvantaged Students, New Directions for Institutional Research, Fall, No. 107*, ed. Alberto F. Cabrera and Steven M. La Nasa, 65–83. San Francisco, CA: Jossey-Bass.

———. 2006. "Studying College Access and Choice: A Proposed Model." In *Higher Education: Handbook of Theory and Research, Volume XXI*, ed. J. C. Smart, 99–157. New York: Springer.

Perna, Laura W., Heather T. Rowan-Kenyon, Scott L. Thomas, Angela Bell, Robert Anderson, and Chunyan Li. 2008. "The Role of College Counseling in Shaping College Opportunity: Variations across High Schools." *Review of Higher Education* 31 (2): 131–159.

Perna, Laura W., and Patricia Steele. 2011. "The Role of Context in Understanding the Contributions of Financial Aid to College Opportunity." *Teachers College Record* 113 (5): 895–933.

Perna, Laura W., and Marvin A. Titus. 2004. "Understanding Differences in the Choice of College Attended: The Role of State Public Policies." *Review of Higher Education* 27 (4): 501–525.

Pham, Chung, and Tracy Keenan. 2011. "Counseling and College Matriculation: Does the Availability of Counseling Affect College-Going Decisions among Highly Qualified First-Generation College-Bound High School Graduates?" *Journal of Applied Economics and Business Research* 1: 12–24.

Planty, Michael, William Hussar, Thomas Snyder, Stephen Provasnik, Grace Kena, Rachel Dinkes, Angelina KewalRamani, and Jana Kemp. 2008. "The Condition of Education, 2008." *NCES 2008-031*, National Center for Education Statistics, U.S. Department of Education, Washington, DC.

Powers, Donald E. 1993. "Coaching for the SAT: Summary of the Summaries and an Update." *Educational Measurement: Issues and Practice* 12 (2): 24–30.

Provasnik, Stephen, Angelina KewalRamani, Mary McLaughlin Coleman, Lauren Gilbertson, Will Herring, and Qingshu Xie. 2007. "Status of Education in Rural America," *NCES 2007-040*, National Center for Education Statistics, U.S. Department of Education, Washington, DC.

Pryor, John H., Sylvia Hurtado, Victor B. Saenz, Jessica S. Korn, José Luis Santos, and William S. Korn. 2006. "The American Freshman National Norms for Fall 2006." Higher Education Research Institute, December, http://www.gseis.ucla.edu/heri/PDFs/06CIRPFS_Norms_Narrative.pdf (accessed February 5, 2007).

Radford, Alexandria Walton, and Nicole Ifill. 2013. "Preparing Students for College: What High Schools Are Doing and How Their Actions Influence Ninth-Graders' College Attitudes, Aspirations, and Plans." National Association for College Admission Counseling, Arlington, VA.

Radford, Alexandria Walton, and Shayna Tasoff. 2009. "Choosing a Postsecondary Institution: Considerations Reported by Students." *NCES 2009-186*, National Center for Education Statistics, U.S. Department of Education, Washington, DC.

Randall, Monica E. 1999. "Survey of College Plans of Maryland High Ability Students." October, Maryland Higher Education Commission, Annapolis, http://www.mhec.state.md.us/publications/research/1999Studies/Surveyof CollegePlansoMDHighAbilityStudents.pdf (accessed September 1, 2011).

Reay, Diane. 1998. "'Always Knowing' and 'Never Being Sure': Familial and Institutional Habituses and Higher Education Choice." *Journal of Education Policy* 13 (4): 519–529.

Rhodes Trust. 2012. "Oxford and the Rhodes Scholarships." http://www.rhodes scholar.org/ (accessed January 21, 2012).

Roderick, Melissa, Jenny Nagaoka, Vanessa Coca, and Eliza Moeller. 2008. "From High School to the Future: Potholes on the Road to College." March, Consortium on Chicago School Research at the University of Chicago.

———. 2009. "From High School to the Future: Making Hard Work Pay Off. The Road to College for Students in CPS's Academically Advanced Programs." April, Consortium on Chicago School Research at the University of Chicago.

Roksa, Josipa, Eric Grodsky, Richard Arum, and Adam Gamoran. 2007. "Changes in Higher Education and Social Stratification in the United States." In *Stratification in Higher Education: A Comparative Study*, ed. Shavit Yossi, Richard Arum, and Adam Gamoran, 165–191. Stanford, CA: Stanford University Press.

Rothstein, Jesse M. 2004. "College Performance Predictions and the SAT." *Journal of Econometrics* 121: 297–317.

Rowan-Kenyon, Heather T., Angela D. Bell, and Laura W. Perna. 2008. "Contextual Influences on Parental Involvement in College Going: Variations by Socioeconomic Class." *Journal of Higher Education* 79 (5): 564–586.

Sagawa, Shirley, and J. B. Schramm. 2008. "High Schools as Launch Pads: How College-Going Culture Improves Graduation Rates in Low-Income High Schools." College Summit, Washington, DC, http://www.collegesummit.org/images/uploads/WhitePaper_new.pdf (accessed June 24, 2012).

Sallie Mae and Gallup. 2008. "How America Pays for College: Sallie Mae's National Study of College Students and Parents." August, http://www.salliemae.com/content/dreams/pdf/AP-Report.pdf (accessed March 2, 2009).

Sallie Mae and Ipsos. 2011. "How America Pays for College 2011." https://www1.salliemae.com/NR/rdonlyres/BAF36839-4913-456E-8883-ACD006B950A5/14952/HowAmericaPaysforCollege_2012.pdf (accessed February 7, 2012).

Sanchez, Rene. 1996. "Colleges Compete for Minority Students by Helping Them Achieve." *Washington Post*, December 28, p. A01.

Sanderson, Allen, Bernard Dugoni, Kenneth Rasinski, and John Taylor. 1996. "National Education Longitudinal Study, 1988–1994 Descriptive Summary Report: With an Essay on Access and Choice in Postsecondary Education." *NCES 96-175*, National Center for Education Statistics, U.S. Department of Education, Washington, DC.

Sanoff, Alvin P. 1999. "A Parent's Plea: Our High Schools Need Better College Counseling." *Chronicle of Higher Education* 45 (23): B7.

Sax, Linda J., Alexander W. Astin, Jennifer A. Lindholm, William S. Korn, Victor B. Saenz, and Kathryn M. Mahoney. 2003. *The American Freshman: National Norms for Fall 2003*. Los Angeles, CA: Higher Education Research Institute, UCLA.

Sewell, William H., and J. Michael Armer. 1966. "Neighborhood Context and College Plans." *American Sociological Review* 31 (2): 159–168.

Shank, Matthew D., and Fred Beasley. 1998. "Gender Effects on the University Selection Process." *Journal of Marketing for Higher Education* 8 (3): 63–71.

Sharpe, Rochelle. 1999. "Education: Beating the Ivy League Odds." *Wall Street Journal*, April 16, p. W1.

Shea, Rachel Hartigan, and David L. Marcus. 2001. "America's Best Colleges: The Competition Is Keener Than Ever; Here's What You Need to Know to Get a Spot at the School You Choose." *U.S. News & World Report* 131 (10): 88–96.

Sherwin, Jay. 2012. "Make Me a Match: Helping Low-Income and First-Generation Students Make Good College Choices." April, New York: MDRC. http://www.mdrc.org/publications/623/policybrief.pdf (accessed June 17, 2012).

Shulman, James L., and William G. Bowen. 2001. *The Game of Life: College Sports and Educational Values*. Princeton, NJ: Princeton University Press.

Skomsvold, Paul, Alexandria Walton Radford, and Lutz Berkner. 2011. "Six-Year Attainment, Persistence, Transfer, Retention, and Withdrawal Rates of Students Who Began Postsecondary Education in 2003–04." *NCES 2011-152*, National Center for Education Statistics, U.S. Department of Education, Washington, DC.

Smart, John C. 1986. "College Effects on Occupational Status Attainment." *Research in Higher Education* 24 (1): 73–95.

Smith, Michael J., and Michael K. Fleming. 2006. "African American Parents in the Search Stage of College Choice: Unintentional Contributions to the Female to Male College Enrollment Gap." *Urban Education* 41 (1): 71–101.

Smith, Tom. 1984. "Recalling Attitudes: An Analysis of Retrospective Questions on the 1982 GSS." *Public Opinion Quarterly* 48 (3): 639–649.

Soares, Joseph A. 2007. *The Power of Privilege: Yale and America's Elite Colleges*. Stanford, CA: Stanford University Press.

———. 2011. *SAT Wars: The Case for Test-Optional College Admissions*. New York: Teacher's College Press.

Solmon, Lewis C. 1975. "The Definition of College Quality and Its Impact on Earnings." *Explorations in Economic Research* 2 (4): 537–587.

Steinberg, Jacques. 2002. *The Gatekeepers: Inside the Admissions Process of a Premier College*. New York: Viking Penguin.

———. 2003. "College-Entrance Preferences for the Well Connected Draw Ire." *New York Times*, February 13, p. A24.

Stevens, Mitchell L. 2007. *Creating a Class: College Admissions and the Education of Elites*. Cambridge, MA: Harvard University Press.

Stringer, William L., Alisa F. Cunningham, Colleen T. O'Brien, and Jamie P. Merisotis. 1998. "It's All Relative: The Role of Parents in College Financing and Enrollment." *New Agenda Series, Volume 1, Number 1*. Indianapolis, IN: USA Group Foundation.

Taylor, Paul, Rich Morin, D'Vera Cohn, and Wendy Wang. 2008. "American Mobility: Who Moves? Who Stays Put? Where's Home?" December 29, Pew Research Center, Washington, DC, http://pewsocialtrends.org/files/2011/04/American-Mobility-Report-updated-12-29-08.pdf (accessed February 10, 2012).

Thomas, Scott L., and Liang Zhang. 2005. "Post-baccalaureate Wage Growth within Four Years of Graduation: The Effects of College Quality and College Major." *Research in Higher Education* 46 (4): 437–459.

Tobin, Eugene M. 2009. "The Modern Evolution of America's Flagship Universities." Appendix in *Crossing the Finish Line: Completing College at America's*

Public Universities, by William G. Bowen, Matthew M. Chingos, and Michael S. McPherson. Princeton, NJ: Princeton University Press.

Tomsho, Robert. 2006. "Saying 'No' to the Ivy League; Families Face Tough Choice as Back-Up Schools Boost Merit Aid for Top Students." *Wall Street Journal*, April 20, p. D1.

Toor, Rachel. 2001. *Admissions Confidential: An Insider's Account of the Elite College Selection Process*. New York: St. Martin's Press.

Tugend, Alina. 2009. "Shortcuts; Maybe It's Time to Rethink the Cost of College Prep." *New York Times*, February 28, http://query.nytimes.com/gst /fullpage.html?res=980DE2DC1E3BF93BA15751C0A96F9C8B63&scp=2& sq=sat+test+prep+cost&st=nyt (accessed May 6, 2010).

Turley, Ruth N. Lopez. 2006. "When Parents Want Children to Stay Home for College." *Research in Higher Education* 47 (7): 823–846.

Turley, Ruth N. Lopez, Martín Santos, and Cecilia Ceja. 2007. "Social Origin and College Opportunity Expectations across Cohorts." *Social Science Research* 36: 1200–1218.

University of California. 2010. "Statewide Eligibility." http://www.universityof california.edu/admissions/undergrad_adm/paths_to_adm/freshman/state _eligibility.html (accessed May 5, 2010).

U.S. Department of Agriculture. 2008. "National School Lunch Program." Food and Nutrition Service, http://www.fns.usda.gov/cnd/lunch/AboutLunch /NSLPFactsheet.pdf (accessed January 16, 2008).

U.S. Department of Education. 2011. "College Navigator." http://nces.ed.gov /collegenavigator/ (accessed July 20, 2011).

U.S. News & World Report. 2006. "America's Best Colleges 2007." Special Report, August 28, 141 (7).

Vars, Frederick E., and William G. Bowen. 1998. "Scholastic Aptitude Test Scores, Race, and Academic Performance in Selective Colleges and Universities." In *The Black-White Test Score Gap*, ed. Christopher Jencks and Meredith Phillips, 457–479. Washington, DC: Brookings Institution Press.

Venezia, Andrea, Micahel W. Kirst, and Anthony L. Antonio. 2003. "Betraying the College Dream: How Disconnected K–12 and Postsecondary Education Systems Undermine Student Aspirations." Stanford Institute for Higher Education Research, Palo Alto, CA, http://www.stanford.edu /group/bridgeproject/betrayingthecollegedream.pdf (accessed September 1, 2011).

Wainer, Howard. 2000. "The SAT as a Social Indicator." In *Drawing Inferences from Self-Selected Samples*, ed. Howard Wainer, 7–22. Mahwah, NJ: Lawrence Erlbaum Associates.

Warwick, Jacquelyn, and Phylis M. Mansfield. 2003. "Perceived Risk in College Selection: Differences in Evaluative Criteria Used by Students and Parents." *Journal of Marketing for Higher Education* 13 (1/2): 101–125.

Wasley, Paula. 2006. "Stanford U. Increases Aid to Cover Tuition for Low-Income Students." *Chronicle of Higher Education* 52 (30): A39.

Weiss, Kenneth R. 1997. "UC Accused of Bias in Admissions; Education: Civil Rights Groups Allege in Federal Complaint that University Has Retained Graduate School Requirements That Favor Whites and Men." *Los Angeles Times*, March 20, p. 3.

White House. 2012a. "College Scorecard." http://www.whitehouse.gov/sites/default /files/image/college-value-profile.pdf (accessed February 4, 2012).

———. 2012b. "President Obama's Blueprint for Keeping College Affordable and within Reach for All Americans." January 27, http://www.whitehouse.gov/the -press-office/2012/01/27/fact-sheet-president-obama-s-blueprint-keeping-col- lege-affordable-and-wi (accessed February 4, 2012).

Whitmire, Richard, and Camille Esch. 2010. "Pathways to the Baccalaureate: How One Community College Is Helping Underprepared Students Succeed." April, New America Foundation, Washington, DC, http://edmoney.newamer ica.net/sites/newamerica.net/files/policydocs/NOVA_Report_Final_2.pdf (accessed September 1, 2011).

Winter, Greg. 2005. "Yale Cuts Expenses for Needy in a Move to Beat Competi- tors." *New York Times*, March 4, p. B5.

Worth, Robert. 2000. "Ivy League Fever." *New York Times*, September 24, West- chester Weekly Desk, p. 14WC1.

Zemsky, Robert, and Penney Oedel. 1983. *The Structure of College Choice.* New York: College Entrance Examination Board.

Zernike, Kate. 2000. "Ease Up, Top Colleges Tell Stressed Applicants." *New York Times*, December 7, p. A1.

Zhang, Liang. 2005a. "Advance to Graduate Education: The Effect of College Quality and Undergraduate Majors." *Review of Higher Education* 28 (3): 313–338.

———. 2005b. "Do Measures of College Quality Matter? The Effect of Col- lege Quality on Graduates' Earnings." *Review of Higher Education* 28 (4): 571–596.

Zwick, Rebecca. 2002. *Fair Game? The Use of Standardized Admissions Tests in Higher Education.* New York: RoutledgeFalmer.

Acknowledgments

I could not have written this book without the hundreds of high school valedictorians who participated with no remuneration in the High School Valedictorian Project (HSVP). All of these students took the time to complete the HSVP survey and fifty-five also gave of themselves by consenting to an interview.

This project greatly benefited from funding given by Princeton University's Center for Migration and Development in the study's initial stages and further financial resources provided by the Princeton Sociology Department and the Andrew W. Mellon Foundation through the National Longitudinal Survey of Freshmen project. MPR Associates also graciously gave me time to work on this manuscript.

Multiple individuals provided feedback over the course of this project. I would like to especially thank Thomas J. Espenshade for his thorough advice on this project and manuscript. I also greatly appreciate the comments provided by Miguel Centeno, Paul DiMaggio, Angel L. Harris, Douglas S. Massey, and anonymous reviewers. Chang Y. Chung, Scott Lynch, and Oscar Torres provided valuable statistical guidance. Elana Broch, Susan Bennett White, other Princeton University Library staff, and various colleagues at MPR assisted the project in locating and retrieving relevant articles and resources. Princeton's survey research director, Ed Freeland, gave constructive advice and support in the implementation of the HSVP web survey. My editor, Elizabeth Branch Dyson, also deserves particular recognition for the guidance she provided in bringing this work to publication.

Lastly, I would like to thank the friends, family, and colleagues who discussed this project with me and encouraged me to pursue it. Most of all, my husband, Zachary M. Radford, needs to be acknowledged for the infinite ways he has supported me throughout this endeavor. I could not have done this without him.

Index